UNDERSTANDING FILM TEXTS

7

For Dom and Rob
Vickie and Olivia

UNDERSTANDING FILM TEXTS

Meaning and Experience

Patrick Phillips

 Publishing

Publisher's Note

The Moving Image is now an integral part of our daily lives, representing an increasing share of our cultural activity. New generations of students know the moving image more intimately and more intensely than their predecessors – but they are not always well served in relating this experience to the academic study of film and television.

'Understanding the Moving Image' is a new series of short orientation texts in the formal study of screen media, with each book offering an introduction to one important topic. All the books will be written at an accessible level, with no assumption of prior academic knowledge on the part of the reader, by authors with teaching experience and an interest/specialism in a particular area.

As befitting a British Film Institute project, the series will privilege the study of the moving image – notably cinema and television. Case materials will focus on texts familiar (and readily available) to the intended readership, without ducking the responsibility to raise awareness of longer traditions and broader horizons. All books will have a structure designed to facilitate learning for the individual reader, while remaining suitable for classroom seminar context.

The books will be useful to the following:
– Post-16 students working for examinations in media and film studies
– Course leaders and teachers from schools to first-year university and adult education
– The general reader with no prior background to the subject.

We are delighted to commence the series with Patrick Phillips' *Understanding Film Texts: Meaning and Experience*, a valuable and insightful introduction to the experience of watching films and analysing their ways of producing meaning.

British Film Institute 2000
publishing@bfi.org.uk

First published in 2000 by the
British Film Institute
21 Stephen Street, London W1P 2LN
The British Film Institute promotes greater understanding of,
and access to, film and moving image culture in the UK.

Copyright © Patrick Phillips 2000
Designed, edited and set by Design Consultants/Siobhan O'Connor, London
Cover design: Squid Inc.
Cover images: (front) *Afterlife* (Hirokazu Kore-eda, 1998; courtesy of ICA Projects); *William Shakespeare's Romeo + Juliet* (Baz Luhrmann, 1996); *Once Were Warriors* (Lee Tamahori, 1994); *Festen* (Thomas Vinterberg, 1998): (back) *The Matrix* (Andy Wachowski, 1999).
Printed in Great Britain by Cromwell Press, Trowbridge, Wiltshire

British Library Cataloguing-in-Publication Data
A catalogue record for this book is available from the British Library
ISBN 0–85170–799–8 pbk
ISBN 0–85170–798–X hbk

Preface

This book was started before and completed after my work in writing the AS and A-Level Film Studies specifications, approved by the UK Qualifications and Curriculum Authority in December 1999. Inevitably, the book reflects key aspects of that specification, especially the emphasis on 'making meaning'. Indeed, this book may be of particular use if you are working towards the AS Film Studies qualification. For the teacher, as for the student, the book requires that you work out from the detail, from the experience of observing, engaging with particular films. The emphasis is on discovery – perhaps leading to 'general principles'. The interactivity generated from the play between main text and margin columns is intended to recognise and highlight our role in 'activating' meanings contained in the film text. It is also intended to encourage reflection on how these are refracted through our personal 'formations' as human beings.

Understanding Film Texts comes out of a range of teaching experiences. I particularly value my time working in the Media Studies Department at Long Road Sixth Form College in Cambridge. I learnt so much from students and colleagues on the value of listening, of learning through doing, of the passion for film that could be released through close analysis of the film text.

Throughout the period of writing, I was teaching first-year BA Film Studies students at Middlesex University. A sense of the need for a book – or series of books – that captured something of the process of 'doing' film studies, especially for those coming from a GNVQ or Access background, or from an A-Level background that did not include the specialist study of film became ever stronger.

Also, throughout this time of writing, I have been teaching part-time adult students in Cambridge on the University of Cambridge Certificate in Film Studies course. A sense of wanting to address the needs of these and other such students coming to film studies from a lifetime of movie-going, but with little or no formal education in the subject, was also a spur to write.

For both first semester undergraduate and extramural students, although for different reasons, the need to provide self-study materials of an appropriate level in an appropriate style is important. It has been my aim both to do this and to address younger students in schools and further education colleges who may use the book in the classroom with a teacher or independently in a learning resource centre. My confidence in believing it is possible to engage with such apparently diverse groups may be misplaced – it is for you, reading this from whatever constituency you represent, to decide. If you love cinema, are fascinated by the film as a complex 'text' and are keen to understand and appreciate more, then this book may provide a launch pad for serious study – whatever experience you bring to the activity of making meaning. I hope so!

Contents

Preface   v

Introduction   ix

Topic Guide   xii

1. Establishing Shots   1

2. Story   17

3. Character   57

4. Spectacle   95

5. Transformations   137

Suggested Further Reading   153

Index   155

Introduction

The term 'film text' is, perhaps, a misleading one. The first thought that may come to mind is that this is the written text – the screenplay. Even thinking about the 'text in performance' is to consider the way in which words have dramatic life breathed in to them by actors. To use the word 'text' at all seems to suggest a move towards emphasising what film has in common with literature and drama, rather than what is distinctive about it as a form of creative expression.

The word 'text' comes from the same Latin root as the word 'textile' – that word is *texere*, meaning to weave. The 'weave' of a film text is complex and requires much more of its audience than is often assumed – as we rapidly process and respond to so many different sources of visual and aural information and patterning, so much sensory stimulation. This book offers an introduction to this 'weave' of images and sound.

The title of this book qualifies the word 'text' by adding the words 'meaning' and 'experience'. The film is never just a textual object, it is an experience.[1] Indeed, the same film text is experienced differently in different viewing circumstances. How we give meaning to the text, how we make meaning, will be determined by our experience of the text and, to use the word in a different way, the experience we bring to the 'text'. Primarily, this is the experience we have as movie-goers, adept at making meaning.[2]

Of course, this book is itself a text – one in the more conventionally understood sense of the word. Indeed, you may perceive it as not just a book, but a textbook. Now a textbook is something else again. The dictionary defines such an object as 'a book containing the main principles of a subject'. You only have to pick up this book and look at its physical dimensions to realise that this cannot possibly be a book containing the main principles of film. Standard textbooks such as David Bordwell and Kristin Thompson's *Film Art: An Introduction* are necessarily more than five or six times bigger than this 'text' you have in your hand. Not all the principles of the subject are covered and those that are not covered with the kind of thoroughness you may reasonably expect from a textbook. So is this not a textbook?

Certainly some of the 'principles' by which films communicate and stimulate are introduced. Also, some of the 'principles' of our role as film spectators, making meaning from what we see and hear, are explored. As you read this, you will also be given a flavour of a whole range of other areas of enquiry and debate, and, hopefully, these will encourage you to take further your studies in film. Perhaps the best I can do is to say that this is a book that throws you into the swimming pool and allows you to discover how far you are already able to swim. Or, to borrow from Gill Branston,[3] it may be helpful to recognise that this book deals primarily in 'ordinary' theory, as opposed to specialist theory. 'Ordinary' theory 'tries to shape an approach to certain kinds of questions about an area you are interested in … why you so enjoyed, or perhaps were unable to enjoy, or even get to see a particular film'.[4] From this engagement with 'ordinary theory', you may be motivated to engage with more academically specialised theoretical approaches to cinema.

The layout of the book allows you to enter into a kind of dialogue – as questions and comments are constantly being thrown in from the margin columns. It is hoped these will provide a much more 'open' reading experience. If you are using the book in a classroom, some of these questions and ideas may be used as the basis for discussion, debate and productive sidetracking. If you are reading the book on your own, these questions and asides may simulate a classroom situation. To quote from Chapter 1 (p. 9), 'the purpose of this book is primarily to encourage you to take your interest in film into more advanced, and probably more formal, kinds of learning. So, for better or worse, the meeting point for this book is imagined to be a fairly relaxed film class where individuals are encouraged to speak and where what they say is considered valuable in the pursuit of knowledge and understanding about the film experience. This film class does not require a mental image of a teacher and rows of tables. It can be conducted in all kinds of settings.'

On the other hand, if you want to avoid the image of a real or a 'virtual' classroom, you can! If you do not wish to be sidetracked, do not wish to be questioned or challenged to think of other examples of this or alternatives ways of doing that, you are free to ignore the material in the margin columns altogether. You may, if you wish, fill the empty spaces in those columns with your own questions and comments.

In reading each of the three main chapters, you will find a loose but common structure. There is an opening section that introduces some of the main issues relating to the chapter's topic. This is followed by several sections that work out of detailed study of particular films, typically two sections on aspects of film communication and two sections on spectator/audience activity in response to this communication. Each chapter then moves towards one or two sections that raise broader issues of debate arising from what has gone before. These sections may be taken as individual units of study.

To get as much as possible out of this book, you will, ideally, have available the films that are the focus for analysis and discussion in chapters 2, 3 and 4. If you do not have direct access to video/DVD copies, you will, I hope, have seen some of these films. And those you have not seen, you may be eager to look out for having read this book. This is not to say that the book is about these particular films – it is not. The book tries to exemplify a set of linked approaches to the study of film texts and our response to them.

The book *is* about these approaches – which are transferable to all those other films that may be much more important to you than the ones chosen here.

The margin material is of three types. One is simply additional information – information that is potentially useful and interesting, but which may have got in the way of the points being made in the main presentation. A second is notes or cross-references, nearly always signposts to somewhere else in the book or to another book or to another film example. A third requires you to be active! Questions are posed that you are invited to answer and, occasionally, suggestions are made for other kinds of things you may do to improve your appreciation and understanding of the area being covered. You may engage with some, all or none of these – it is completely up to you.

Endnotes

1. Christopher Wilkins, writing about the use of the concept of 'text', says this: 'Appropriate for dealing with works of literature … it has never been adequate for film or television. Its use tends to obscure the facts that film and television are both works and experience – constructed, made, interpreted and consumed by people.' In Christine Gledhill & Linda Williams (eds), *Reinventing Film Studies* (London: Arnold, 2000), p. 219.

2. Geoffrey Nowell Smith writes: 'It is easier to say why films mean than how. Films mean because people want them to mean. Meaning is not something inert, a passive attribute of books, films, computer programs, or other objects. Rather it is the result of a process whereby people "make sense" of something with which they are confronted.' ibid., p. 10.

3. Gill Branston, ibid., pp. 22–6.

4. Gill Branston, ibid., p. 24.

Topic Guide

At a point fairly early in the writing of this book, I thought how much better it would work as a web site with hyper-links. Without hyper-links, however, I realised that the reader would have to keep several fingers in other pages with a constant flicking back and forth – like playing an accordion. Knowing that this would send me crazy, I felt it unfair to inflict it on others! So, at face value, the book has a fairly conventional structure: you can start at the beginning and finish at the end. You do not, however, have to do this. You can read the chapters in (just about) any sequence. More complicatedly, you may track what were earlier described as 'principles of the subject' across the chapters using the tables below (section number followed by page reference). The margin column 'signposting', together with the index, should prevent you from getting lost!

1. Film Communication and Film Aesthetics

Narrative		Genre		Signification		Mise-en-Scene		Editing	
2.1.a	17–21	2.1.b	21–4	2.4	34–9	2.4	34–9	2.2	27–32
2.1.b	21–4	4.3	103–13	2.6	48	3.2	65–9	2.5	39–45
2.2	27–32			3.2	65–9	4.5	118–26	4.3	103–13
2.5	39–45			4.2	103–4			4.4	113–18
2.6.a	46–8							4.5	118–26
2.6.b	48–52								
4.4	113–18								
4.5	118–26								

Cinematography And Staging		Sound: Dialogue		Sound: Music/Noise		Performance	
3.5	76–81	2.3	32–4	4.2	100–3	3.1	57–65
4.3	103–13	3.3	69–74			3.4	74–6
4.4	113–18					4.2	100–3
4.5	118–26					4.4	113–18
4.6	126–32						

2. Audiences and Response

Meaning and Response		Active Spectatorship		Messages and Values	
1.6	9–12	1.5	7–9	2.6.b	48–52
2.2	27–32	2.1.c	25–7	3.1	57–65
2.6.a	46–8	2.6.a	46–8	3.2	65–9
3.6	81–5	3.5	76–81	3.7	85–8
3.7	85–8	3.6	81–5		
3.8	88–92	4.6	126–32		
3.9	92–4	4.7	132–6		
4.6	126–32	5.1	140–3		
5.4	149–52				

3. Issues and Debates

Issues in Evaluation		Issues in Realism		Ideological Debate		Cinema Experience		Film Studies: Directions	
2.7	52–5	4.7	132–6	2.6.b	48–52	4.1	95–100	1.2	3–4
3.7	88–92	5.1	137–40	3.7	85–8	4.4	113–18	1.3	4–5
3.8	92–94	5.2	140–3			4.5	126–32	1.4	5–6
		5.3	143–7			4.6	126–32	1.6	9–12
						5.1	137–40	1.8	13–15
						5.4	149–52	4.7	132–6
								5.4	149–52

1. Establishing Shots

This introductory chapter raises questions of language in relation to our interest in films and the cinema experience. A model is presented to identify different factors involved in our response to films and a programme for the following chapters is set out, together with some of the issues to be developed.

1.1 Film talk: just part of the cinema event

We come out of a cinema wanting to talk. We want to share impressions, sort out our own reactions, debate what happened and what it all meant, and then make some sort of judgment. This social, negotiated response is one of the pleasures provided by the cinematic experience. It can be a sophisticated activity even if it occurs at the pub or on the bus using the language of everyday conversation.

We want to talk about how convincing we found the story – the twists in the plot, the motivation of the characters and the extent to which the ending brought the story and the issues it raised to a satisfactory close.

> *So, when Jackie Brown said to Max that she's never used him, are we supposed to believe her? And why didn't he go off with her to Spain at the end?*

We refer to heightened moments in the film – moments of spectacle or suspense, or emotional intensity – and may use them as the basis for talking about the film's overall capacity to engage our interest.

Pam Grier in Quentin Tarantino's *Jackie Brown* (USA, 1998). See p. 5 for comment on the additional meanings associated with Pam Grier that the director was clearly conscious of when casting her in the lead role.

What was really disturbing was how quick and unannounced the shootings were. The guy, what was his name – Beaumont – that Samuel L. Jackson kills in the boot of his car near the beginning. Oh, and De Niro shooting Melanie was almost as bad as that guy getting shot by Travolta in the back of the car in Pulp Fiction! *And then De Niro getting it. Well, I guess it was inevitable, but I was disappointed. It came right in a sassy, funny conversation. Maybe this is what the film is about somehow – the casualness of death in this gangster world. But why is it so funny?*

We bring to the conversation an ability to place the film by type and explicitly or implicitly compare it with other films.

Jackie Brown *is like Tarantino's other films – listen to the dialogue, that sick humour ... But it seems a lot more conventional in some ways than his other movies. I suppose it's a bit like Scorsese's* Goodfellas, *a lot of emphasis on character and then, bam, somebody gets it. But I suppose in* Goodfellas *there's some honour; here, everybody is out for themselves.*

We are able to describe the impact of certain roles and perform-ances, usually in terms of believability or appropriateness, but also explicitly or implicity by reference to other films.

Pam Grier was great and Samuel L. Jackson was riveting. But I most enjoyed De Niro, who hardly said anything. He was kind of dumb and yet had a sense of the right way for crooks to behave. And wasn't the use of Michael Keaton funny? He jumps out saying something like 'Can I help?'. And we all go, 'That's Michael Keaton!'

In discussing our response we often make reference to the expectations we had before buying a ticket. These would have been created by a combination of the promoted image of the film through other media, reviews, and word of mouth.

I felt I had to see this movie because it was the 'new Tarantino' movie. The reviews I read were OK, but I wasn't led to expect this to be as amazing as Pulp Fiction. *And I suppose it wasn't. But as a regular gangster movie it was thoroughly enjoyable. The thing that I was most interested in was all this stuff about it being a 'black' movie directed by a white guy. Spike Lee and Denzel Washington hated all this use of the word 'nigger'. I don't know, it seemed natural to me in the context of Samuel L. Jackson saying it. Or is it Tarantino just trying to be provocative?*

Explication and **critical judgment** are the two principal components in this kind of conversation.

At its simplest, explication involves simply sorting out what happened and why – *comprehension*.

Our critical judgments tend to be based on the film's capacity to engage our interest in the story and its characters, and to satisfy expectations. We have a natural tendency towards *evaluation*.

It is important to emphasise that real skills are on display here. These skills, like those of being able to view a film meaningfully in the first place, are learnt through experience and through our everyday immersion in a society where the movies are a very significant cultural presence.

Much, however, is repressed in this kind of conversation.

1.2 Film talk: getting heavy

While it is socially acceptable to discuss explicit meaning, debating, for example, the choices made by characters or the twists of the plot, there is usually the need for caution in pushing the conversation towards the exploration of implicit meaning. The anti-intellectual door clicks shut. Looking for 'deeper meaning' is something for the classroom; it is an activity carried out only by groups of people who have agreed to 'permit' themselves to do so. Yet **making meaning** at a whole range of levels is something we are all capable of doing. We do it moment-by-moment throughout a film and in our reflections afterwards. We can develop and refine these skills we already possess, but perhaps do not acknowledge.

There is another kind of engagement with film that is difficult to talk about. While we are watching a film, we can experience moments of **intense feeling** – indeed, this is what makes the film event so remarkable, different in intensity and engagement from other films. These feelings may be triggered by something fairly explicit in the film, such as the fictional re-enactment of some personal experience. They may be

▶ In what ways do you make meaning when you watch a film? ●

triggered by some much more subliminal stimulus in the film which moves us to tears or laughter.

Sometimes we discover capacities for pleasure and fascination in scenes that we would never admit to outside the movie theatre, perhaps involving the representation of 'taboo' subjects (most often representations of sex or violence) and the desires that these subjects induce. Sometimes we find resistances to certain scenes (or to whole movies), although we might have difficulty putting the reasons for these into words.

Sometimes we think about the strangeness of the film experience. How can it be so intense, so absorbing when we know that we are simply watching images projected onto a screen? Questioning the whole basis of our interaction with what we see and hear may be no more than a passing thought. But, if we pursue these questions, we move from problems posed by a particular film – such as 'What does it mean?' and 'Did I like it?' – to the problems posed by cinema itself. How does cinema work its effects on us? What is our role? What is cinema?

To go much further, we would need to think more abstractly – drawing on sociological, psychological and philosophical ideas. We would move into **film theory**. In many respects, we may already hold to particular theories about cinema, about the movie experience, although they we may never have formulated them clearly into words.

1.3 Finding a language

While recognising the social restraints on our film conversation, it is important also to consider the limitations of our language. Even in a situation of trust with friends, we may feel reluctant to talk about more complex levels of meaning or more complex kinds of response because we feel we do not have a language (concepts, terminology, etc.) adequate to the task.

Perhaps the principal function of education is to give us a language that is capable of shaping and articulating what we already know and experience, but cannot adequately communicate. If we are keen to bring more to our conversations about film, we will learn this 'language', the discourse of film studies. Of course, this runs the risk of closing a vicious circle because, in beginning to use more

▶ What kinds of pleasures do you hope for when you choose to watch a film? ●

▶ What for you is the single most amazing thing about the cinema, about how it works as a medium for storytelling and holding our interest?

The French film theorist Christian Metz once said that films are difficult to explain because they are easy to understand. Is this your experience? ●

specialist forms of language, we find we can only practise it within the specialist community which uses that language – other film studies students.

There is another problem with language – any language, in fact. It does our thinking for us. The **discourse** of film studies requires us to conceive of film in its terms. What I mean by this is that the kind of analysis we undertake will be driven in part by the language available to us. The discourse of film studies will lead us to particular kinds of description, particular kinds of analysis determined by the categories it provides.

1.4 The knowledge

Education gives us more than language systems – it also provides us with bodies of knowledge (although we can often teach ourselves these). In a ten-minute conversation about the movie before shifting to all the other things we want to share with our friends, we may be wary not just about the depth of our discussion, but also its breadth. Some comparison with similar recent films will tend to stop short of 'film buffery', although fan gossip is often a lively ingredient. To attempt to place the movie in context within **film history** would certainly be considered a specialist activity.

To some extent, we are also aware of our roles as consumers and that film exists in a commercial marketplace. Today, Hollywood film budgets are flaunted and publicity campaigns are extensive. How far we question the choice of films available to us will depend on how satisfied we are with what we have. Film studies can provide answers to questions about the **cinema business** (film finance, production, distribution and exhibition). These may be particularly important if we are concerned about the variety and choice of films available to us. In turn, we are more likely to be concerned about variety and choice, the more we are knowledgeable about the history of film and the diversity of films from different national cinemas, different cultures. We will be anxious to see different kinds of film flourishing. We may want the opportunity to see them exhibited more often at a local cinema or available at the video store or more commonly shown on television. Our response to issues in the study of the cinema business may be provoked by very personal concerns we have as consumers and fans.

► What are some of the discourses you have learnt through your education – either in school or outside? Do you recognise what is being said here about a discourse 'doing our thinking for us'? ●
For more on discourse, see Chapter 2 (pp. 48–52)

The 'film buff' is, typically, a person who can give you the most obscure information on a film.
► What's your film buff specialism? ●

The film buff and the film historian are better placed to identify any **intertextual** features in a film. That is when a film invites links to be made with other films, perhaps from an earlier period in film history. These may be based on quoting a sequence of shots or some lines of dialogue. Sometimes it is a vaguer kind of relationship – as when a film pays *hommage* to somebody from an earlier time in film history. For example, the actress Pam Grier's presence in *Jackie Brown* is an homage both to her and to the blaxploitation movies in which she starred in the 1970s.
► Can you recall a film that gave you particular pleasure because of its intertextual features or because of its *hommage* to some film or star or director from an earlier time in film history? ●

▶ Can you identify one source of frustration – even anger – which you feel as a movie-goer as a result of commercial decisions made within the film industry? ●
The very limited distribution and exhibition in the United Kingdom of a highly acclaimed Japanese film is referred to in Chapter 5 (see pp. 147–9).

▶ Recall a sequence from a film that you have seen recently in which you were really impressed by some of its formal features – perhaps its shot composition and cinematography, or its editing and use of sound. Is it possible to enjoy a film primarily for its form and style, or is story the crucial factor? ●

Here is an example of increased critical appreciation:

Increased knowledge:
'I didn't know that Saul Bass [graphic artist] and Bernard Hermann [composer] had such creative input to the shower sequence in Hitchcock's *Psycho*?'
Critical work:
Let us look again at the sequence and see how it works – visually and aurally.
Shift in appreciation:
'Having looked in detail at the montage of shots and the precise way in which chords of music seem literally to "strike", I can see why people rate this as one of the most successful horror scenes in cinema.'

Knowledge of **film forms and styles** is once again something we develop from early childhood. We learn through experience how movies work as forms of communication. Our preoccupation, however, is with story and we assume the film's form (its editing, composition, camera work) serves the purpose of the story. The film's form may, to all intents and purposes, seem *invisible*. Having said this, contemporary popular films, as well as so-called 'art' films, commonly make us aware of the *expressive* use of techniques to give maximum impact to specific moments in a film. Indeed, many 'event' films such as *Star Wars – Episode 1* attract audiences at least as much because of their display of film techniques and effects as because of their story and characters.

As we begin to become aware of different kinds of film from the past and from other cinema traditions than Hollywood, we become more sensitive to creative choices made by director, cinematographer, designer, editor and so on. To focus a conversation primarily on the formal features of a film again indicates some level of expertise, rather than an 'ordinary' social response.

Focusing mainly on the creative choices made by filmmakers shifts film into the visual arts. We become aware of the 'poetics' of film (from the Greek *poesis*, literally the 'making'). As we become more interested in film form and style, we begin to recognise that they cannot be separated from the film's content; form and style are part of the content of the film, part of the meaning. Our response is to the whole experience offered by the film.

Knowledge – of film history, of the cinema business, of film form and style – increases our capacity for **critical appreciation**. 'Appreciation' is often assumed to be positive. It develops out of our increased knowledge and insight. Criticism, by contrast, is assumed to be negative. In practice, good critical work should start in neutral, with an open question: Let us see if this works? In the process of answering this question, our appreciation of the film, or at least of the part we are studying, changes. By the time you finish this book, you should be much more confident about asking the questions which are vital for critical work – and so for developing your appreciation.

1.5 It may not feel like work, but …

Critical 'work', however, is not the only activity with which we are concerned. The film event itself – turning up at the cinema (or renting the video), sitting in front of the screen and putting yourself in the position of spectator require work which cannot in itself be described as critical. (Although, of course, you will have exercised some critical choice in making these decisions.) Let us be a little more clear about the kind of work we do as spectators of a movie.

First, and most obviously, we work as **information processors**, dealing with all the messages contained in the complex communication system which makes up a typical movie. We must 'decode' both visual and aural information. Just think what visual communication we have to work with in *William Shakespeare's Romeo and Juliet*. Just think of the work we are asked to do in a typical sequence which crosscuts between the two versions of the central character in *Sliding Doors*. We must make connections, recognise differences. We must constantly adjust our sense of time and space. The film experience happens less on the screen than in our heads – it is a remarkably complex mental experience. The point has already been made that most of the basic comprehension skills we need to make sense of a film are learnt from childhood onwards in our regular and frequent exposure to movies. At the same time, it has to be said that the 'language' of commercial cinema is a particularly easy one to pick up and follow. (Why is this?)

Secondly, although it is almost simultaneous, having processed the information, we respond by **giving attention** – directing our interest. This is most likely to focus on the events and characters, although our interest may extend to thinking about the film's style and the techniques used by those who have contributed to the film – director, designer, cinematographer, actor, composer and so on. Thus, we may experience the movie relatively more 'affectively' – that is, through our feelings – or relatively more 'cognitively' – that is, through our intellects. In practice, we experience the movie event continuously and repeatedly in both modes, even if we are not thinking consciously about style and technique. Even at the level of story, we are responding both to the emotions and to the information we are given.

Thirdly, and inevitably, we become involved moment by moment in **interpreting** the film. This takes us back to what

You will find a study of *Sliding Doors* in Chapter 2 and a study of *William Shakespeare's Romeo and Juliet* in Chapter 4.

This revisits Christian Metz's idea referred to on p. 4.

▶ Why do we give more of our attention, commit ourselves more, to some movies than to others? ●

▶ Think of a film you have seen in which your interpretation was at odds with that of other people. What 'agenda' determined your particular and personal interpretation? ●

▶ Think of a film of which you have a very definite evaluation. What criteria did you use in arriving at this evaluation? ●

One of the concerns expressed by people when they take up the study of film is whether their pleasure as fans will be destroyed. One way of looking at this is to consider 'affective' and 'cognitive' responses as two ends of a spectrum.

Affective ◄───────► Cognitive
(emotion)   (intellect)

As 'critics' working towards greater 'appreciation', it may be said that we shift towards the cognitive end of the scale. However, the critical appreciation we arrive at will be cold and detached indeed if it leaves behind the emotions that will almost certainly be at the heart of the film. This book wishes to promote as strongly as it can an 'holistic' approach – that is, one which recognises the cognitive and the affective as part of a single experience.

Pleasure is found anywhere along this affective–cognitive spectrum. It is a mistake to believe that the more we engage intellectually, the less we can 'enjoy' a film. If the film stands up to our critical appreciation, it will be enjoyed even more. Of course, if it does not – if, in the course of looking at it with our heads rather than our hearts, we recognise it as shallow and fake – then we will (rightly) like it less.

Titanic is perhaps a useful film for the exploration of these issues.

was said earlier about making meaning. One interesting set of questions surrounds the extent to which we interpret a film collectively as an audience – more or less arriving at the same understanding of what we have seen. Another surrounds the extent to which each of us interprets a film very personally as a spectator bringing a very personal 'agenda' to the movies.

Fourthly, we make overall judgments which occur after the movie has finished, but which are a synthesis of our activity during the film. We cannot resist **evaluating** the film in relation to the kind of experience it has provided – 'I like this'; 'No, I can't stand that.' What sorts of judgments do we make? We respond positively or negatively to twists in the plot; to the traits of characters (and the actors portraying them); to setting and music. Simultaneously, we respond positively or negatively to the structure of the story, the pace and rhythm created by editing, the positions we are put in as an audience for participating in the story. Our judgments will vary in kind, and will tend to reflect the affective – cognitive shifts that occur constantly in our viewing activity. This particularly applies to the way we form judgments on the film's 'attitude', its specific take on the world it represents to us. We may have a gut feeling that the film is disagreeable to us in its development of a particular theme or idea, but which we only become conscious of and think through in our minds by the end of the film, or even well after the end.

In particular, we will respond in relation to the kind of pleasure we think we have been offered. It is important not to think of pleasure as any one thing. Different individuals will go into a movie auditorium with different desires that they wish to have satisfied. These desires may be for exciting action, sexual stimulation, aesthetic delight or all of these and more. Our desire may be for a film that provides comfort and reassurance – a film that portrays life as we want it to be using conventions of storytelling with which we are totally familiar. Alternatively, our desire may be for a film that challenges us to look at some aspect of life and the world in new and different ways, perhaps using storytelling techniques which deliberately surprise and unsettle us. So, our evaluation will be in relation to the criteria we employ.

By this fourth stage, we have moved out of the cinema. Ideally, we should consider all the different contexts in which this evaluative work occurs. It really would be an unmanageable task, however, if we were to try to take account of all the more common situations, public and private, where we might pursue our interest in the film experience – from chatting in the video store with a fellow fan to exchanging ideas across cyberspace.

Referring back to what was said at the beginning about 'film talk' and 'finding a language', the purpose of this book is primarily to encourage you to take you interest in film into more advanced, and probably more formal, kinds of learning. So, for better or worse, the meeting point for this book is imagined to be a fairly relaxed film class where individuals are encouraged to speak and where what they say is considered valuable in the pursuit of knowledge and understanding about the film experience. This film class does not require a mental image of a teacher and rows of tables. It can be conducted in all kinds of settings. Its defining characteristic is that it is purposeful and wishes to be reasonably systematic in the way in which it conducts its investigations. It is a film class that may even consist only of you and me.

1.6 Film studies – how did you find it?

In our classroom – real or virtual – it is important to recognise the range of key inputs which determine meaning and response in our film viewing. One is the film itself as a 'text' made up of image and sound. This study of the **film text** is the principal focus of this book.

The type of close textual analysis will differ according to the **critical approach** we adopt. The range and sophistication of the critical approaches we can deploy in the analysis of a film will be an indication of our experience and 'competence'. This competence will come from informal or formal learning.

In linking film to one or more critical approaches, we must take account of what may be the 'fashion' of the moment in film studies. This will tend to determine both the kind of film text we think worth studying and the kinds of critical approaches worth applying. These 'inputs' can be presented as shown at the top of the following page.

Much work in film studies (and certainly a lot of work in literature studies) stops here. But it is vitally important that we at least recognise that this is just part of the picture. There are other studies that inform and extend the study of film texts.

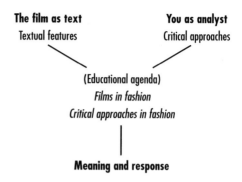

The film as text   **You as analyst**
Textual features   Critical approaches

(Educational agenda)
Films in fashion
Critical approaches in fashion

Meaning and response

However, the meaning and our response to a film will be influenced by factors other than those 'internal' to the film itself. For example, our response may be partly determined by the 'image' created in advance by the industry's promotion and marketing. Our response may reflect the 'image' of the movie we have picked up from the broader culture. In other words, as well as an 'internal' life as text, films have a public, 'external' existence within culture.

Also, we create meaning from our distinctive and sometimes highly personal reactions. We have each been formed by a particular combination of life experiences, values and beliefs. It is inevitable that they will be present in the intensely personal experience of watching a film in the darkness of a movie auditorium.

At a wider level still, social values (ideological and, particularly, hegemonic beliefs and attitudes) will colour both the film as cultural object and our personal response as spectators.

Let us present these two 'inputs' as follows:

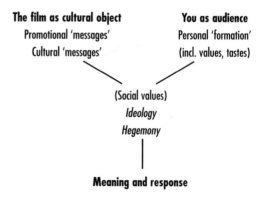

The film as cultural object   **You as audience**
Promotional 'messages'   Personal 'formation'
Cultural 'messages'   (incl. values, tastes)

(Social values)
Ideology
Hegemony

Meaning and response

For a working description of what we mean by *ideology* and *hegemony*, see the next chapter (pp. 48–50).

The approach to film studies proposed here is one that takes account of all the factors above – textual, critical, cultural and personal. This approach sees the film as both a text for close study and an artefact existing in culture. It sees you and me as both critics and audience members. All of these factors combined 'generate' meaning and response.

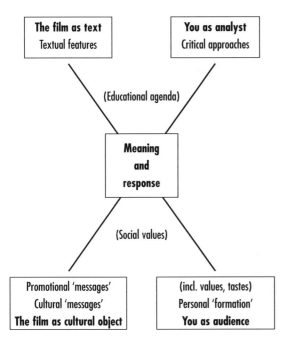

What makes this view even more complex is that not only can we draw lines of intersection towards the centre, but we can also draw lines all around and across this diagram. Everything is connected to everything else.

Before you become too perplexed, let me intervene. This book certainly wishes to encourage you to take this 'whole' view. At the same time, it offers itself as an introduction to the study of the film text – and the infinite possibilities generated by the model just presented will have to be reined in. In the chapters that follow, you will find a traditional bias towards the top half of the model – that is, towards critical 'work' and analysis.

Coming out of the cinema, we are comfortable about asking casually, 'How did you find it?' The proposal here is that we take exactly this question into the slightly more

▶ In order to bring this diagram to life, put an actual film in the centre. What kind of study would you want to make of this film? Draw up a list of questions you would want to ask from around the four 'corners': film as text; film as cultural object; you as audience; you as analyst.

Now choose another – and quite different – film from the first. Again, place it within the diagram. What questions would you want to ask this time? Are they the same questions as for your first film? Are they quite different ones? ●

You are encouraged as you work through this book to hold on to the personal and social interests that have motivated you to want to learn more in the first place. You should continuously reflect on how meaning and response are created through the interaction of all kinds of different 'inputs'. In your further thinking, reading and studying, you will, hopefully, make more of these connections.

formal setting of a classroom and adopt a somewhat more systematic approach. There should be no inhibitions about the kinds of answers we give, however, as *all* responses are of interest and deserve further consideration. They may vary from 'I thought the editing and music were really brilliant in the final sequence' to 'I don't think it was value for money – especially in relation to all the hype' to 'I couldn't help thinking of my boyfriend every time that …'

1.7 The programme

This book is of necessity highly selective in its focus. 'How was it for you?' will be asked in relation to just three of the pleasures offered by films: story, character and spectacle.

Although no specific theme is pursued throughout the book, two broad, and sometimes overlapping themes do recur. One is romance and sexuality; the other – sometimes merely an extension of the first – is the family. You may want to take the opportunity to develop more interesting comparisons between some of these films – particularly in relation to their messages and values. Certainly you will find the films exploring these broad subjects – the family, sexual romance – cover a variety of genres and some of them are surprisingly violent!

Chapter 2 considers ways in which the cinematic **story** is told and the ways in which meaning and response are generated through this very distinctive storytelling medium. A study will be made of an old favourite (I hope you agree!), *E.T. – The Extra Terrestrial*. This Spielberg/Hollywood movie will be set alongside a very different film, an American-financed film with a British setting, *Sliding Doors*.

Chapter 3 looks primarily at **character** and performance and, again, how we engage with them in relation to meaning and response. The films which provide the basis for this study are the British film *Secrets and Lies* and the New Zealand film *Once Were Warriors*.

Chapter 4 is mainly concerned with **spectacle** and our response to cinema as a medium of visual and aural display. Focus will be on the Hong Kong supernatural martial arts movie *A Chinese Ghost Story* and *William Shakespeare's Romeo and Juliet*.

Chapter 5, as the concluding chapter, begins to open up the study, pulling together ideas on making meaning in

The programme: video/DVD references

VIDEO (PAL) – UK REFERENCES

E.T. – The Extraterrestrial	0445283
Sliding Doors	VHR4587
Secrets and Lies	CC7830
Once Were Warriors	EVS1171
William Shakespeare's Romeo and Juliet	4143S
Chinese Ghost Story	HK016
The Matrix	S017665
Festen	BL18
After Life	ICAV1042

DVD (Territory 2)

E.T. – The Extraterrestrial	n/a
Sliding Doors	n/a
Secrets and Lies	VCD0026
Once Were Warriors	EDV9022
William Shakespeare's Romeo and Juliet	04143DVD
A Chinese Ghost Story	n/a
The Matrix	D017737
Festen	n/a
After Life	n/a

relation to issues of realism and make-believe. The focus is on some of the ways in which cinema can be seen as a medium of **transformation**. Brief reference is made to three films in very different styles, on very different budgets and coming out of very different cinema cultures. These are the Hollywood blockbuster *The Matrix*, the Danish 'Dogme 95' film *Festen* and the critically acclaimed Japanese film *After Life*. As though by chance, another recurring theme emerges by the end of the book, one that I guess I ought to warn you about from the beginning: virtual presences – ghosts!

Choosing films for a short introductory book such as this requires a careful juggling of different priorities. In relation to studying the film text, it is important to include examples of films that operate according the familiar conventions of popular commercial cinema.

If only for reasons of contrast, it is also important to include at least one film that operates according to different principles. It is also useful to have some contrast between the films in terms of the commercial, cultural and social contexts in which they can be placed. This contrast may include looking at films from different national cinemas and/or from different production sectors – the large-scale complex production and the small 'independent' production, for example. It may also include looking at examples of film from different historical periods (although in this book the choice has been made to consider only films made since the early 1980s).

In relation to story, character and spectacle, it is valuable to include different kinds of cultural representation. This is also important in testing our personal response against stories and human situations some of which may be more, some less immediately recognisable to us.

1.8 So far, then ...

What I hope I have done in this introductory chapter is to provide some establishing shots for what is to follow. Let us draw together some of these.

To take up film studies involves acknowledging:

- how much you **already know** about how films work;

- what skills of analysis you **already possess** and use.

At the same time, it also involves recognising:

This book does not want to encourage a crude and often artificial distinction between a kind of cinema described loosely as 'Hollywood' and the majority of the remainder described as 'alternative'. Nor does it want to encourage that crude distinction between 'multiplex' and 'art-house' films.

▶ Look at the list of films on the facing page. Try to categorise them in different ways that seem to make sense to you. When you have finished, think about the categories you have used. Why these categories? Where do they come from? ●

Establishing shots are to be found at the very beginning of a movie or at the beginning of a major new sequence involving a change of location. For an example, see the description of the opening of *Sliding Doors* (p. 41).
▶ What is your favourite sequence of establishing shots? ●

- how our ability to **make meaning** can improve through our developing experience as 'readers' of film texts;

- how our ability to think through our **response** to a film can become more complex in relation to our developing understanding of how films work to communicate and how we, as film spectators, 'work' with the film.

This book has to start somewhere. It will assume that you already are able to make sense of movies and enjoy them both intellectually and emotionally. What is offered in the chapters that follow are a number of 'springboards' to personal reflection and further, more in-depth study of film.

Film studies offers the opportunity to gain **additional knowledge** of:

- film form and style;

- cinema institutions, including their historical dimensions;

- critical approaches and theories developed for the analysis of films and the cinema experience.

There is the opportunity to gain **additional skills** in:

- applying knowledge so you can develop a more complex understanding and appreciation of the meaning contained in a film and your response to it;

- applying a specialist language useful for articulating more effectively what we see and what we think.

More specifically, the **'work'** of watching a film needs to be considered in its four aspects:

- processing information;

- directing attention;

- interpreting – in relation to some explicit or implicit agenda;

- evaluating – in relation to some explicit or implicit criteria.

The book will imagine participation in an informal and interactive film class. This will require you be active in your thinking and honest in your personal reflection. In particular, you will be asked repeatedly, directly and indirectly, to refer

As you read on, you will recognise that this book concentrates on film form and style, especially as they inform our study of the film 'text'. By the time you have reached the final chapter, you will begin to have some feel for the kinds of critical approaches and theories you may want to study further. What the book is only able to address through the occasional reference is your interest in cinema institutions, such as Hollywood, or your interest in cinema history.

to your own **experience** of film-going and of cinema as a medium.

The focus of this book will be on three central areas of pleasure and interest within the fiction film:

- story
- character
- spectacle

together with a fourth, which provides the subject of the shorter final chapter:

- transformations.

The exploration will keep slipping from particular films to questions of cinema itself – what is it as a medium of creative expression and personal response? It will soon become clear that the main interest is not in *what* meanings we make so much as in *how* we make them. This requires a close study of how we interact with the film text. Focusing on the *how* means that the choice of films is not so important. What is important is the transferability of the approach used in this book to films other than those discussed – you find this book. The films chosen stand in for all the films you might actually want to consider after putting the book down – and writing your own response to the films that fascinate you.

2. Story

This chapter attempts to build an overview of film narrative *and includes some discussion of* genre. *The pleasures provided by narrative are outlined and illustrated by the study of two films,* **E.T. – The Extraterrestrial** *(United States, 1982) and* **Sliding Doors** *(United States/United Kingdom, 1998). There is a particular emphasis on* visual storytelling *in these films, recognising the central importance of* mise en scène *and editing. The final part of the chapter explores the values and attitudes contained within film story, with* discourse *and* hegemony *introduced as important concepts. Finally, issues of* evaluation *are raised. The more we consider our own work as 'meaning makers', the more difficult it is to generalise about what may be considered a 'good' or a 'bad' film.*

2.1a Take one: stories, plots and narration

We have a strong desire for stories and every day we encounter them, most commonly in conversation (including gossip) and in our contact with the news media. We also encounter stories that are more artfully crafted – by novelists, dramatists and film-makers.

A story takes bits of information and strings them together in **time** (usually in chronological form, i.e. this happened, then this, then this). This stringing together usually involves **causality** (this happened which led to this happening which led to this happening). Also, the story will take place in locations, physical places or – to put it more abstractly – in **'space'**.

▶ Why? Why are stories so important to us? ●

'We can consider a narrative to be a chain of events in cause–effect relationship occurring in time and space.' (Bordwell and Thompson, Film Art, 5th edn, p. 90)

▶ The kind of story which appears in the news, a 'news story', is the most likely to be accepted as true. Should it be? ●

▶ Think of a story you have told. What did you exaggerate and why? ●

▶ Compare the kind of story told in a 'realistic' television soap opera with the kind of story told in, say, Japanese Anime. Are these two kinds of storytelling entirely different? ●

▶ Think about how you retell part of your life, say your childhood between the ages of five and ten, as 'history'. What do you do in order to turn those years of your life into a story? ●

▶ Recall two films, preferably ones you know well: one with a straightforward narrative that starts at the beginning of the story and finishes at the end; the other with a more complex plot organisation.

Note down the main sections of each film in the order in which they occur. When you have done this, reflect on why you think the two films were constructed as they were. ●

(You may find it useful to read Section 2.2 on p. 28 before doing this.)

These stories may be 'true' in the sense that they recount things that have happened in the world (for example, television news). They may be partly true, but some significant details may have been altered to give greater interest or shock value (for example, a tabloid press version of events designed to increase drama and the sensational). They may be completely fictitious, although based loosely on the kinds of events and emotions that are recognisably part of the world in which we live. For example, in television soap operas, fictional characters show emotions and undergo life experiences that we can easily recognise to the extent that some viewers so identify with characters that they write to them as if they were real people. At the other end of the spectrum, there are much more fantastic fictions which derive from our fertile and weird imaginations. For example, action comics take us into a different dimension of imaginative storytelling.

The French have a useful general word for story – *histoire*. For English speakers, this clearly triggers thoughts of that specific kind of story which we call 'history'. We may assume history to be a clear example of the first kind of story referred to in the previous paragraph, that is, an account of things that have happened in the world. This does not mean, however, that history just tells itself. Events, characters and information all need to be organised into a narrative. Not everything can be included, so selection becomes important. Those details that are included will have been chosen because they support a particular narrative construction. All storytelling is a history – even if the story is fictitious – and will demonstrate the characteristics of selection and construction.

To go back to what was said at the beginning of this section, two key influences on this construction are time and causality.

Time is experienced as linear (past ➤ present ➤ future). From starting to read this sentence until the end of it, a second from now, time has moved forward. Stories most often seem to duplicate this forward movement, although they do not always do this. The way the 'bits' of the story are arranged – plotted – often goes against the linearity of the story, as in when we skip backwards and forwards between events. How a story is organised may be very complicated. I could, for example, start somewhere near the end and then use flashbacks to recount events that have occurred earlier (one of the most distinctive elements of film storytelling). My purpose will be to create additional interest for my audience. The arrangement of the story is the plot. To take a very well known example, *Pulp Fiction* has a story that is not the same as the plot, that is, the story is not presented chronologically on screen. If you wish to recount *Pulp Fiction* to a friend, you have the choice of starting at the beginning of the story or at the beginning of the plot.

Plot is usually less than the story, in that plot will not include everything that is in the story. By inference, we build up a fuller picture than that provided by the plot. We may, for example, be able to recount what happened before the actions of the plot begin or what happens in parallel time, but is not shown to us. This is our first encounter with the hugely important recognition that we actively make meaning, fleshing out the plot into the full story. It is also our first opportunity to acknowledge how skilled we are in taking what we are given and constructing further story information. In a film such as *Pulp Fiction*, we develop a fuller story in our minds from the plot we are given.

▶ Can you clearly see the distinction between story and plot? ●

Stories form within **narrative structures**. We can say that stories have a beginning and an end – and, whether very long or very short, a middle section. This may seem so obvious as to be hardly worth stating. When we start asking questions, however, we can begin to see how important are some of the decisions made by the storyteller. Why start here? Why finish there? Why include this in the middle? There are many answers to these three questions, but most basically they are about the management of information (knowledge) and emotion (feeling). The process of **narration** is an important means by which we are teased, misled, held in suspense, released from suspense – in other words, an important component of the rollercoaster ride of watching a movie.

▶ Let us go back to the story of your own childhood, some time between the ages of five and ten.
Reflect on why you started where you did and why you chose to finish at a certain point. ●

'Narration, the plot's way of distributing story information in order to achieve specific effects. Narration is the moment-by-moment process that guides us in building the story out of the plot.'
(Bordwell and Thompson, Film Art, 5th edn, p. 102)

The starting point for the story will be the point shortly before or at which some event occurs to change the people and/or environment of a particular place. In plotting the story, the storyteller may introduce two parallel lines of development, or construct a plot in which one main plot is supported by one or more sub-plots designed to give the story more texture. The end point will be the point the storyteller considers appropriate for 'closing' the story. The

In narrative theory, we often refer to an initial **equilibrium** which is broken by some event (such as violence breaking out in a community) –. That equilibrium has to be restored or a new one created to take the place of the one that has been lost.

Hollywood-type films have been characterised as having a high degree of closure, where all the strands of the story are tied up. In fact, it is quite common today for films to have something less than complete closure – some elements of the story will be resolved, but others are left open.

▶ In the two films you have so far been thinking about, what is the initial equilibrium that is destroyed? What new equilibrium is put in place at the end? Do either or both of your films have 'open' endings – or are they examples of conventional narrative 'closure'? ●

▶ Going back to the notes you made on the main sections of your two films above, can you identify a three-act structure? Be precise in defining the breaks. (Often they are surprisingly evenly spaced. In a 90-minute film, the act breaks are, more or less, at 30 and 60 minutes.) ●

sub-plots will most often be drawn back into the main plot at the point of closure. Audience curiosity/anxiety in relation to the suspense element will be satisfied and some sort of order/stability will be established or re-established.

Often the middle section provides us with further complications to the initial problem. Sub-plots may develop and, in the process, reveal connections with one another and with the main plot.

To a surprising degree, Hollywood took on board the three-act structure of the nineteenth-century stage melodrama when feature-length films first began to be produced. This three act structure – initial disruption; complication; resolution and closure – is the basic narrative structure of many, many films. As you will see in sections 2 and 3 below, it is still possible to identify this three-act structure in contemporary films.

So, as a film-maker, I have a story in my head and the first really fundamental thing I have to do is work out a time-based structure. The second thing I need to do is to locate the story in space; I need to give the story physical form in terms of locations and actors. For example, I can set a story as a western or as a sci-fi movie. The same events with the same character types can be placed in very different fictional worlds, dressed in different costumes with a different type of dialogue and a different kind of musical soundtrack. To use a more specialist word, the **diegesis** can change, but the basic story remain the same.

As well as time and space, I have to consider something else. However simple or complex the plot used to tell a story, 'and then …' remains the common phrase which drives narrative forward in time. But 'and then …' is not enough to create interest in itself. All a time-based linear account will do is create a list of events. We need 'because' as well. We need motivation, explanation – and not just in stories told by historians.

'And then … because' is the basis of storytelling; this is what hooks the audience. Both create the desire for knowledge, to know more. A story plays on our natural curiosity.

Sometimes the 'because' is assumed in the 'and then …'. For example:

The general lost the battle and then committed suicide.

We are most likely to infer that the second event was the result of the first; however, the more information we have about the general, the less confident we will be about the inference we make. If we also knew his wife had just left him or that he had been diagnosed with a terminal illness, causality would be less clear. Maybe the poor guy killed himself for all these reasons! The important point is that we need reasons for things happening. If we have a choice of possible reasons, we can make the story more our own by choosing the explanation we prefer and take delight in arguing our view against that of a friend who prefers a different explanation.

This alerts us to something else that is very important about a story – its **instability**. This is not to say that the story itself changes each time we encounter it. As a written text, as a film, it is 'fixed' for all time – and yet it 'moves'. Stories change at the point of reception, at the point at which listeners, viewers, readers make that story their own. No kind of story is immune to this – not 'news', not 'history', not *Austin Powers*, not *The Matrix*.

But we are getting ahead of ourselves here. Let us consider a little more what are some of the key elements for the storyteller.

2.1b Take two: less abstract

Our interest in a story (and, in fact, a large part of its 'instability') will depend to a very important degree on its **protagonists** – the characters. Characters are sufficiently important for the whole of the next chapter to be devoted to them. What needs to be said briefly here is that characters are nearly always the 'agents' of the story – that is, what they do provides the causality, leads to the next 'and then …'. Sometimes there will be a non-human agent in a story – such as a huge iceberg or a meteorite shower – but, within this premise, human characters will determine what direction the drama takes. In their decisions and actions – in what they do – characters reveal who they are, what their strengths and weaknesses are. Also, a storyteller will work to exploit a natural human interest in character in order to guarantee interest in the story as a whole. The storyteller needs to have created some interest in our suicidal general, prompted a particular viewpoint – whether sympathy or repulsion – if we are to respond to his plight.

▶ Why do we infer things when engaging with stories? ●

▶ If a film storyteller can be certain that an audience will always be making inferences from the information which they are provided with– that is, is always on the look-out to make more story from the available plot – how may the screenwriter and director exploit this? ●

▶ We most often experience a sense of a story's 'instability' over time. Consider again the two contrasting films you were invited to think about earlier.

Have the meanings of either of them changed over time? Did you understand and respond to either of them very differently on second viewing, compared with the way you understood and responded the first time? ●

I am sailing close to very risky, very deep waters when using The Matrix *as an example. After all, this film asks some challenging questions about the way in which we accept the story/histoire of the world which we think we are living in – when, in fact, there is another and quite different story/histoire to be told by those few people who remain capable of seeing beyond appearances. See Chapter 5, p. 140.*

Restricted and unrestricted narration
Hitchcock provides us with a useful, if frequently referred to, example to illustrate this distinction. He asks whether it is better to film a sequence involving a bomb explosion by means of restricted narrative, so we are as ignorant of the presence of the bomb as are the potential victims, or whether it is better to use unrestricted narrative so that we know what the potential victims do not, namely that there is a bomb ticking away beneath their feet.
▶ What do you think? Which is better – restricted or unrestricted narrative? ●
For an excellent example of the second option, see Pontecorvo's film Battle of Algiers *(Italy/Algeria, 1966).*

▶ What is your favourite flashback movie? ●
I think it is hard to find better examples than some of the classic Hollywood film noirs of the 1940s such as Double Indemnity *and* Out of the Past.

Running time is a more interesting subject than may appear at first sight. **Here are three points, each of which you may try to explain**:
• In relation to what was said about film taking over the three-act structure of the nineteenth-century play, it is clear that film wished to replicate the social practice of going to the theatre. From around 1915, movie 'palaces' were built that looked like the grandest of theatres and offered programmes that ran more or less for the same length of time as theatre productions.
• At different times in film history, films have been relatively shorter or relatively longer. Throughout the late 1990s, for example, major Hollywood films became much longer.
• Films differ in length in relation to the cinema out of which they come. Indian popular cinema, for example, has generally produced films that are on average a third longer than standard Hollywood films.

Our interest will also depend on whether the story has **suspense**. All kinds of stories – although some more than others, such as action movies – encourage us to hang in for the next bit of information. The suicide of the general can either just happen or be exploited as an opportunity for both the creation of suspense and character sympathy. In designing the narration, fine calculations need to be made about what information to release to the audience and what to hold back. The most common way of doing this is by shifting between **unrestricted** and **restricted** narration.

Unrestricted narration is when we see everything, including much more than the characters themselves. We hold an advantage – the suspense is generated precisely by the fact that we know something that the character does not. Restricted narration is when we only have partial access to what is going on. (It may also mean that we share the character's false information.) The flashback is a particularly interesting and fairly commonly used tool of film narration. Not only does this reorder the chronology of the story, but it also exploits restricted narrative to control the audience access to information.

Besides these fundamentals of narrative organisation and management, what else is of importance? One of the most obvious is that film narratives must work to a more or less normative understanding between producers and audiences about the **running time** for a movie. (Hollywood films are usually between 90 and 120 minutes in length.) This is the result primarily of commercial considerations, such as production costs and exhibition programmes. This, like other imposed restrictions, is not necessarily a bad thing. It forces a certain tightness, a discipline, in the process of selection and construction of narrative material.

Formal conventions are also of great significance. Human communication is undoubtedly more likely to succeed where communicator and audience share an understanding of the 'rules' or 'codes' within which they are operating. This is particularly clear in the media. Television news will present a news item in a certain recognisable form. The account of a football match on the back page of a tabloid newspaper will be in a familiar form. This form will include familiar character types, familiar situations and familiar language, as well as a familiar overall 'packaging' or structure. Storytellers and audiences will live in a society in which they share a range of **genres**, or storytelling forms. Both the creator and the receiver of the story use their knowledge of genres in making meaning. The storyteller will exploit the conventions of genre as a convenient way to 'package' the story and, in doing this, communicate quickly and effectively significant story information to the audience. In fact, so familiar are genre conventions that significant amounts of story can be missed out of the plot altogether. This is because the audience in its meaning-making activity is so familiar with the genre form being used. Audience members will feel confident in their assumptions and inferences, in 'processing' information that they are given.

Originality in a story is important; however, as an ingredient, it must be used sparingly. If there is too much originality, the audience may lose its bearings. Generally, commercial films are made up of a large 'base' of generic convention, with a small but telling 'twist' of originality. To put it another way, popular film storytelling is largely repetition with just enough variation to give the film its own identity and surprise element. (Although often even the surprise element is predictable and based on convention.) Interestingly, the pleasure for the audience is as much in the conventional base as in the surprise twist.

Storytelling is, then, highly conventional. The conventions differ for different kinds of stories, but those of any particular kind will be instantly recognisable to its fans. The conventions that structure even a story on the *Jerry Springer Show* (for all its apparent spontaneity) are clearly recognisable to those who become familiar with them through repeated viewing. The conventions of the classical tragedy in literature are recognisable to those who spend any time watching and reading plays such as *Romeo and Juliet* (the 1996 film version of which we will look at closely in Chapter 4).

Despite the different conventions of different kinds of stories, the vast majority have much in common. To summarise, a film narrative:

- is time-based;

- occurs in space (location);

- emphasises causality;

▶ As a storyteller (whether historian or football reporter or gossip), we face the challenge of putting our stories into recognisable forms.
What do we gain? What do we lose? ●

A useful concept for considering how both film-makers and audiences rely on familiar, conventional forms in storytelling is schemata (see pp. 130–3).

▶ Reflect yet again on the two films you have been working on so far in this chapter. How far do they typify this characteristic of storytelling: a large degree of repetition of conventions, with a small amount of variation? What genres do they belong to? What are some of the key characteristics of these genres? Is either film a mixed (hybrid) genre film? ●

The conventions of our favourite genres, be they horror or sci-fi, romantic comedy or the musical, the western or the thriller, become familiar to us as we immerse ourselves in film — and television — narrative). For this reason, this book will assume your familiarity with film genres and, unlike other film books, will not devote a large amount of space to them.

This idea of a **commercial aesthetic** is not as odd as it sounds. Other than cinema, consider the commercial aesthetic that is at the heart of, for example, fashion, design and architecture. In a closer parallel to cinema storytelling, consider how much the publishing business makes calculations about best-sellers.

A commercial aesthetic is one in which artistic choices are tied up with issues of what will work to attract and hold the attention of mass audiences. For example, the relationship between narrative and running time (p. 22) is a commercial aesthetic issue. More broadly, the whole visual 'language' of popular cinema can be seen to have developed in relation to what works best for a relaxed audience looking for a pleasurable night out.

For many, the compromise between art and commerce is positive proof that films must be third rate (or worse!) – certainly as 'texts' for serious study. Let me try to defend the commercial aesthetic.

First, I would prefer to say that 'creative negotiation' is a more productive phrase than 'compromise', a word that only suggests loss. Secondly, it is worth remembering what was said in relation to the running time issue about how artistic work of all kinds benefits from the discipline of boundaries, limitations – even if some of these are imposed for commercial reasons. Thirdly, if the commercial aesthetic is about producing films that are sufficiently pleasurable to attract an audience and thereby make a profit, why should this prevent such films from being great works of art?

▶ How do you feel about art that is also 'commercial'? More specifically, what do you feel about the practice of organising previews and carefully analysing feedback in order to see whether the audience likes what the film-makers have produced? Do you find this a shocking betrayal of the film-makers and their right to determine the film's final cut? ●

- creates interest in its protagonists (characters), who will nearly always be the principle causal agents;

- has a narrative structure: a beginning, a middle and an end (although not necessarily conforming to the chronology of the story);

- depends upon the audience to make meaning by fleshing out the plot into story;

- uses narration in order to hold back or manage knowledge and emotion in ways that create active audience involvement in what will happen and why;

- conforms to the requirements of producers and audiences, for example, in regard to running time;

- works within the conventions of a genre form, determining limits to originality, but providing recognition for the audience.

So what makes these factors distinctive to film? Surely much of what has been said here, and throughout this section so far, could equally apply to the novel or theatre or radio drama? Well, the most obvious and distinctive characteristic of film is that it is a visual form of storytelling – however important dialogue may be. Film storytelling manipulates time and space in ways that are specific to cinema as a visual medium, as we will see when we now consider in detail two of the key tools of **visual storytelling**, *mise en scène* and editing.

Narrative film has evolved not in the abstract, but in response to the real needs of real audiences for a form of visual storytelling that ensures comprehensibility and pleasure. Popular film is an aesthetic form – that is, it is concerned with the artistic arrangement of its parts in order to create a pleasing effect. It must be a 'pleasing effect', however, for the majority of typical movie-goers. As a commercial activity, film storytelling must be profitable – and profit comes from meeting the pleasure needs of the audience. It is as calculated as it needs to be – including the re-editing of entire sequences after preview audiences' feedback on what they do not like. Within the context of cinema (but not just cinema), it is useful to regard storytelling as a **commercial aesthetic** – an art form designed to give pleasure in order to make profit.

2.1c Take three: pleasures

Before we move on to the specific study of two films, we should consider what the pleasures of film story are. Here I outline four sources of pleasure – and follow them up with some thoughts on realism in relation to pleasure.

Again, the issue arises as to whether these forms of pleasure are common to all forms of storytelling. Think how each of the following forms of pleasure is distinctive to narrative film.

- Real life seems shapeless. One of the pleasures of story is an artistic one, a 'shaping' of messy human experience into something neater. This **shaping** is an aesthetic pleasure and an intellectual one. Out of this shaping come two further pleasures, pleasures which actually pull in contrary directions. There is the desire in the audience to want more – more emotion, more spectacle, more stimulation of the emotions and the intellect. And there is the equally strong desire for the story to be over, or resolved – to have satisfied the desire to know what happens and why in the moment of 'closure'.

  ▶ Consider either of the films you have been thinking about during this section. Is there a particular pleasure because of the 'shape' the film narrative gives to human experience? What are the qualities that make you want the film to continue? What are the impulses that make you hope it will end? ●

  Again, you may wish to compare the two films.

- Real life is not often very intense or exciting. A second pleasure of story is to simulate (or perhaps I mean stimulate?) a more 'dramatic' existence. We are offered the opportunity to try out experiences and undergo states of feeling that are often extraordinary in relation to our daily lives. These are forms of sophisticated **imaginative 'play'** in which we willingly participate. We buy into (pleasurable) anxiety!

  ▶ What kinds of 'simulation' do your films offer you? Are they pleasurable? In particular, think about the idea that things that cause us anxiety, fear or sadness can be actually described as 'pleasurable'. ●

  We return to ideas of 'play' at the end of Chapter 4

- As real life is most of the time fairly shapeless (beyond perhaps a sense of a daily routine) and unremarkable, and, because we are caught up inside it, we are unable to find clear points of focus for **reflection** about that life. A third pleasure of story is that it focuses issues and gives us the opportunity to generalise from its particular details. We recognise within a particular story the dramatisation of broader issues, values and states of being. We may simultaneously see the general nature of these – and their very personal application to our own lives. (See the final section of this chapter, pp. 52–5.)

  ▶ Consider either or both your chosen films in terms of what they offer you as a focus for reflection. Think about how we 'personalise' issues, making them ours. (How much of this work is actually ours – are we just controlled by the way in which the film works on us?) ●

▶ What desires do your two films 'stage'? Is this something you feel uneasy about – the idea that, in the movies, we in some sense 'give permission' for our fantasy lives to run wild?

    Examine the fantasies either of your two films triggered. (You do not have to go public on this!) ●

For more on realism, see Chapter 3 (pp. 88–90) and Chapter 4 (pp. 130–1) and, less directly, the whole of Chapter 5

E.T. – The Extraterrestrial: how does the audience 'agree' to the realism of this film?

▶ Consider a film that has not worked for you, one which you simply found 'unrealistic'. Why was this?

    Analyse some of the things which you feel prevented an 'agreement' between you and the imaginative world of the film. ●

- Also, because real life is most of the time fairly shapeless and unremarkable, we are as human beings endlessly desiring. A fourth pleasure of story is that it can stage our **desires**, play out our fantasies. A story can never fulfil our desire (which may be one reason we come back for more and more stories), but we are content that our desire is staged and experience the pleasure of a performance that gives an outlet to our imaginative (and sometimes deeply personal) self.

For all of the above pleasures to work, to actually be experienced by the audience, the story will have to be 'realistic'. Now, this word will haunt us throughout the book (and beyond if you pursue your interest in film studies). This is not the place to go into debates about **realism**, but let me just say here that a story need not necessarily be realistic in the sense of being 'likely' or plausible in relation to the world we know. In fact, we often seek out the story experience for the unlikely and the implausible! The story will have to be realistic on its own terms. If a future world is created, for example, it must establish and retain its own kind of imaginative coherence and consistency. If a film opts to work according to a particular set of (genre) conventions, it does so trusting that the audience, as participants in the storytelling event, has already agreed to these conventions. What seems important to ensure that an audience 'agrees' to the story's realism is that characters have 'realistic' emotions and that events trigger *feelings* that are realistic – that is, which are recognisably human. On this basis, an animated cartoon such as *The Lion King* can be described as 'realistic'. The human emotions displayed by the characters allow the audience to identify with the feeling of each dramatic situation. It creates its own internally consistent world. It works according to conventions 'agreed' upon with the audience. An awareness of the bond between the teller, the tale and its audience is very important. This is particularly so in relation to understanding the terms in which we engage in the imaginative play of consuming stories.

    In what follows, we are going to try to expand on some of the things that have been outlined in this opening section by reference to two quite different films, *E.T. – The Extraterrestrial* and *Sliding Doors*. The emphasis will be first on using the two films to exemplify and expand what has been said so far about narrative design (section 2.2). This will be followed by some investigation of the importance of dialogue in narrative (section 2.3) before moving much more specifically to ideas of visual storytelling by reference to *mise en scène* (section 2.4) and editing (section 2.5).

2.2. Narrative design

In both the examples we are going to look at, the story, as told through plot, moves forwards in a straightforward chrono-logical fashion. Of course, plot leaves out much of the story – which we fill in ourselves as discussed earlier. In these two examples, this should not be too demanding since the plots we are going to consider do not cut up the story into segments and radically reorder them in the manner of, say, *Pulp Fiction*. There are no significant flashbacks. Having said this, however, the second example, *Sliding Doors*, draws attention to its own telling and is much more complicated in its structure than the first, *E.T. – The Extraterrestrial*.

As in all stories, 'what if' motivates the storytelling in *E.T.* What if an extraterrestrial creature is left behind when its companions visit Earth (well, California at least). What if this creature finds refuge in a suburban home while the scientific establishment tries to track it down? What if a ten-year-old boy called Elliot<u>T</u> becomes such a close friend of the creature that a symbiotic relationship develops? What if Elliott's brother and sister are drawn in to this secret? What if the creature is super-intelligent and quickly learns to talk, able to say, among other things, 'E.T. phone home,'? What if it can construct a communication system out of household bits and pieces capable of communicating with some distant planet? What if it falls ill, is tracked down by the government scientists, is put in laboratory-like conditions and dies? What if, responding to Elliott's words, it comes back from the dead? What if Elliott, his brother and their friends, riding BMX bikes, can save the creature from the scientists? What if BMX bikes can fly? What if, in an emotional farewell, Elliott is able to see the creature depart in a rescue spaceship? Crazier stories have been told!

A film story must be one that can be visualised. *E.T.* is a very visual story (we will explore this more closely in the next section of this chapter). It also helps if the story can be made

Remember what was stated earlier (pp. 23–4). A film narrative:
- is time-based;
- occurs in space (location);
- emphasises causality;
- creates interest in its protagonists (characters), who will nearly always be the principle causal agents;
- has a narrative structure: a beginning, a middle and an end (although not necessarily conforming to the chronology of the story);
- depends upon the audience to make meaning by fleshing out the plot into story;
- uses narration in order to hold back or manage knowledge and emotion in ways that create active audience involvement in what will happen and why;
- conforms to the requirements of producers and audiences, for example, in regard to running time;
- works within the conventions of a genre form, determining limits to originality, but providing recognition for the audience.

E.T. – The Extra-Terrestrial is the kind of film that is maybe overfamiliar to us. It has become, as its director Steven Spielberg anticipated, a 'Christmas TV movie', a movie like *The Wizard of Oz* or *It's a Wonderful Life* that fits in with the feel-good, family-orientated mood of Christmas. It is a film we may associate with childhood, a film to 'grow out of' as our movie tastes mature. It is certainly a perfect example of the commercial aesthetic which underpins popular cinema. On the one hand, it is a critically acclaimed film, making an extraordinary impact when it premiered at the Cannes Film Festival in 1982 and voted 25th in the American Film Institute list of Greatest American Films of all Time in 1998. On the other hand, such was its commercial success that it was earning Spielberg alone more than a $1 million a day each day during the period of its initial release. It was also the first film to make (even) more in video sales than at the cinema box office.

Here and throughout the book, time references may be slightly different on your video recorder. I have used the same kind of domestic video equipment to which I am assuming you have access. Of course, DVD offers greater accuracy and consistency.

You may want to divide the story up in another way – perhaps into a different three sections; perhaps into more sections or less. Also, please feel free to give each sequence a different name, one which captures the main point for you.

▶ Over what time period does the story of *E.T.* occur? What are the indicators of story time? ●

▶ Looking at any of the three 'parts' as presented here, identify examples of 'cause' and 'effect'. Perhaps the effect is immediate; perhaps it is delayed until much later in the film. ●

▶ How does the story create interest in its main characters? ●

▶ Does the story seem familiar in the way it develops? Can you think of other stories, and a 'pattern' to these stories, which *E.T.* follows? ●

▶ What particular examples from *E.T.* come to mind when thinking about how the story provides – and holds back – knowledge which we are eager to have? Is *E.T.* more of a restricted or unrestricted narrative? ●

to conform to the conventional shape' of a commercial narrative film. *E.T.* does so in its 'classic' three-act structure (see the first section, p. x). The first third sets up the story. The second third creates complications and challenges. The final third sorts them out and brings the story to what we have already described as 'closure'.

Here is the briefest of outlines of *E.T.* Please note that the names given to each 'act' and the sequences which make up these acts are my own, not the screenwriter's.

E.T. STORY OUTLINE
00.00–01.05   Opening credits

First part (33.33) – Setting up the story
1.	01.05	Marooned
2.	07.28	Family 1 (the 'coyote')
2a.		• Picking up the pizza
2b.		• Surrounding the log store
3.	11.48	First sighting
4.	14.07	On the trail
5.	15.40	Family 2 (making Halloween plans)
6.	18.19	First acquaintance
7.	24.11	Developments
7a.		• Elliott and E.T.
7b.		• Plus Mike and Gertie

Second part (39.37) – Challenges and complications
8.	34.38	Threat remains
9.	35.05	Children and E.T. develop friendship
10.	39.19	Symbiosis – ET and the frogs
11.	48.12	Learning to talk
11a.		• with Gertie
11b.		• and Elliott: phone home
12.	53.20	Developments
12a.		• Mike and Elliott monitored
12b.		• Gertie's bedtime story
13.	57.49	Halloween
13a.		• Dressing up
13b.		• Flying across the moon
14.	68.18	Lost and found
15.	72.00	Sickness and house invasion

Third Part (31.27) – Death, Resurrection, Ascension

16	74.15	Quarantine and death
16a.		• Dawn arrival of scientific 'army'
16b.		• Night – quarantine
16c.		• E.T. treatment and death
17.	84.20	Resurrection
18.	91.52	Rescue and ascension
18a.		• The chase
18b.		• Spaceship farewell

105.42–107.30   Closing credits

E.T. is a film with surprisingly weak causality. (See p. 32.) As a 'fairy story', however, this may be considered a strength. Do we always need explanations?

Sliding Doors, like *E.T.*, tells a simple story in a linear form. It focuses on Helen, who at the beginning of the film is sacked from her public relations job in London. She takes the tube home, but just misses one train and because of a delay on the line is forced to take a taxi. Someone attempts to mug her; she falls and cuts her head. A taxi driver takes her to hospital. Meanwhile, her boyfriend Gerry, who is trying to complete his first novel, is in bed with his ex-girlfriend, American business executive Lydia. When Helen gets home, Lydia is just driving off. Gerry takes Helen out that night to a restaurant/bar called Bertorelli's to get drunk.

The next day, Helen decides to take temporary work as a waitress at Bertorelli's in the evenings and delivering sandwiches by day. Lydia is insistent that Gerry leave Helen. Helen is sufficiently suspicious of her boyfriend to follow him, but is reassured that he is going to the library as he claims. Gerry is guilty and wants to confess, but Helen falls asleep on him before he can do so.

Helen faints while waitressing. Gerry is away for the weekend with Lydia. When Gerry comes back and presents her with flowers, Helen is more convinced he is seeing someone else. She tells her friend, Anna, that she is pregnant.

Lydia, in frustration, finishes with Gerry, but then finds out she is pregnant, too. In revenge, she calls Helen to her flat on the pretext of a job interview, while also asking Gerry to be there. When Gerry, not Lydia, opens the door, Helen runs off.

▶ Is there anything about the story which you notice when it is presented as an abstract summary that you were not aware of while watching the film? ●

▶ Take the story elements of *E.T.* as presented here and produce a different narrative design. For example, you could go for a narration made up of flashbacks. When you have produced your version, think about how it might be a very different experience for the audience from the version created by Steven Spielberg and Melissa Mathison, the screenwriter. ●

▶ Summarise the pleasures *E.T.* provides you with as a film story. ●

Sliding Doors was a commercial hit in 1998, appealing both to a popular audience taste for romantic comedy/melodrama and to critics interested in its unusually 'daring' narrative form. The film's success shows, I think, that, after 100 years of cinema, both storytellers and audiences have become enormously skilled and sophisticated. This is a commercial movie (partly financed by British companies, but also with significant investment by two US companies, Miramax and Paramount) and cast a then upcoming star, Gwyneth Paltrow. Yet it assumes a relationship between film-makers and audience that is very 'knowing' of film as a story-telling medium. We are encouraged both to be 'inside' the film world, fully wrapped up in the emotional drama(s) and 'outside' looking in on it, smiling at the film as a constructed object employing techniques of which we are only too aware. Perhaps you could compare the film with *Groundhog Day* (Ramis, US, 1993). You may also consider whether *Sliding Doors* has been surpassed in its use of a particular kind of narrative construction by the 1999 German thriller *Run Lola Run* (Twyker, Germany, 1998).

Gerry follows and, in the struggle, Helen falls down the stairs. She is rushed to hospital. She recovers and tells Gerry to leave her hospital room and never come back. When she is discharged, she takes the hospital lift. She drops her earring and a man picks it up. She is able to make a Monty Python reference which surprises him.

The film ends at this point. Not much of a story!

What gained huge attention for this film was another great 'What if …?', a 'what if' we may ask ourselves frequently in our everyday lives. 'What if I had caught that train …?' *Sliding Doors* tells a parallel story of Helen catching the tube rather than missing it and follows the cause-and-effect chain which ensues.

Here, in summary form, is the narrative of the story just outlined, that of the Helen who misses the tube train.

SLIDING DOORS STORY OUTLINE

(Note: All the sequences marked* crosscut between Helen 1 and (blonde) Helen 2. Some of them in fact give proportionally much more time to Helen 2.)

First part (32.36) – Setting up the story

1.	00.00	Establishes Helen's situation
2.	01.52	PR company meeting
3.	03.09	Catching tube (2.29)*
		(including 'replay' sequence ➝ Helen 2)
4.	05.48	Mugging *
5.	10.23	Gerry at home *
6.	17.26	Bertorelli's: getting drunk *
7.	24.38	Recovery *
		• waitress/sandwich deliveries/makes love for the first time in two months

Second part (45.16) – Complications

8.	32.37	Developments *
		• H follows G to library
		• H on her deliveries is told off by Lydia
		• H falls asleep before he can confess to her
9.	44.18	Rowing *
10.	51.38	Fainting *

As with the plot summary of E.T., the headings used here are mine, not those of the screenwriter. And again, as with E.T., you may wish to divide the film up differently. For example, can you see a more equal three-act structure than I have been able to identify?

▶ From this point, add the story for Helen 2, who *catches* the train, using the same sequence division as here. ●

11. 61.29   (H at Bertorelli's; G with L at hotel)
               Distance
               (G buys H flowers)
12. 69.42   Discovery *
               (H tells Anna she is pregnant)

Third part (13.41) – Two accidents: a death and a recovery
13. 77.54   Accident and unconsciousness *

Helen 2's story finishes here.

14. 87.38   Recovery
               (H tells G to go; in hospital lift, H meets James)

Closing credits (91.15)

▶ Sequence by sequence, how close are Helen 2's experiences to Helen 1's? ●

Causality in Sliding Doors appears to be very strong. Things happen 'because …'. In fact, many of the developments in the story (and not just the one at the tube station at the beginning) depend on chance. This is the main underlying idea of the film – how our lives may be very different depending on one simple event such as catching or failing to catch a train.

After her mugging, Helen says to Gerry (16.24):

If I'd just caught that bloody train.

His reply is:

You don't want to go wondering things like that you know … em … if only this and what if that, you know – alarming …

In fact, we will find lots of examples of the same sort of thing in *Sliding Doors*. This is not so much the 'what if' question as the 'what if instead'. At how many other, unacknowledged, points in the story could everything have turned out differently if not for a chance event or avoidance of an event? For example, what if Helen 1 had got home from the hospital after the mugging two minutes earlier and found Gerry with Lydia? What if Helen 2, having caught the tube and met James, had not decided to get off after him at his stop to apologise for being unresponsive to his conversation?

Too many chance events are, arguably, bad for a story. Chance is too easy a solution in storytelling. It can blow apart what we have begun to call the 'agreement' between

▶ Compare the way *Sliding Doors* works as a narrative structure with *Run Lola Run* mentioned above. They work in different genres. Despite this, is it possible to say which is more successful in its storytelling and why? ●

Earlier you read this:

… a story need not necessarily be realistic in the sense of being 'likely' or plausible in relation to the world we know. In fact, we often seek out the story experience for the unlikely and the implausible! The story will have to be realistic on its own terms. If a future world is created, for example, it must establish and retain its own kind of imaginative coherence and consistency. If a film opts to work according to a particular set of (genre) conventions, it does so trusting that the audience, as participants in the storytelling event, has already agreed to these conventions. What seems important to ensure that an audience 'agrees' to the story's realism is that characters have 'realistic' emotions and that events trigger *feelings* that are realistic – that is, which are recognisably human. *(See p. 26)*

▶ Does *Sliding Doors* work on these terms? ●
▶ Does *E.T.* work on these terms? ●

▶ Compare *E.T.* with another contemporary fairy tale – perhaps *Edward Scissorhands* (Burton, United States, 1990). ●

There is more on dialogue in the next chapter.

storyteller and audience. Does *Sliding Doors* get away with it? There are certainly weaknesses by 'realistic' standards. Can you identify some examples? Do they bother you? If not, this may be because of your particular level of tolerance for the genre within which the story is contained. It is a romantic comedy – and, in comedy, chance (even farcical chance such as someone leaving the split second before someone else arrives) is acceptable to an audience. We set different standards when we place ourselves within the conventional rule–based world of genre cinema.

By comparison with *Sliding Doors*, *E.T.* is surprisingly less concerned with causality. There is other information we may want, but the film simply does not give it to us. At a less important level, but important in relation to the logic of cause and effect, we may wonder why Elliott appeared to suffer no punishment after the frog incident at school. More important questions left unanswered include:

• Why is E.T. left behind at the beginning – what is he doing?
• Why does Elliott pursue E.T. when he is obviously scared?
• Why does E.T. fall ill?
• What brings about E.T.'s resurrection from the dead?

We seem to be invited to take these things on trust. They just happen – like in a fairy tale. It certainly falls well below the tightly plotted cause-and-effect structure of many Hollywood films. It is interesting to read William Kotzwinkle's novelisation of the film. The novel (written after the film) attempts to 'fill in' information, but perhaps this is unnecessary. 'Imagine the impossible,' as in one of the fairy tales, Elliott's mother tells his sister, Gertie. As with *Sliding Doors*, our demands of a film story will depend on the genre we recognise the film as working in – in the case of *E.T.*, the contemporary fairy story.

2.3. Storytelling and dialogue

Although the emphasis in this chapter is on visual story-telling, dialogue is important. Crucial story and character information is communicated verbally. This is true of *Sliding Doors*. Just consider how much information we pick up through listening to the dialogue in the very first scene when Helen is fired from the public relations company. Rather

E.T. – The Extraterrestrial: Elliott protests, 'Dad would believe me'.

more awkwardly, think of those scenes where characters tell each other things they must already know – for our benefit. For example, the first time we encounter Lydia and Gerry together, they helpfully tell us the history of their relationship while talking to one another!

Compared with watching *Sliding Doors*, we are much less dependent on dialogue information in *E.T.* One of the few scenes which is an exception to this is the second occasion on which the family are gathered around their dining table at night (Scene 5 – 15.40). Here we find out a number of pieces of information which add interest to characters or anticipate future dramatic action. We find out that Elliott's father has left home and gone 'to Mexico with Sally'. There is clearly the implication that without his dad, Elliott is a less supported, more lonely child. 'Dad would believe me.' We also learn that the family are getting ready for Halloween – this prepares us for a key scene of the film. Of less obvious significance at this point in the film is when Elliott says of the creature he has seen, 'They'll give it a lobotomy or do experiments on it or something.'

Other dialogue is of little significance in explaining more fully the events of the story – although it gives character detail and adds humour. An example of the first is the information that the sympathetic scientist himself has been waiting for an extra-terrestrial since the age of ten. An example of humour is Elliott's great line, 'How can you explain school to a higher being?' (scene 10) When Michael has to drive the getaway truck (scene 18), he says, 'I've never

In a very useful article in the periodical *Film Quarterly* (vol. 52 no. 3, Spring 99), Todd Berliner identifies five functions of dialogue in commercial Hollywood-style movies.
   Dialogue:

1. either advances the plot or supplies relevant information
2. moves in a direct line, often motivated by the need to establish the victory of one character over another

In addition:

3. characters communicate effectively
4. characters do not adjust what they say – they speak flawlessly
5. except when something is wrong – then a character starts slurring or stuttering or in some way becomes inarticulate

Berliner shows that film dialogue is conventional and pragmatic, rather than realistic. For example, in real life, people rarely speak so clearly or are so to the point!

▶ Find examples from *Sliding Doors* (in particular) and *E.T.* to illustrate each of these five points about dialogue. Also, consider how realistic or artificial you find the dialogue to be. ●

These scene references are mine – see pp. 28–9.

A few pages earlier I described the third act of E.T. (rather mischievously!) as "Death, Resurrection and Ascension". For what it is worth, Spielberg dismissed Christian interpretations of the film.

Compare this Christ story with that offered by The Matrix *– see Chapter 5*

Anthropologists and psychoanalysts have encouraged theories of storytelling which identify 'archetypal' patterns. In other words, templates of stories which exist in different cultures and over vast periods of human history. *E.T.* may unconsciously reflect other stories from other cultures and other times. What do you think?

▶ If you feel strongly that a film means something unintended by the film's makers, are you wrong? In other words, who has power in determining meaning? *This is a* very *important question!* ●

driven forward.' But this itself is only funny because it has been anticipated visually earlier in the film when he clumsily backs the family station wagon down the drive (scene 7). Perhaps the best example of this interplay between verbal information and the visual is when Elliott tells us, 'Grown-ups can't see him.' (scene 7). His mother then shows how true this is as E.T. hides in toy cupboards and most comically walks around the kitchen (scene 11), the mother slamming the refrigerator door in his face at one point, with Gertie saying, 'I think you've killed him.'

Perhaps one place where dialogue does serve a different and potentially important purpose is in offering the audience a way of 'reading' the film. Elliott cuts his finger (scene 12) and it is made better by E.T.'s finger beam. In the next bedroom, we hear Elliott's mother reading to his kid sister: 'She thinks she'll get well again if she believes in fairies.' Getting well from a mysterious illness – and needing to 'believe' – captures, of course, the central drama of the film. (Just as, in a comic vein, Gerry's comment to Helen about catching or missing trains – You don't want to go wondering things like that you know … em … if only this and what if that, you know – alarming …' acknowledges the central dramatic premise of *Sliding Doors*.)

By contrast, some 'readings' have no basis in the dialogue. A reading of *E.T.* which sees a direct parallel with the story of Jesus Christ is one we may choose to impose from our creativity as members of the audience – and meaning makers. His coming down to Earth, his message of love and gentleness, his temptation, his death, resurrection and ascension back to where he came from can be 'activated' by us if we choose and become an interpretation of the film. There is nothing in the dialogue, however, that specifically directs us to do so. This kind of 'reading' derives purely from what we see as the story unfolds and the extent to which we may want to project this Christ story onto it.

2.4 *E.T.* and the visual story: *mise en scène*

Visual storytelling was the essence of cinema before the coming of the 'talkies' at the end of the 1920s. Audiences made meaning from the images they were given.

Much has been written about the experience of silent cinema for audiences. One view is that the silent film audience was more free to make the story their own. The powerful images, the accompanying music (silent cinema was not in fact silent) and the relatively few intertitles meant that audiences 'filled in' detail from their own imaginations – and this contributed to both a more 'open' space for the spectator's imagination to move within and a more intense personal response.

Melissa Mathison, the screenwriter (and associate producer), and Spielberg tell *E.T.* as a story through moving images – with what little dialogue there is working primarily as reinforcement of visual information. The story unfolds using the two principle forms of cinematic expression – *mise en scène* and editing. In this section, and with reference to *E.T.*, I wish to concentrate on the first of these.

Mise en scène is the term used to describe everything that is in the frame – all the detail that makes up the image. Essentially, it is what we see. *Mise en scène* is the result of the work of a combination of people, including art director, set designer and costume designer. *Mise en scène* includes both the vastness of a studio set and a tiny prop crucial to the plot development. It includes lavish costumes and subtle make-up.

At one remove, *mise en scène* also necessarily involves the work of the cinematographer, who lights and photographs the *mise en scène*. The kind of shot (angle, distance, focus) will affect what and how we see, as will any distinctive 'look' which is created through lighting. (Cinematography has famously been described as 'painting in light'.) For example, a characteristic of many sequences in *E.T.* is a mistiness in the *mise en scène* – even indoors. This is enhanced by rear lighting – from back windows, from inside doorways, even from the family refrigerator. Why do you think the director and cinematographer went for this kind of look?

Perhaps the most taken-for-granted aspect of *mise en scène* is the actors. Actors contribute very significantly to *mise en scène*. They convey meaning through their physical appearance and through their movement, as well as through the words they speak. Some actors convey meanings that come from their familiarity in a particular kind of role. Beyond this, some actors – stars – convey meanings that derive from the off-screen knowledge the audience has about them.

Although we are going to look at editing in the next section, it is impossible not to refer to its importance here.

▶ Are we more actively involved in a film in which we have to get information from the visuals – rather than from the soundtrack? For example, is *E.T.* a more 'active' experience for the audience because relatively little story information is conveyed through speech compared even with *Sliding Doors*? ●

Let us anticipate here some of the work we will be doing on character in the next chapter.

▶ Consider *Sliding Doors*: what information do we learn about characters such as James, Gerry, Lydia, Anna and Russell from the way they dress? How much different is Helen 2 after her 'makeover' halfway through the movie? ●

▶ Are there sequences in *Sliding Doors* where set design provides us with character information? ●

▶ Thinking about locations, three (possibly) trivial questions:
• Why do you think Helen and James went to an American-style diner?
• Why is the Albert Bridge over the River Thames used, and used several times?
• Why do you think the hospital chosen at the end was such a modern-looking one? ●

▶ Consider the physical appearances of the actors who play James, Gerry, Lydia, Anna and Russell in *Sliding Doors*. How important is casting? ●

▶ Does our recognition of Gwyneth Paltrow in *Sliding Doors* add additional levels of meaning? Imagine other stars in the role of Helen. In each case, how might the character change? ●

▶ *E.T.* does not use movie stars. Besides keeping the film's budget lower, what may be gained from not casting stars?

A pan is a camera movement.

There is more on cinematography in Chapter 4.

Our attention is most often drawn to what is significant in the *mise en scène* by director, set designer and cinematographer. One question you must ask yourself as someone making meaning from the study of *mise en scène* is how far to go in identifying significance. For example, is one of these two features (that is, truncated shots of human bodies and camera panning) more significant and important to interrogate than the other? How do you decide?

Editing combines the images of the *mise en scène*, thus determining the order and frequency with which we see them. Editing exploits the natural tendency of the human brain to 'make sense'. We see a set of images in an edited sequence and we immediately, automatically, set to work, making meaning out of them by establishing links and connections. (This becomes as automatic and 'natural' to us as making moving images out of twenty-four still photographs passing in front of our eyes every second!)

If we consider the first sequence from *E.T.*, we gain some sense of the effectiveness of cinema as a visual storytelling medium. Nearly seventy separate edits occur (at an average rate of one every five-and-a-half seconds). From the first shot of Scene 1 (of the night sky with a vertical pan down to a forest) to the first shot of Scene 2 (the driveway of the family home) takes just less than six and a half minutes.

Editing, along with cinematography, is the main means by which suspense is created, especially from the point in the sequence when the 'hunters' of E.T. arrive in a swirl of headlamps and torches. Watch this sequence of the film, pausing briefly between shots to consider how story information is communicated. In addition, consider how cinematography and set design are able to signify mood throughout the sequence.

The more we study *mise en scène*, the more we begin to identify intriguing details. Here, for example, are a couple of odd features from this opening sequence. We only see humans represented by parts of their bodies – their feet, or their arms and hands, or their waists – Why? And does this happen elsewhere in the movie? A lot of the shots involve pans. Have you noticed that after the first vertical pan referred to above, every camera movement in this scene goes in the same direction, from right to left – can you think of a possible reason for this?

Before looking at another scene in detail, let us consider how *mise en scène* 'patterns' the story, helps to give it some shape. In general, *mise en scène* does this by containing images that recur during the movie, encouraging the audience to see a kind of 'weave', the repetitions becoming a **motif**. For example, E.T. is repeatedly associated with soft toys or with fancy-dress disguises or pumpkin heads. (Why do you think this is?)

Sometimes recurring features in the *mise en scène* encourage the audience to think about a meaning running through this pattern of repetition and variation. For example, several times a red light is prominent in the design of the *mise en scène*. (What does it mean?) Sometimes an image serves to anticipate a future event – as when the famous first BMX 'flight' across the face of the moon prepares us for the victorious conclusion to the chase sequence near the end.

E.T. – The Extraterrestrial: the BMX flight across the moon, anticipates the escape flight at the end of the film.

Of course, it may be that 'meaning' is not so simple as 'This equals that'. If we take the pot of flowers that is introduced in Scene 9, then it is pretty clear that this object within the *mise en scène* communicates story information purely visually. It tells us that E.T. has the power to revitalise nature. It also serves as an indicator of E.T.'s health. But why a pot of flowers to do this rather than some other object?

If we work on the basis that nothing in the *mise en scène* that we notice should ever be regarded as 'meaningless', let us look at a specific composition in sequence 12 (approx. 55.05). Gertie's mum is telling her the fairy story. There is a sunflower-shaped single light in the top left of the frame, as well as the normal bedside lamp on the right of the frame. Why?

Or let us take a more substantial but linked example from Scene 7 (approx. 33.20). The three children look towards the camera in what represents E.T.'s point of view from the toy cupboard in Elliott's bedroom. Behind them and very prominent both as a design feature and as a light source is a flower-shaped window. It shines down from behind the children and takes on the quality, like the sunflower in Scene 12, not just of a flower, but also of a star. Here the *mise en scène* offers an image for the audience that does not provide additional story information, but it does enrich the sequence. How?

▶ In some ways, important aspects of a film's meaning can be captured in single images. Select three images from the film, using a video pause control, which in your view communicate a lot about the film's story and mood. Talk about each of them in as much detail as you can. ●

What quickly becomes clear is that in working with *mise en scène*, we work with **'signs'**. A single frame, like a photograph, is a complex meaning system in which each detail signifies (sign-ifies). Shot composition will tend to draw our eyes to particularly significant (sign-ificant) details for our understanding of the story. An image of a flower communicates to us at one level quite simply. It is what it is, a physical object we know from our own experience of everyday living. But the flower considered as a sign may have other meanings – as in E.T. when it becomes an indicator of E.T.'s power and health. Even then, these are meanings we can collectively share as an

The science of signs – semiotics – is important for the study of all forms of human communication, including film. We will build up some understanding of signs as 'signifiers' of meaning over the next three chapters. We will consider not just visual signs, but also aural signs – speech, music, noise.

The great value of semiotics is that it draws attention to our active role in making meaning. We have an instinctive need to relate the signifier (the image/word/sound) to a signified (a mental concept).

Beyond this we recognise that a signifier works at more than one level of signification. Take the example of the flower in E.T.

Signifier – image of flower

Signified (first-level meaning/denotation) – botanical object

Signified (second-level meaning/connotation) – indicator of E.T.'s health or symbol of natural beauty opposed to a certain kind of ugly science.

Whereas the first-level meaning (the denotative meaning) will be agreed by everyone, the second-level meaning (the connotative meaning) is more open, dependent on our imaginations, our mental associations.

▶ Return to the three images you selected and begin to think in terms of signifier/signified and in terms of first-level meaning/second-level meaning. ●

For more on semiotics, see p. 48, as well as Chapter 3, pp. 65–8 and Chapter 4, pp. 103–4.

▶ Like so much in films, we can take shot composition for granted. Consider what is gained by the simple decision to place Mike in front of the television monitor where we can see his brother. ●

▶ Did you notice this kind of 'layering' of visual information between foreground, middle distance and background in the three images you were looking at a little while ago? ●

audience. But what of the colour of the flower – yellow or red is itself a sign, perhaps with a varying significance for different people.

In contrast with these 'flower' examples, Let us look finally at what was identified as the beginning of the 'Act Three' (74.15). Here, the *mise en scène* does contribute direct story information. The machinery of the scientific and governmental establishment has caught up with E.T. The first we see is the emergence over the brow of a hill at sunset of an army of scientists. The shot is sinister, frightening, coming immediately after the invasion of the family home by men in spacesuits. We then see E.T. alone, lying on the kitchen floor. His position conveys helplessness, intensified by his repetition of the word 'home' to the spacesuited figure who says nothing – we hear only the awful sound of breathing apparatus. At this point, the sequence cuts back to the procession of scientists, now rolling out plastic coverings in front of them. The scene then cuts to night and acetylene torches being used to construct an entire camp around the family home. The welding equipment is harsh; so, too, are the red-and-blue flashing police car lights.

A very specific piece of story information follows. We see the middle part of the body of what we assume is a scientist putting on an anti-contamination suit. The shot dwells on his keys. We realise this person has been after E.T. since the first sequence of the film.

There follows a number of interior shots, rubber gloves, suits, apparatus, all reinforcing the inhuman qualities of this 'operation'. Gertie and Mike are questioned. The latter is positioned so that we can see his brother behind him on a television monitor, stretched out on a bed. There is a very interesting piece of dialogue at this point. It is one of the few places where dialogue reinforces or 'anchors' our reading of visual information:

MIKE: *It communicates through Elliott.*
SCIENTIST: *Elliott thinks its thoughts.*
MIKE: *No, Elliott feels its feelings.*

The contrast between cold, scientific thinking and the warmth of feeling represented by E.T. is clear. So what we have here is an extended example of *mise en scène* communicating not just story information, but also ideas – a theme running through the film about 'good' science and 'bad' science. 'Good' science is improvisational (such as E.T.'s DIY construction of his interstellar communication system). 'Good' science is full of wonder (like E.T. putting balls in the air to show the children his home.) Feeling is privileged over thought. It is possible, of course, to argue with this and say the film is simple-minded in promoting a charming, miraculous kind of fairy-tale science! The point to emphasise here, however, is the power of *mise en scène* in communicating (signifying) information, ideas and feelings.

2.5 *Sliding Doors* and the visual story: editing

While emphasising *mise en scène* in *E.T.*, it is important to recognise that editing is just as important. Indeed, editing is important in any film made up of more than one shot! Editing works for the film as a whole (what we will call the **'macro' functions**), joining together the main sequences of the film into the overall narrative. Editing also works within the sequence (what we will call the **'micro' functions**), controlling spatial relations, managing the passing of time and, more generally, linking and contrasting shots in order to affect the audience in some way. An excellent example of the use of editing in driving the story forwards while also creating suspense and generating ideas ('meanings') for the audience is what I have identified as sequence 10 of *E.T.*, 'The Symbiosis Scene' – beginning 39.19 (see overleaf). Looking closely at a sequence such as this one, we begin to appreciate how flexible is the language of film as a storytelling medium and, in particular, how editing is central to this language.

In moving back to *Sliding Doors*, we encounter a story that could only be told through editing. Its basic idea is conceived and realised because editing as a film-making tool exists. (Is editing the very basis of the medium of cinema?)

If we go back to the earlier examination of the overall narrative structure of *Sliding Doors*, the plot summary (pp. 30–1) of Helen 1's story takes a simple linear form. If this story was all we had, we might talk about the editing as providing basic continuity. **Continuity editing** is actually a particular kind of editing which is designed to create a 'flow' of images which appears so natural and obvious that the editing itself is described as 'seamless' and even as 'invisible'. If we look at a short sequence, such as the attempted mugging,

▶ What is achieved in this sequence through crosscutting? ●

▶ In this sequence, how does editing and specifically crosscutting create drama and comedy, and develop key ideas? ●

▶ How active must you be as a spectator to make meaning from this sequence of shots? ●

▶ What examples of intertextuality can you find in this sequence? (See p. 5) ●

E.T. (39 min. 19 sec.)
SCENE 10 – SYMBIOSIS SCENE – ELLIOTT, ET AND THE FROGS

39.19 Home: exterior overhead long shot: leaving for school: *'How do you explain school to a higher being?'* (left-to-right pan)

39.34 Walking towards school. Conversation with friends: *'Where's your goblin; he's a spaceman.'* *'Uranus'* quip.

40.10 On bus throwing paper.

40.20 Home, Gertie does not want to leave: mother suspicious, goes back upstairs, but cannot see E.T. among dolls.

41.10 Classroom – the back of the teacher – ET doodles 'E.T.'. Girl looking.

41.37 Home. E.T. leaves cupboard – dog.

42.05 Classroom: Teacher preparing class for dissection – the scalpel very sharp – little blood.

42.20 Home: Into refrigerator. Dog anticipates – potato salad.

43.00 Classroom – Elliott burps.

43.15 Home: E.T. walks into wall.

43.23 Classroom: Elliott tries to keep eyes open – teacher saying that the frog's heart will still beat.

43.32 Home. E.T. walks into another kitchen cupboard.

43.35 Classroom. Elliott drifting off.

43.40 Home. E.T. collapses.

43.43 Classroom. Elliott slides under desk.

43.47 Home. Can opens.

43.49 Classroom. Elliott revitalised.

43.53 Home. E.T. drinking.

43.58 Classroom. Elliott looks to blonde girl – she turns away.

44.02 Home: E.T. on child's spelling computer – *Tom & Jerry*/flying saucer

44.29 Classroom: Teacher hands out chloroform – again only torso of male adult. Elliott looks at frog and says 'Hi!'

45.24 Home: E.T. hand on table – sci-fi comic strip 'help, help' Sesame Street – telephone

46.29 Classroom: Elliott says, *'Save him.'* – *'Run for your life, run for the river.'* (SERIES OF SHOTS as Elliott upturns all the jars.)

47.03 Home: E.T. with the electric circuit of a toy computer – John Ford's film *The Quiet Man* on television.

47.25 Classroom: Frogs around the feet of plain girl with ponytail.

47.31 Home: Television – Maureen O'Hara in *The Quiet Man*.

47.34 Classroom: The other blonde girl on chair as frogs play about her feet.

47.37 Home: *The Quiet Man* – John Wayne chases O'Hara and pulls her back.

47.41 Classroom: Elliott reaches out to girl.

47.42 Home: *The Quiet Man* – Wayne pulls back.

47.45 Classroom: Elliott pulls back.

47.48 Home: *The Quiet Man* – Wayne pulls close.

47.49 Classroom: Elliott pulls close.

47.50 Home: *The Quiet Man* – Wayne kisses – E.T. reaction shot.

47.55 Classroom: Elliott kisses girl.

47.59 Home: E.T. reaction.

48.03 Classroom: Elliott pulled away.

48.04 Classroom: Hands of other pupils throwing frogs out of window.

48.10 School, floor-level shot: Feet of girl – no fear as frogs jump around. Elliott is led away.

a series of shots are joined together to give the impression of continuous action in a given physical space. However, in this particular example (and throughout *Sliding Doors* – which is untypical as a commercial narrative realist film), the editing is drawn to our attention and therefore becomes 'visible'. Interspersed throughout this mugging sequence are three shots of Helen 2 with James on the tube (including a traveller listening to a band called 'Elastic Thrombosis'). Once we have this kind of crosscutting between two physical locations and two different sets of characters, the audience becomes much more conscious of editing as an active component in the storytelling.

Another kind of editing which draws attention to itself can be found in the very first sequence of *Sliding Doors*. Here we have a **montage** of sixteen shots (each held for an average of 5 seconds). After two establishing shots which tell the audience we are in London, we see Helen rapidly move from flat to lift to tube station to sandwich bar to off-licence to public relations company. An edit will often abbreviate time – creating an *ellipsis*. (So, for example, Helen goes down the stairs of her home and in the next shot she is coming out of a lift). An edit will often change the physical space (again, as in the example just given). However, when this happens ten or more times in quick succession, we are much more obviously aware of the editing mechanism.

In fact, an audience accepts editing not because it is 'invisible' – it obviously is not – but because it is the accepted basis of film's communication system. The conventions of editing can be thought of rather like the conventions that make writing possible. We shift from sentence to sentence, from paragraph to paragraph, simply because we have learnt from education and experience to do so. Similarly, we are not fazed by a cut which takes us to a different viewing position within a scene or may take us to a different time or to a different physical space.

Before looking at editing at the service of narrative structure (what was referred to above as 'macro' editing), Let us look at examples of ordinary editing procedures within a particular sequence (the 'micro' level). The very simplest sequences in the film are those between Gerry and his friend Russell at a pub – there are four of them in total, all belonging to the Helen 1 narrative.

It is important to note the 'rule' on which the shooting of scenes such as this are based. In the first shot, we establish that Russell is on the left, Gerry on the right. If we imagine that we are looking down from overhead and draw a circle around them, it is possible to put the camera anywhere in the semicircle in front of them, but nowhere in the semicircle behind them. If we put the camera anywhere in the back semicircle, Gerry would appear on the left and Russell on the right. In classical continuity editing, this is thought to disorientate the audience. This is called the 180° rule. It works to ensure that editing produces not just continuity in time, but coherence in physical space.

▶ **How important is the 180° rule?**
Some non-Hollywood cinema, such as classical Japanese cinema, developed a film 'language' that moved right around the 360° 'circle' confident that this would cause no difficulty for the spectators in getting their bearings within the physical space of the action.

Shot/reverse-shot editing may be used to exemplify the argument that many of the basic features of film form/film language work so well because they duplicate our normal mental activity.
▶ What do you think of this idea that film form conforms to our everyday mental processing of experience? ●

'Interpolate' means to insert something into a text. It implies malpractice, even cheating. 'Interpellation' is a rarely used word, usually meaning an interruption. Strictly speaking it would seem that the word 'interpolate' is the more accurate in capturing the idea of the film spectator drawn into the imaginary space of the film's drama. Film studies prefers 'interpellate' which has an obsolete meaning — to summons. The idea is that the spectator is summoned into a viewing position which it is impossible to resist. Another film studies word used alongside interpellate

---

The first is in Sequence 6 (18 min. 18 secs), and is cut into the Bertorelli's bar episodes (where both Helens go to drink). There are just three shots:

1. Side-on two-person shot with Russell on the left and Gerry on the right. This is the establishing shot and is used just once at the beginning.

2. Over Gerry's shoulder looking at Russell.

3. Reverse of this – but closer to Gerry without Russell's shoulder in view.

Shot 2 and Shot 3 alternate; each is used eleven times. (Why, incidentally, is shot 3 a one-person shot with a relatively closer view of Gerry than shot 2 gives us of Russell?). The cuts between Shot 2 and Shot 3 are motivated by lines of dialogue. In other words, the edit involves cutting to the listener a split second before he replies. Generally, in this shot/reverse-shot routine we are given a shot of the speaker, rather than the listener – although this is not always the case. This rapid shifting is something we take for granted as the most common, conventional way in which dialogue sequences are filmed, both on film and television. The twenty-three edits are not invisible, but they do not intrude on our watching; indeed, they enable us to follow the conversation intently.

Consider how important are the routines of editing of dialogue cues in drawing the audience into the drama. This is, after all one of the most fundamental differences between the theatre and film. In the theatre, we are in one fixed position, perhaps some distance away from the actors. In film, we have a much closer and consequently more intimate kind of engagement. We are **interpellated** into the fictional world, sometimes positioned it seems in the space between characters, sometimes swinging from one character's point-of-view to another's.

A slightly more complicated but just as routine example is when Helen 2 and James are on a boat with the Albert Bridge illuminated behind them (In Sequence 9, 47 min. 41 secs). Although this scene lasts nearly four minutes, there are only seven different shots, three of which are used only once and one only twice; however, one is used five times, one eighteen times and one nineteen times.

The scene begins with a shot of the moon (shot 1). There is a cut to a long shot of a boat in which are James and Helen

2, with the Albert Bridge behind the boat (shot 2). This then moves to a slightly closer (medium shot) of James and Helen 2 (shot 3) and then to a slightly closer shot still (a medium close shot) (shot 4). This, in turn, shifts to a medium close-up of James (shot 5) and then a medium close-up of Helen 2 (shot 6). These two shots are used alternately, as in the example of Gerry and Russell in the pub. Interspersed into this are four medium two-person shots (shot 4) and one longer two-person shot (shot 3). At the very end, there is a close two-person shot as they kiss (shot 8)

Editing has a number of functions. The examples we have just looked at confirm two of these:

- to create within a scene the 'reality effect' of continuous time and coherent physical space;

- to draw in the spectator through the interplay of separate shots.

In addition to these, there are two other major functions of editing which may operate within or between scenes (which we have already identified in the *E.T.* frog dissection scene):

- to create potential meaning through linking two shots – encouraging the audience to make mental connections; and

- to create drama, particularly suspense, through providing or withholding information.

And then, of course, editing at the macro level is the cement that holds together the bricks of the structure as a whole.

Let us look at Sequence 10 of *Sliding Doors* (beginning at 51 min. 38 secs.). This is immediately after Helen 2's romantic river scene and what she describes as her 'big lapse of concentration' when she goes to bed with James.

The sequence begins with a dramatic contrast made up of three shots:

1. Helen 1 in the sandwich bar doing her daytime job
2. Lydia's sports car outside the house prompting Gerry to comment that if she wanted to be any more obvious she would advertise in *Adulterer's Weekly*
3. Helen 1 delivering sandwiches

What does the editing achieve here?

---

is the French word 'suture' – to stitch. The spectator is stitched into the film text – the 'weave' (see p. ix).

▶ How is continuity of time maintained across the shots? ●
▶ How is coherence of space maintained? ●
▶ How does the editing contribute to audience involvement? ●
▶ Taking the same eight shots, might you have edited them differently? ●

We then have three contrasting locations:

4. Exterior of the Grove House Hotel (Gerry and Lydia's destination)
5. Exterior of Clive's Bar and Restaurant (Helen 2 has organised the opening event)
6. Interior of Bertorelli's (where Helen 1 is doing her evening job)

What does the editing do here?

Starting with the last shot referred to (shot 6), there is a 3 minute 27 second sequence which crosscuts between Bertorelli's and Clive's – that is, between the experiences of Helen 1 and Helen 2. The dramatic event that marks Helen 2's evening is the unexpected arrival of Gerry. (How small a world is the London of this film!) Having talked to him, Helen 2 feels quite faint. A very rapid crosscutting involving fifteen shots links Helen 2 with Helen 1. In Bertorelli's, Helen 1 nearly falls in a faint. The crosscutting continues with Helen 1 walking left out of the frame in one shot and Helen 2 walking right out of the frame in the next. This is repeated until Helen 2 has rejoined the party and Helen 1 is in the restaurant kitchen trying to phone Gerry. This kind of crosscutting is common throughout *Sliding Doors*. What is achieved by telling the story using this kind of editing?

Finally, if we include the last shot of Helen 1 in the restaurant kitchen trying to phone and the empty hotel room that follows it, there is further parallelism created. The film cuts to Helen 2 telling Anna that James is away. There is then a shot of James in a hotel room nearly – but not quite – making a phone call (we assume to Helen 2). This is followed by a daytime scene at the Grove House Hotel where Gerry and Lydia are staying – a scene in which Gerry has to ring off because of the noise Lydia is making before Helen 1 can tell him that she is pregnant.

Looking at this sequence as a whole, we can see how editing creates both specific dramatic effects – specific meanings – and, more generally, pushes forward the narrative. In fact, editing is the means by which the film develops in time and through different physical spaces from its beginning to its end.

Sliding Doors: The beginning and end of a major cross-cutting sequence in which both Helen 1, working as a waitress, and Helen 2, working on her first independent public relations project, almost faint. Note image 6 in which Helen 1 emerges out of Helen 2 in the fade from one shot into the next.

A common criticism of film, especially commercial, popular film, is that the audience is helpless – in a position of complete dependence on the narration – and therefore 'passive'.

You may ask why film – and television – is singled out for this criticism since we are just as helpless to intervene in listening to a piece of music or in reading a novel or in watching a performance of a play!

▶ Why do you think there has long been this particular prejudice against the viewing of the moving image as an activity requiring our intelligence, imagination and humanity? ●

▶ Can you think of other examples of this in *E.T.* and *Sliding Doors*? ●

2.6.a The film storyteller and the audience – *histoire*

In the previous sections, we have emphasised the work of film-makers. They work with *mise en scène* and editing to create meaning. And, more broadly, we have considered the story itself as a designed narrative structure, conceived and brought to the screen by the film's makers. As members of the audience, we are controlled, teased and (perhaps) satisfied by a narration that is presented to us already complete. Certainly we cannot actively intervene to change any component of a shot or any edited sequence, or the overall trajectory of the narrative. At the same time, the question keeps resurfacing about our active roles in making meaning. This section explores further the relationship between two different meaning makers – those who produce the film text and those who, as audience, 'activate' this text in consuming it.

One area that we have already touched upon is the choice between employing restricted and unrestricted narrative (see p. 22). The audience is clearly in a position of dependency in the access narration gives us to story information. In terms of audience engagement, it is perhaps useful to think of this as a game – a game in which the rules can be altered only by one side. This does not, however, mean that the other side surrenders into passivity – if they did, they would probably end up saying, 'We don't want to play.' The very opposite happens! The other side – the audience – becomes more alert, more quick-witted each time the goal posts are shifted. It is part of the fun of engaging with the film.

For example, in *Sliding Doors*, we have an apparently unrestricted view of James with a woman whom we quickly assume to be his wife (unrestricted at least in relation to Helen 2, who does not have access to this information as we do). We are tempted into the reasonable conclusion that James is a lying two-timer! In fact, our knowledge is restricted in that we only find out late in the narrative that they are separated and she has been around to support James in caring for his sick mother. This restriction of information within a fairly unrestricted narrative is an example of the constant shifting and manoeuvring that goes on between storyteller and audience.

Yes, we surrender to narration – but we do so willingly and for reasons other than because we want to spend two hours as cabbages! In the process of surrendering to 'it', we surrender to 'they' who are the source of the narration. But who are 'they'? Where does narration come from?

What or who is the source of film narration? In relation to commercial films, made to provide pleasure in return for financial profit, there are several answers to this:

- It comes from the creative individuals who write screenplays, produce, direct, design, shoot and edit.

    Creativity suggests personal expression and, in particular, we may look for the 'signature' of the director. These creative individuals may, however, be working in a calculated way to maximise profits on their film – their creativity is in satisfying an audience rather than in personal expression.

- It comes from a 'system', which in the case of both films studied in this chapter, can be described as rooted in a particular 'mode of production'.

    This is the standard professional practice of commercial film-making – as in other areas of human activity, there is a routine, accepted way of doing it. The product will bear the imprint of the standard 'professional practice' of cinema as a commercial and industrial institution.

- Drawing together the first two, we can talk about film story as deriving from conventions of storytelling which are convenient both for film-makers and the 'system' of production.

    These conventions are most often described in terms of genres. These provide 'templates' for storytelling (see p. 22–3).

- Most immediately, however, in the act of watching a film, the audience may feel that, with the absence of any personal voice, an 'I', the film in fact comes from nowhere. It simply is.

    Through its mode of telling, narrative realist film succeeds in hiding its source.

Let us revisit *E.T.* and *Sliding Doors* asking the question: where does it feel that the narration is coming from? The only obvious answer is 'from cinema'. Cinema as a medium of human communication, and more specifically here as a medium for storytelling, is the origin of the story. I remember when, aged five, I saw my first western at a cinema. Afterwards, I asked my dad to take me behind the screen to

Projected onto the screen is the illusion of presence. It is not surprising that, from the earliest attempts to theorise about the nature of the film medium, reference has been made to Plato's cave. I became a Platonist at the age of five when I discovered that the cowboys and Indians were mere projections, and that this world I had been in for the previous two hours was made up of tricks of light. The real world was somewhere else! 'Presence' is actually absence. (Yet again, consider the ideas in *The Matrix* and see also section 5.3 on pp. 143–7.)

On p. 38, the concepts signifier/signified were introduced. A signifier conjures up a mental image of something. The signified is the mental image. The 'real' thing, the referent of the signifier/signified is absent. For example, an image of an apple conjures up a mental concept 'apple' but any real apple is absent. This semiotic equivalent of Plato's cave – of mental images but physical absence – helps to justify descriptions of cinema as a 'dream' medium. I actually prefer the idea of cinema as a 'ghostly' medium. An image (signifier) may create the mental concept of Marilyn Monroe (signified) – but the real Marilyn Monroe is absent. Indeed the fact that the real Marilyn Monroe is dead precisely suggest to me this medium of ghosts!

▶ Is it easier to watch and respond to *E.T.* as simply 'there', as histoire, than it is with *Sliding Doors*? ●

What I mean here is that a discourse will operate, often it would appear 'naturally', to favour one position, one value system, over another. For example, much work has been done to demonstrate how the English language prioritises male 'he' and excludes female 'she' in everyday communication. Interestingly, similar work has been done to demonstrate that standard Hollywood-style film form prioritises the 'male look', the male way of seeing the world, over the female. (But this is for another book!)

see the horses, wagons and particularly the cowboys and Indians (I cannot remember what this film was). I was unable to acknowledge the nature of the medium: strips of film moving through a machine which projects them onto a screen at a speed which gives the illusion of realistic movement. I could not imagine that the source of the story was a projector.

As members of an audience, we are positioned between the apparatus of the projector behind us and the screen in front of us. In addition, in a modern auditorium, we will enjoy the effect of stereo sound. The size of the screen, the darkness, the sound – all work collectively to produce an irresistible 'presence'. And we are caught up right in the middle of it. Unless we are consciously looking out for, say, the characteristic features of a Spielberg movie, or are particularly interested in parallel editing, or are particularly drawn to observe how generic conventions are being used, we accept the film as simply 'there'. Narration appears as *histoire* – as an impersonal 'telling'.

Is this a bad thing? Well, a film narration is, like all other forms of narration, actually a **discourse**, the result of choices that both reflect and determine a clear set of messages and values. If we approach the viewing of a film as simply 'there', accept it as histoire, we are not acknowledging its identity as discourse.

2.6.b The film storyteller and the audience – discourse

Discourse is a complex and far-reaching concept which we have only touched upon superficially in Chapter 1 (see pp. 4–5). At its broadest, it refers to the way in which something is told not just in terms of its specific language (whether verbal or visual), but also in terms of what it prioritises. Discourses are both general and specific. So, narrative realist cinema is a discursive form, a particular kind of human expression which represents the world in a certain way, employs a particular kind of visual 'language'. Within narrative realist cinema as a whole, particular genres have their own more specific discourses. For example, the sci-fi film is preoccupied with themes of science and control; the romance is preoccupied with themes of sexuality, gender and often property relations. These ideas are either implicit – taken for granted within the way the story is conceived – or explicit in that the film actively promotes certain values, attitudes and beliefs.

In *E.T.*, the narration adopts certain 'positions'. Here are some of them:

- State-sponsored science is sinister and out of sympathy with the wonder of the universe.

- Schools perpetuate the kinds of values demonstrated by the scientific state – and liberation is needed from its practices.

- Mums do a good job in keeping things going domestically, but boys need fathers.

- Girls, especially sisters, are a nuisance or scream a lot; boys do things – such as expertly ride BMX bikes.

Making deductions from this, we may conclude that the narration derives from an anti-establishment, liberal, male source. The film may simply be 'there', but choices have been made which give a certain identity to the narration. It does not, of course, answer the question of where the narration comes from. (But it may give some clues!) What it does is confirm that story is a discursive activity and comes from somewhere rather than nowhere.

Similarly, in *Sliding Doors*, the narration adopts 'positions', principally on its main subjects, sexuality and relationships:

- Moral principles should inform a relationship – lying and cheating are bad, and you ultimately pay the consequences.

- Women who retain their sensitivity and vulnerability are likely to be hurt, but they are also likely to meet a sensitive (good) man eventually

- Women who do not retain their sensitivity and vulnerability are monsters.

- Women work and can be successful in what they do – but this falls away into insignificance if they do not have love.

- Fate/chance is significant in life.

This implies that the narration is rooted in a traditional set of moral attitudes. At the very least, we can begin to recognise a tension between these moral attitudes and the film's apparent endorsement of the idea of career woman.

It is useful to set out values contained in a film as binary opposites, such as for *E.T.*:

Miraculous science	Institutional science
Boys	Girls
Childhood	Adulthood
Family	State
'Free' education	School

This kind of binary analysis does not just open up the study of the film's messages and values. It also opens up an additional way of studying the 'deep' structure that underpins a story.

▶ See how far you can extend the above list, then do the same thing for *Sliding Doors*. ●

Claude Levi-Strauss, the French anthropologist, indirectly contributed much to the study of film narrative and genre. He argued that all societies tell stories to resolve imaginatively the contradictions at the heart of a society that in reality cannot be resolved. These can be presented as binary opposites. For example, in our society we are encouraged simultaneously to 'be free' and to be conformist citizens of the state. It is the central tension in many different genres – from the western to the melodrama. Storytellers work the 'borders' between these irreconcilable opposites, producing imaginative narratives that give the illusion that these opposites can be successfully negotiated.

Fundamentally, discourses contain (and reveal) the power relations existing in society, whether between men and women, rich and poor, white and black, powerful and powerless.

▶ When you go to the cinema, do you want to be challenged or reassured? ●

The concept of discourse is closely connected with another key concept, **hegemony**. Hegemony is the taken-for-granted 'common-sense' outlook on some aspect of human reality shared by the vast majority of people within a society. Hegemony helps us to understand the illusion that commonly shared attitudes and values, ways of making sense of our world, appear to come from nowhere.

If we take narrative realist cinema as a discourse, then that discourse determines a common-sense view of what a film is. One of these characteristics is that it disguises its discursiveness by pretending to be simply 'there'. As a result of being simply there, the discourses it takes up from the wider society – discourses about law and order and sexuality, for example – are themselves seen as non-discursive, as natural, as taken for granted. Like the films we have been discussing, these core values of society appear to come from nowhere – they simply are! This leads to a compounding of the criticism levelled against popular cinema (and other media) that not only does it disguise its own discursive form, but it also 'naturalises' these profoundly significant social and political discourses.

The set of assumptions around discourse and hegemony suggest that people ought to think critically about the constructed nature of reality and the value systems that fundamentally influence our lives. From a commercial perspective, however, the very opposite may appear to be the case. People do not want to think critically about their 'constructed' reality. They pay for entertainment, release from the concerns of their lives. They may well want the security of hegemonic values within familiar discourses.

Let us summarise. We need to add to the points made in part (a) of this section. Narration is never just 'there', however much it may give this impression.

• First, to go back to a very important point made at the beginning of this chapter, narration will always be the result of a process of selection and construction. As the sections on *mise en scène* and editing have shown, this selection and construction is complex, operating at the most minute levels of the film text.

• Secondly, narration is ideological as a consequence of the choices made – that is, it prefers certain values and beliefs, promotes a certain 'attitude' over others.

- Thirdly, narration is discourse, but disguises its discourse as history. In other words, it appears simply to 'be'.

So where does narration come from? It comes from *all* the possible sources listed in part (a) – the film-makers, the mode of production, generic conventions. And these, in turn, come out of and reflect broader values central to the culture in which they operate. These values often appear as so obvious that they hardly seem like values at all.

Narration is experienced by the audience who sit in the space between projector and screen. Again, we ask the question: is this a passive activity?

In part (a), the answer was a defiant 'no', based on the argument that moment-by-moment within a narrative film we are necessarily active meaning makers as we work to process the information provided. In light of the distinction between histoire and discourse, however, and in light of our discussion of hegemony, this now needs to be made more complex. We need to distinguish between our 'first-level' activity and our 'second-level' activity.

At a first level of engagement – in narrative events, the film's *histoire* – we actively work to make sense of what is going on. Our response to events will be an expression of our personalities and attitudes, while conscious that we are involved in the 'game' of film narration. It is the reason we go to the movies – it is a pleasurable interaction between ourselves and the film.

However, at a second level of engagement – in the film's messages and values, the film's discourse – we may or may not be 'active'. There are a number of possibilities:

1. We may identify the film's discourse and actively wrestle with it, thinking through points of agreement and disagreement.

2. We may identify the film's discourse and choose to be fairly relaxed about it, comfortable with a 'first-level' participation in the film's *histoire*.

3. We may fail to identify the discourse, it disappearing within the film's *histoire*.

It is the last of these possibilities that supports the ongoing argument that film-going can be dangerous for our ideological

The 'escapism' of popular film may often include the 'staging' of our anti-hegemonic desires and fantasies. We may enjoy a film with an apparently oppositional attitude to the state and its institutions. So many popular films are popular precisely because they adopt an 'attitude' towards school, the state or whatever that is critical – nearly always setting these institutions against individualism, personal freedom. (See the note above on Levi-Strauss, p. 49.)

It is debatable whether 'playing' with an alternative set of ideas is a genuinely challenging experience for the audience. It may be seen as just another form of temporary escapism, an opportunity to spend two hours with the pleasurable fantasy of being free, of rejecting the system. Afterwards we return to the unchanged actual world having 'played' with the fantasy – and, ironically, more refreshed to go on living within our actual world. In other words, we make do with a periodic simulation of 'breaking free'.

▶ Does a film such as *Thelma and Louise* work in this way? ●

▶ Do you think it is possible to make a distinction between a genuinely oppositional film and one that is just offering a fantasy of escape? For example, can *E.T.* be seen as an 'oppositional' film in any real sense? ●

▶ Reflect again on the films you selected at the beginning of this chapter. How did you respond to them at this 'second level of engagement'?

Do you feel that, in fact, point 3 here best expresses your position and that you now want to return to these films to reconsider issues of discourse and hegemony? ●

▶ Reflect again on what was said about cinema pleasure on p. 8. Does the discipline of film studies risk taking the pleasure out of movie-going? ●

Having nearly got to the end of this chapter, you are strongly recommended to read Robert McKee's *Story* (New York, Harper Collins, 1997). This recommendation comes not because this book is the last word in film story construction (although it is written in a style that suggests that it is!). It is well worth reading because it will sharpen your awareness of the pragmatics of commercial storytelling. Its frightening assertiveness captures the 'voice' of the hard-headed script department at a studio.

health! The point I want to make here is that it has less to do with questions of active/passive spectating. It has to do either with the choices we make (as in points 1 and 2) or the level of competence – education – we bring to the screening event (as in point 3).

2.7. From response to evaluation

This last point about our level of competence as spectators is clearly important when we consider questions of evaluation. We may go on the rollercoaster ride offered by the narrative without any conscious sense of what makes the roller coaster work – the ways in which the 'thrills' are carefully manipulated. This is a raw experience. As we become more knowledgeable about film, the techniques used in constructing story through plot and in constructing individual sequences to achieve certain effects become more visible to us. We may enjoy the film more (or less) as a result. What we identify in the structure, the mechanism of the story, may strike us as smart and effective, or heavy-handed and clichéd.

Also, at the level of the narrative as a whole, we may ask whether the central problems, which are the engine room of the story and of our involvement, are presented and resolved satisfactorily. These problems are nearly always based on some kind of 'no-win' paradox. The central problem of *E.T.* is the escape story that is the focus for a friendship. The paradoxical problem is a common one in escape movies. The escapee needs a friend to help; if the friend helps him to escape, he loses the friend. The central problem of *Sliding Doors* is the identification and pursuit of true, as opposed to false, love. The paradox of the film is that the lover needs chance to be on her side, but if she depends on chance she can never be sure whether what she has found is right.

Does the film gain and satisfy our interest through the skilful telling of its story, through the presentation of an engaging central paradox? Does the simple linear structure of *E.T.* with its often weak causality strengthen or weaken the film's impact for you – and why? Does the complexity of *Sliding Doors*, the parallelism, the dependence on chance (lots of chance!) satisfy your appetite for a story which not only holds your interest, but also stimulates you? Or do you find the basic idea of *Sliding Doors* silly and the way it is pursued ridiculous? Or something in between?

Beyond our response to the structure and mechanisms of film story, we can ask other, much broader questions – such as was the story worth telling? What does it offer which the audience can take away as a 'gain' in their lives? For example, does it allow the audience to reflect on some aspect of human experience in an interesting way? Does the film story inspire through the qualities revealed by its characters and the message contained in its resolution? Does the film prompt an escape to a more imaginative level of experience? Is it enough to say that the film allowed a pleasant two hours to pass in which our minds are distracted from all the things that normally preoccupy us?

Rooted in a commercial aesthetic (see p. 24), film producers and distributors may well tell us that a 'good' film story is one that satisfies the demands (the desires) of a very large, general audience. Since both the films we have been looking at in this chapter were conceived as 'commercial' products, it seems most appropriate that we measure them in these terms. This seems further reinforced by the fact that the vast majority of an audience will respond fairly uniformly to a film – in terms of laughing in the same places and gasping with horror in the same places – telling us much about the shared experience of film communication.

This shared, communal activity should not, however, disguise the fact that lots of private narratives are going on, each fascinating – and only partly controllable by the film text. Each of us enters the space provided by the narration as individuals. We respond sometimes in predictable, fairly uniform and regulated ways to stimulus material in the film carefully calculated by the film's makers. We also respond to stimulus we find in the film that is quite outside the 'management' of the film text. As individuals, we will always make personal the film experience.

This is where relatively more objective criteria concerning a well-crafted film story begin to merge with rather more subjective criteria relating to what you or I specifically – as distinct (even unique!) human beings – might be looking for when we go to the movies.

You may find the story of a ten-year-old boy living in small town in California and befriending an extra-terrestrial enchanting and moving because the story has triggered a set of memories about childhood or fantasies about the

Critics of popular culture would certainly be uncomfortable about regarding escapism as a positive quality.

▶ The crudest form of consumer criticism is counting box-office income. A film is (obviously!) a good film the more money it makes.

Is this a reasonable position to take? ●

Scene from *E.T. – The Extraterrestrial*: preparing to phone home – how do we respond to this fantasy and why?

miraculous. You may find the story of a young professional woman cheated on by her partner as really painful for reasons far in excess of the qualities to be located in the screenplay or the acting or the editing. You may find her recovery (twice!) as inspirational far in excess of what the story offers. In all these examples, your response will be in relation to all kinds of personal factors – with the film operating primarily as a stimulus for your own imaginative 'work'.

For example, what particular reasons do you have for liking/disliking the frog liberation sequence in *E.T.*? What particular reasons do you have for liking/disliking the fainting sequence in *Sliding Doors*? Your own personality must colour your response. You may hate the idea of dissection (and school) and take great pleasure in the frogs' anarchic escape. On the other hand, you may be the kind of person who takes a delight in cutting up frogs and may be disappointed! You may enjoy the complications to the story that develop in the *Sliding Doors* fainting sequence and delight in having to guess even further in what direction Helen's life (lives) is going.

This leads us to a sense of the film's 'attitude' and takes us back to issues raised in the previous section about the film's discourse. This will usually be cumulative, our gut response to a range of details across the film as a whole. Do we like these films for what we perceive as sympathetic attitudes towards values that we hold ourselves? Do we dislike these films because their messages and values work against our own? The point of focus for such questions is often the ending – how the film resolves the problems, 'closes' the issues it has raised. This is the moment when we may feel most helpless as an audience; yet also the moment of maximum critical alertness. We know what we want. We know we are going to be upset if we do not get it.

At all levels at which we 'work' with a film, we must be as rigorously honest with ourselves. What did I really think, feel at this particular point? Attempting to ask why may teach you a lot about yourself as well as about film.

So when is a film story a good story? We need to determine criteria for answering this question. A story may be considered excellent by one set of criteria (for example, its plotting and the use of narrative devices) and lousy by another (for example, its messages and values). When our own personal appropriation of the film is taken into account – that is, when we make the film our own in responding to it – evaluation becomes a very difficult thing to unravel. We may find ourselves in the embarrassing position of liking a film that is not at all skilfully made; or of disliking a film which is universally admired. Can you think of examples of each?

Often we find ourselves working very hard on behalf of the film. We hate to be bored, hate to feel that our investment in the cinema ticket or the video rental has been a waste of money. The film as a 'text' should be just the starting point for an evaluation of the film as an 'experience' in which a whole range of social, cultural and personal factors have to be taken into account.

► Consider your personal response to these two moments from the endings of the films:

In *E.T.*, the group of boys is being chased by the police. They come to a road block. What options do they have left? None it would seem. They will be apprehended; E.T. will be put back under the clinical control of the scientists. And then they fly. The boys on their BMXs fly off into the sky, landing at a miraculous rendezvous point with E.T.'s rescue spaceship.

In *Sliding Doors*, Helen leaves her (private?) hospital room, recovered from her fall. In the lift, she drops her earrings (again) and a stranger we know as James (again) picks them up.

► At the end of these films, do you feel pleasure, delight? Do you feel satisfied as a spectator? ●

► Overall, what are the strengths and weaknesses of *E.T.* as a film story? ●

► Overall, what are the strengths and weaknesses of *Sliding Doors* as a film story? ●

Further issues of film evaluation are discussed in section 3.9 (pp. 92–4).

3. Character

This chapter introduces a number of approaches to character study in film, including an emphasis on performance. *The visual is again emphasised in relation to detailed discussion of **Secrets and Lies** (United Kingdom, 1996) and **Once Were Warriors** (New Zealand, 1994), as well as further exploration of* dialogue. *The intimacy of our contact with screen characters is considered in relation to* voyeurism, *and this extends to a study of the relationship between our* alignment *through the film text with characters and our* allegiance *to those characters. Characters are considered as offering opportunities for our* imaginative 'play' *and this extends to a comparison of* 'realist' *and* 'psychological' *approaches in exploring response. Characters are seen as ideologically significant, with discussion centring on the* messages *and values* they convey. *In the final part, issues of* evaluation *are related to questions of audience* competence.

3.1 Characters – what are they?

Character is central to story – as we have seen in the previous chapter. Stories of all kinds – including film stories – are about the lives of characters, usually of the human variety; characters move the story forwards through their actions; and characters provide perhaps the principal focus for our involvement as 'active' spectators.

It is useful to begin by distinguishing between character and **characterisation**. The latter is a 'list' of features that make up the person, some of which will be exploited more

Sliding Doors is apparently based on 'blind chance'. In fact, many of the key developments in the stories of both Helen 1 and Helen 2 are related to how her/their character responds to circumstances. Perhaps there is some middle ground here: we are constantly the victims of blind chance, but how we respond to this 'chance' will be determined by our character.

▶ What do you think? ●

▶ Think of a film which deals with a central character whose actions are bad, illegal or perhaps immoral (such as someone who murders), but with whom we sympathise with in relation to our understanding and empathy with their past.

     On balance, how far does knowledge of their past influence our response to their later actions? ●

▶ Think about a favourite film:
Do the central characters generate the action?
Do the central characters change or remain the same?
Do we learn more about them as the film proceeds?
Are there things we learn about them which help explain why they do what they do? ●

than others in the development of a story. Those which are emphasised – the person's greed or generosity, cowardice or bravery – will be the characteristics that define 'character' for the audience. This is because these key characteristics will be the one's that determine what a character *does* in a particular situation. Ultimately, **character** in the movies is always about what people do – or fail to do. So, character is intimately related to action, to causality, especially in popular cinema.

In western literature, there is a strong emphasis on the idea that 'character is fate', that who we are determines what we do, what life decisions we make. At a simple level, if I am a person who lacks self-confidence and has a low self-image, and I meet someone whom I find ravishingly desirable, I am less likely to *do* something that might develop a relationship with that person than if I am self-assured and have a high self-image. Here it is possible to talk about a fate that precedes character – the fate of the physical features I am blessed with, the kind of society I am born into, the childhood experiences that have formed my character, etc. In a story, this information about a character may lead to sympathy for, or at least understanding of, their actions, but it does not alter the fact that their character is what it is, does what it does. This sense of character, determined by fate (or, if you prefer, chance) informs much film drama, as it does literature.

When talking about a movie, we often talk about how a character changes, becomes a different (usually better) person. When this happens, it is nearly always the result of some single major event in their life – an event usually dramatised in the movie. The way we may change through the accumulation of small experiences over a lifetime or simply through the gradual process of maturation is not the kind of change that films can handle very well or that those who approve scripts are usually very interested in. Character change needs to be in relation to major events, to dramatic conflict.

In fact, very often a character does not change at all. The audience simply accumulates more information about them. Our understanding of them changes. But this, too, is action-dependent. We learn new and different things about a character as we discover what they are capable of doing – or, very often, as they themselves discover what they are capable of doing. This again relates back to what we looked at in the last chapter about story and plot. Plot controls the supply of knowledge for carefully calculated dramatic reasons. One of the most important areas of knowledge control centres on character. Carefully managing the way character is revealed to the audience is one of the main functions of the carefully structured plot. Conscious control or regulation of how much we know – and when – is a skill the film storyteller needs to possess. We are given as much information as we need to engage with the story, gain our bearings and commit ourselves to emotions and values. At the same time, we have information withheld from us in order to create uncertainty, anxiety – suspense.

▶ Think of a film that illustrates this balance between revealing and withholding character information. What purposes are served by this careful control over information? Does it help construct a more interesting film? ●

But who are we talking about when we refer to a character? Let us return to the question of when is a character a character. A lot of bit parts in the movies involve figures performing some kind of narrative function – the messenger, the driver, the security guard may do something without their action requiring any understanding of their character. These figures may be given some recognisable trait, a distinctive mannerism, but this does not make a character.

A character, as opposed to a figure who simply performs a narrative function, will have a set of characteristics and, in realist narrative, these will usually be seen to connect directly or indirectly with the decisions they make and the actions they perform, especially in dramatic situations. Of these features, the most obvious is that they will have a history, will have come from somewhere, will have have had life experiences. If little or nothing is revealed to us about this, then we will at least have the features of their present, a place where they now live, a lifestyle that they now enjoy.

In passing, let's not forget our own character and its role in the film – as a maker of meaning. The decisions we make, what we do in the act of watching a film will be determined by who we are, where we come from, etc.

Information about someone's past is most easily communicated verbally – and is a common feature of written texts, especially novels and biographies. In the theatre, too, parts are written so that crucial aspects of a character's past or present may be revealed through monologues and dialogues. This also happens often in movies, but other methods may be used, such as the visual flashback sequence. Information about someone's present is more commonly communicated visually through *mise en scène*. 'Signifiers' (see p. 37) such as the kind of clothes the character wears, how they furnish their house or the kind of car they drive may be important indicators of the 'whole' person. (They function as 'indexical' signs – see p. 65). We make meaning from them both by

Sometimes the flashback history of a person's life takes the form of a montage sequence. My favourite is when Don Lockwood (Gene Kelly) is asked at a Hollywood premiere in Singin' in the Rain to talk about how he became a star. After the false modesty of 'not in front of all these people', he narrates his struggle to stardom which takes the form of a montage of short comic scenes.

▶ **Do you have a memorable example of a flashback providing character information?** ●

For more on this, see section 4.4, p. 113

The commutation test is a useful exercise.

Take a favourite film (perhaps the same one you were working on above) and try recasting the three or four central roles with other actors/actresses.

What immediately becomes clear is that different actors bring distinctive qualities to a role – each actor in their physical body, mannerisms, speech and star persona 'signifies' something different.

You have already been asked to consider the consequences of a different star playing Helen in *Sliding Doors* (p. 35).

▶ Think of some examples of casting which have worked surprisingly well. Think of some you think have been disastrous. ●

▶ Have you seen a film adaptation of a favourite novel or play? If so, what was your reaction in watching the film adaptation to the 'fixing' of a character in the form of a particular actor/actress? ●

reference to our knowledge of the world and from our knowledge of the conventions of film storytelling, especially genre.

As well as a past history and a present lifestyle, we look for information and understanding from the physical being of the character – their body. The most revealing part of the body (unless you are a reflexologist!) is the face. One of the most important and distinctive things the cinema brought to human story telling was the close-up. It became possible to communicate a character in a face.

Since the body and particularly the face communicate so much, then, within visual storytelling, **casting** and **performance** are of crucial importance. In reading literature, we create an image in our mind of a character. In the movies, that image is fixed in place by the actor. People sometimes reject a movie adaptation of one of their favourite novels because the casting failed to meet their mental image of a key character. People sometimes read a book after seeing the movie adaptation and can only see a particular character in the form of the actor or actress who played that role in the film and has subsequently defined or 'fixed' the character forever in the reader's mind. In Chapter 4, we consider a screen adaptation of literature – *Shakespeare's Romeo and Juliet*. Is Leonardo DiCaprio an acceptable physical embodiment of the Romeo that may have existed in your mind from reading the play first?

Casting and performance are often held in interesting opposition. Film directors will sometimes cast an 'unknown', perhaps someone who has never acted before, because they look right for the part. The risk is that they cannot 'perform'. On the other hand, a very experienced actor or actress may have to work incredibly hard to overcome their physical mismatch with the character they are playing or the 'baggage' their star persona brings to the part. Sometimes this works (and Oscars are awarded); sometimes it fails and audiences are forced to endure a couple of hours of mild embarrassment on behalf of the performer.

Movie performance is different from theatre performance in a number of ways in addition to the obvious one of theatre being 'live'. Perhaps the two most important are these. First, the theatre actor has to project a performance out into an auditorium where people's relative distance from them cannot change. By contrast, a movie actor can play to a camera less than a metre away from them – and know that that is how close the audience will be in the cinema. This may significantly affect the style of acting. (In what ways, do you think?) Secondly, the theatre actor will most commonly work out of a tradition we can refer to as **impersonation**. He or she will create or 'build' from their repertoire of voices, mannerisms and so on a character who may be very different from the person they themselves are. The movie actor, particularly in popular commercial cinema, is more likely to work out of **personification**. He or she will not so much build a character as simply *be* that character. The voice, mannerisms and so on required for the role are simple theirs. Another way of describing this is to say that the movie actor 'em-bodies' the role.

This second point is particularly important in relation to stars. While character actors in the movies (an interesting phrase!) may well be much closer to the theatre tradition of impersonation, the star may well simply personify the character. What I mean here is that some kinds of acting require the skills of turning yourself into someone quite different; others require that the person/image the actor already possesses is simply carried over into the role. In simple terms, some stars play themselves or, to be more accurate, some stars play their own star image.

This needs major qualification in one obvious respect. Many stars today – such as Nicolas Cage, Al Pacino, Robert De Niro, Meryl Streep – prefer to be admired for their acting skills, for their ability to impersonate. Such stars work out of a tradition of screen acting known as 'The Method'. This requires that they identify intensely with the role – perhaps spending weeks living exactly like their character would live, perhaps physically altering their bodies through exercise or body-building programmes. Most of all, method acting requires that the actor works out of a deep psychological association with the person they are playing which appears to go far beyond surface impersonation using voice and mannerism. It is debatable, however, whether you can call the result 'impersonation'. Some argue that method acting is better seen as a particularly extreme kind of 'personification' in which not just the body, but also the psychology and personal life experiences of the actor become one with the character.

For more on star study, see Chapter 4 where stars are considered within the context of cinema spectacle

▶ Think of a star who clearly exemplifies this idea of 'personifying' a character by simply bringing their star image to the role. ●
My examples would be Hugh Grant and particularly Julia Roberts in Notting Hill.

▶ Do you agree that these stars are good examples of stars who cross this line between 'personification' and 'impersonation'?
What about – to take a sample – John Travolta, Melanie Griffiths, Sean Connery, Geena Davis, Tom Hanks, Denzel Washington? ●
The last two are particularly interesting because they take on a variety of roles. How would you describe Tom Hanks's performances in Forrest Gump, Philadelphia *and* Saving Private Ryan, *respectively? How would you describe Denzel Washington's performances in* Malcolm X, Philadelphia, Devil in a Blue Dress *and* The Hurricane?

▶ Do you agree? If so, why do you think this is? What about, say, De Niro or Pacino? ●

It is interesting to study performance in film studies, not least because what may seem very realistic in one historical period becomes less so in another.

▶ This begs the question of how we should talk about stars:

- as real people?
- as the roles they play?
- as distinctive screen presences?
- as hyper-real people who circulate within a media construction of them? ●

See section 4.4 for more on this

It is usually films that have been classified as 'classics' and where characters are seen as more than just 'types' that the intense study of character seems appropriate – characters such as Charles Foster Kane in *Citizen Kane*, Ethan Edwards in *The Searchers*, Jake La Motta in *Raging Bull* and Lester Burnham in *American Beauty*.

▶ Is one of the reasons films achieve 'classic' status the depth and complexity of characterisation to be found in them? ●

As a footnote to what has been said about performance, it is interesting to note that the films just mentioned achieve their depth and complexity in performance – through the work of Orson Welles, John Wayne, Robert De Niro and Kevin Spacey, respectively. This begs the question of whether the distinction between 'impersonation' and 'personification' is really very helpful.

▶ Do these stars (and others) work right across this range of impersonation ◀—▶ personification? ●

▶ I am very conscious that all the examples here are of male roles/male stars. What equivalent female roles/female stars would you nominate? ●

One of the interesting critical issues is that 'The Method' often ends up looking less realistic than normal screen acting. If we look now at the early 'stars' of method acting, such as Marlon Brando, their performances appear contrived, artificial.

While star study has become an established part of film studies, character study has not. This does not mean that film studies ignores character, merely that character has become the focus for studies in representation, narrative, genre, audience and spectatorship. The assumption that storytelling in popular culture (including most film) is simply formulaic and routine, with a natural tendency towards cliché and stereotype, has led to a very uncertain and ambivalent approach to character – when compared with, for example, equivalent work in the academic study of literature.

Film characters are often thought to lack depth and complexity, their main interest being 'symptomatic' – that is, they are 'symptoms' of some broader type of human predicament or behaviour pattern which they represent. As we saw in Chapter 2 (pp. 23), stories are essentially repetitions of generic formulae with just enough 'variation' to distinguish one story from another. As an extension of this, characters may be seen as stock 'types' without the subtleties and ambiguities we find in more 'serious' literature – or even in so-called art-house movies. A common approach to the study of character in popular film has been to construct a model of the 'type' from a large number of film examples and then take a particular character to demonstrate how it may be an interesting 'variation' on this type. The character is a seen as a **structure** rather than a reality that could walk off the screen and into real life.

This discomfort in talking about characters as people, even though we bring such a strong level of human engagement to them, is possibly intensified by three things very specific to movies and television. Two have already been touched upon.

First, characterisation is as much visual as it is verbal. So we are forced to find ways of talking about character which include the visual, not just the words of dialogue and description on the written page.

Secondly – and linked to this – is the intimate relationship between the character role, casting and performance. There is a 'real' person in this equation – the actor. In the theatre, we can still keep role and actor apart by virtue of the fact that, in the past and in the future, the role has been and will be reinterpreted by other actors. In the movies, however, the role and the actor are nearly always forever one (give or take the occasional remake).

Thirdly, specific to film and television is the way in which our relationship to characters is controlled by cinematography and editing – in other words, by the apparatus and techniques of the medium. As viewers (spectators) of a movie, our relationship to any particular character can be significantly affected by the way they are presented to us. For example, our relationship will be significantly different depending on whether they are presented to us largely in long shot or close-up, or whether the film is edited in such a way as to create a particular dramatic intimacy between the spectator and the character.

The basis of this book is the making of meaning. So, we must ask some direct questions about how meaning is made by those involved in the film's creation and by us in our response.

- How is character constructed visually?

- How is character constructed through dialogue?

- How is a character constructed through performance?

- What is the significance of the position we are put in as spectators for responding to character?

- To what extent is our response to character out of the control of those who make the film?

In terms of evaluation, we must ask when a character 'works' for us – in other words, when a character is believable, convincing and intensifies the necessary 'agreement' between film and audience referred to in Chapter 2 (pp. 26). We must also reflect on how and why characters give us pleasure – and what kinds of pleasure.

Perhaps character matters too much to audiences – and from an academic point of view it has been important for film studies to establish a cool, clinical distance between the critical analyst and the character in question. On the other hand, responding to characters as if they are real people with real histories and real psychologies is a normal and

▶ Consider a film, perhaps one not usually thought of as having great distinction, where you think the characters deserve serious study because of their psychological depth, complexity and ambiguity. ●

We return to this question of how we evaluate whether or not a character 'works' in section 3.9 (p. 92)

▶ Who is your favourite star? What do you think is the basis of your fandom?

Consider a contemporary star with a large fan following whom you do not like. What do you think is the appeal of this star to his/her fans? Why do you not respond to this appeal? ●

This discussion is picked up again in section 3.6 (p. 81)

In studying these two films, you may find it useful to produce representations of their narrative structures – through the numbering and labelling of sequences along the lines of those offered in Chapter 2 for E.T. and Sliding Doors. (see pp. 28–9 and 30–1)

pleasurable activity for audiences. We immerse ourselves in the fictional world the film offers us and let our imaginations take off in whatever unpredictable direction the particular interaction between film text and spectator dictates.

This opens up a very interesting and important distinction between different kinds of film study. If our approach to film studies has a primary focus on **textual studies**, we come to it as a constructed object to be deconstructed using formal analytical and critical means. In the process, we will learn a lot about how that film works. One of the elements of the film we will probably want to deconstruct is character and its representation in the body of an actor or actress. We may end up with a dissected corpse. If our approach to film studies has a primary focus on audiences and on what people do with films socially, culturally and personally, we are more interested in **response studies**. We will want to know how a character works its effect on the audience, creating a strong relationship based, perhaps, on desire or repulsion. We will want to know the relationship between character, performance and fandom. In turn, we may wish to know the relationship between fandom and the attitudes, styles and values that are significant within the culture at that moment.

Is it possible to synthesise these approaches? On the one hand, can we accept that a character most certainly is a textual construct of interest to us primarily in relation to its formal elements? On the other, can we also capture something of the way that textual construct is animated in the moment of reception by real people (us!) with our interest in how and why we appropriate film characters for our imaginative and social needs?

The two films which will provide the focus for our investigation come from outside the Hollywood production system and deal with conflict within the family. One of them, *Once Were Warriors*, although made in New Zealand, adopts a recognisable Hollywood style – in fact, it has been seen as a further example of the American 'hood' movies of the late 1980s and early 1990s such as *Boyz 'n the Hood* and *Menace 2 Society*. It is a film directed by Lee Tamahori who, prior to *Once Were Warriors*, was best known as the director of television commercials in his homeland. The other, *Secrets and Lies*, is a British film made in a more low-key style characteristic of British television drama. It was directed by

Mike Leigh, who is well known for his distinctive approach to building character and performance out of improvisation with his actors.

3.2 Visual character

Perhaps the most common experience we have of 'visual character' is in photography and painting – especially portraiture. From a single image, carefully constructed and executed with skill, we can gain a complex insight into the person who is the subject of that portrait. To extend the idea raised in Chapter 2 (pp. 37–8), we actively 'decode' the portrait, making meaning from what is signified by physical features, gestures and more abstract elements of the portrait such as angle of view and lighting. We respond to the **iconic** – the simple physical 'presence' of the image, still and in front of us for our reflection. A portrait, however, may have other potential sources of meaning. An **indexical** meaning will also be present. Some characteristic or characteristics will denote the 'whole' person – this may be some aspect of their dress or hairstyle, for example. Beyond this, a single person may be an index for a whole group of people. For example, the face of an individual fisherman may encourage us to think about the general category of 'fishermen'. In such a case, we go from a particular person to a whole category of people and their way of existence. In the process, we go from a person to an idea, even a whole set of ideas.

There is a subtle but important difference between this process and stereotyping. The **stereotype** is a form of 'shorthand' used in communication to suggest quickly (and sometimes lazily!) a category of person. In *Secrets and Lies*, in the carefully composed images, we are sometimes seeing with fresh eyes – the familiar is made less familiar. I am suggesting that here we are drawn to respond actively – working with the indexical qualities of the image to make meaning. One of the basic characteristics of art is the way in which the familiar is defamiliarised so that we see things we might otherwise take for granted in new ways. The stereotype does the opposite, exploiting and confirming a conventionally accepted set of attributes belonging to the subject of the representation. In what follows – not just in our exploration of *Secrets and Lies*, but also *Once Were Warriors* – you may find it useful (and challenging) to consider the fine line between the stereo-

The possibility of clothes as an 'index' of character has already been referred to on p. 57

This was the basis of Italian Neo-Realism in the 1940s. In referring to the example of a fisherman, I think particularly of La Terra Trema *(Visconti, Italy, 1947).*

▶ Can you think of any examples of a similar process in a film you have seen – a transformation from the individual to the general? ●

Let me give a simple example of the way photography defamiliarises. Every day I walk past an old tree at the corner of my local park, without thinking anything about it. One day I go into the local library where there is an exhibition of photographs. I see a black-and-white photograph of the tree, composed and framed by the photographer. Looking at the image creates an entirely new relationship to that tree. I see it aesthetically; I see it as an object of wonder. I see less – because it is not the actual tree – but I see more than if I were casually walking past it.

For more on defamiliarisation, see overleaf.

Secrets and Lies: Maurice as director/photographer.

For reference, the portraits taken in the two sequences are as follows:

Sequence 1 (beginning 12. 10)	
Family group	Little boy
Boxer	Woman in fishnet tights
Nurse	Group of five businessmen
Mum and baby	**Sequence 2 (beginning 15.42)**
Dog	Graduate
Cat	Long smiling man and short serious woman
Potential bridegroom	Mixed couple
Magician	Elderly mother and daughter
Three young women	Smiling couple
Three children in ballet costume	

▶ Do you think that Maurice's (Mike Leigh's) photographs are just exploiting stereotypes, or is there a defamiliarising process going on here in which we are invited to respond actively to the images we are given?

In relation to this, you may wish to think about the technical qualities of the images – composition, lighting, angle, etc. ●

Certainly Maurice's brilliance as a 'director' deserves some appreciation!

typical and its defamiliarisation; the conversion from a character 'type' to a distinctive individualised character.

Secrets and Lies has a photographer as one of its central characters. Maurice specialises in portrait and wedding photography. On three separate occasions we are presented with sequences of portraits as he works in his studio. Here, and in his wedding photography, much is revealed about Maurice himself – his patience, his generosity, his sensitivity, his distinctive charm in usually getting his subjects to smile. (Although in contrast with the visual, which we are concentrating on here, this information about Maurice is mostly conveyed verbally – by what he says off-screen which is directed at the subjects of his portraits.)

The iconic and the indexical meanings of the image are very clearly exemplified in the sequences beginning at 12 min. 10 sec. and again at 15.42. The power of the visual image appears to depend on three things: the physical person and what they wear; their pose; and the animation they bring to the shoot. Each of these is a mixture of the distinctive and the predictable. The iconic 'thereness' of the image may present us with the distinctive – but unknowable. By contrast, the indexical anchors this in social and cultural meanings that we can access easily. So, the way a person dresses allows us to 'place' them along with lots of other people who dress in this way. If the first level of meaning simply involves us mentally recording what is in front of our eyes, the second level requires us to make connections, mental associations. In the process, we are actively looking for what we might loosely call 'stereotypical' features, features that will give us a handle on the whole person. Beyond this, we may feel we can then place the person within their society.

Every genre has its character types and, in some genres, these characters are easily 'indexed' by costume and mannerism. Working within a commercial cinema and wishing to communicate effectively with an audience, screenwriter, director and actor must create a character from a familiar base model, but add (sometimes quite small) distinctive traits. This is another aspect of the repetition and variation which sustains commercial cinema. In the case of character, the crucial factors are often how the character is photographed (com-'posed') and performed ('animated').

In *Secrets and Lies*, the studio portraits heighten our awareness of the fact that we 'read' visual images of characters

In both *Secrets and Lies* and *Once were Warriors*, there are many useful examples of how an 'index' of character is provided by how someone dresses (including hairstyle and make-up) or by their gesture and body movement or by their home environment. (All of these are aspects of the film's *mise en scène*.)

Here is one particularly vivid example of each in the final lengthy scene of Roxanne's birthday in *Secrets and Lies*:

- Jane's costume
- Paul's facial expression and body movement
- Monica's home – so proudly shown off

And these from *Once Were Warriors*:

- Nig's costume – including the tattooed body as part of that costume.
- Beth's facial expression and body movement, especially when she is under stress – revealed in simply actions such as lighting a cigarette.
- The 'hood' of South Auckland, especially the areas of waste land alongside and under urban road systems which contrast so powerfully with the opening shot of the film – the traditional rural beauty of New Zealand – presented as an advertising hoarding.

As a footnote to this last example, the traditional shot of rural New Zealand with which the film begins is an excellent example of the defamiliarising of a stereotype, in this case the stereotypical visualisation of New Zealand. The camera pulls back to (a) draw attention to the fact that we have only been looking at a photographic representation and (b) show that that representation is in striking contrast to the urban neighbourhood in which it is located.

You can follow up these ideas on character presentation in sections 4.4 (pp. 113–18) and 4.5 (pp. 118–26).

Once Were Warriors: from a billboard image of a beautiful rural location to this image of Beth – the opening shot of the film draws attention to the very different representation of New Zealand that awaits us.

throughout the film. Some significant portraits are interspersed through the movie. For example, consider:

> *Hortense sitting in her flat in right profile (11 min. 24 sec.); Cynthia pushing up her breasts in front of the mirror (30.40); Maurice sitting in a pub looking straight ahead with a large portrait painting behind him (49.18); Maurice in the back pew of a church waiting to take some wedding pictures – followed immediately by Monica sitting on the stairs at home (53.58); Cynthia and Roxanne sitting in their living room (77.44).*

We are given time as an audience not only to think about the situations these individuals are confronted with, but also more generally to reflect on who they are as human beings. To go back to what was said a few paragraphs earlier, in dwelling

Secrets and Lies: Hortense takes Cynthia's call.

▶ By this stage are you clear about:

• the iconic sign
• the indexical sign
• the symbolic sign?

Try to find a further example of each from either of the two films we are looking at in this chapter. ●

The association of tattoos, commonly referred to as *moko*, with gang violence was a cause of great concern in sections of the Maori community. Indeed, as we will see in section 3.7 (p. 85), all kinds of concerns were expressed about the political, social and cultural representation of Maori culture in *Once Were Warriors*.

▶ Which film, *Secrets and Lies* or *Once Were Warriors*, leaves us with more of a sense of the interior lives of its main characters? ●

And, of course, this kind of moment is rarely silent – the visual image will be supported by ambient sound or a music track.

---

on characters such as Cynthia and Roxanne outside of any dramatic scene, the audience is invited to reflect on them as people with an interior life.

There is one 'portrait' image which particularly deserves attention in *Secrets and Lies*. It is not a still portrait, but invites the kind of reflection we have been talking about. Hortense has phoned Cynthia to tell her that she is her daughter. Cynthia, after initially responding by saying she does not want to meet her, now phones back. Hortense has been having a bath. She comes to the phone (64.00) wearing white face cream to talk as a black woman to the white mother she has never seen. Your reaction to this as *mise en scène* may be an interesting indicator of your taste in movie direction generally. Is this a clever, ironic visual comment? Is it a visual overstatement, unnecessary on top of the pain we already know the two characters are experiencing? Is it simply comic? What it certainly does is provide us with an example of the third generally recognised kind of 'signification' alongside the iconic and the indexical. This is the **symbolic**, a visual image which represents an abstract idea. Clearly the image of Hortense with her whitened face is encouraging us to think about issues of racial identity here and thus representing an abstract idea visually.

The visualising of the male body is a vivid example of the symbolic in *Once Were Warriors*. Jake and his two older sons define themselves through their physical bodies and the actions their bodies express. Jake, 'Jake the Muss', externalises his passions and demons in his muscular body. His eldest son, Nig, does so through the Maori tattoos which his father, for complex reasons, loathes. His second son, Boogie, finds ways of establishing an inner strength, of internalising the kind of power his father can only communicate through his fists. He does this in learning the discipline of the traditional warrior chants and dances while in the youth custody centre.

A particular challenge in film (and television) presentations is to find a means of communicating the interior life of a character. In novels, we can have direct access to what a character is thinking and feeling through interior monologues, streams of consciousness, where we can read on the written page what they think and feel. Of course, film can do this to some extent through voice-over in which the character is able to articulate what is going on in their heads – an interior monologue spoken over images. This is verbal communication – although the images we see while listening to a voice-over will nearly always enrich it, either by reinforcing what we hear or, sometimes, by presenting a contrast for dramatic, ironic or comic effect.

What is of particular interest to us here, however, is how a character's inner self can be communicated visually. We look into an actor's face and 'see' the person within. The iconic becomes an index of aspects of their interior life. In practice, this depends on two kinds of performance – that of the actor and that of the camera. These will be supported by the *mise en scène* of location (a landscape, an interior). One example from *Secrets and Lies* is when Maurice has been invited to make his own dinner. (The complete dialogue for the sequence follows on p. xx.) The shot we are given of him is from a high angle and we physically move closer to where he is wedged into a corner of the room. His long suffering, his loneliness, his exhaustion are caught by this shot. It is achieved both in the actor's performance and in the cinematography.

In acknowledging the work of a number of creative people responsible for the visual richness of character presentation – actor, cinematographer, designer, director – we must also recognise how much the meaning-making is our work. We constantly hypothesise based on the evidence available to us. We use our natural perceptiveness and critical intelligence to relate different kinds of information. We engage in this processing constantly and automatically.

3.3. Talking character

In emphasising the visual in film storytelling, this does not mean we should ignore the spoken word. Speech is important in providing character information, as we have already seen in Chapter 2, section 3.

Characters can tell us what kind of people they are from single lines of dialogue. For example, what do we learn of Maurice's character in *Secrets and Lies* from these comments:

> *Children are playing noisily outside Maurice and Monica's six-bedroom suburban home. Maurice says, 'Well at least they can play outside.'* (04.10)

Roxanne and Paul have gone to the bus stop following Cynthia's revelation about Hortense at the birthday party:

Secrets and Lies: The interior life in a visual image – Maurice at the end of the sequence from which the dialogue is quoted on pp. 71–2.

▶ With a couple of friends, look at some still frames of a character, either from one of the two films we are exploring here or from a film of your choice, and share what each of you 'sees'. Talk through any disagreements in what you 'see' and try to explain them. ●

▶ Think of a film in which you have been particularly caught up with a character grappling with their emotions and feelings. Can you locate a moment in which the film seems to encourage us to look inside the mind and heart of a character through purely visual means? ●

Obviously dialogue needs 'performing'. In practice, it is difficult to look at the dialogue separate from the performances (see Section 3.4 below). It is interesting in this regard to speculate on why people buy film screenplays to read. My own feeling is that the printed word becomes a trigger for recalling performances as much as it offers its own pleasures as a written text.

It is also very important to recognise that the performances need filming. The point has already been made that figure composition and set design are important, as are the choices made by the cinematographer in terms of angle, height and so on of the shot.

In fact, perhaps this question is the wrong way round. What does dialogue add to the visual information? Which dominates: the visual or the verbal? A famous study in 1974 by Colin McCabe asked this question in relation to the American thriller *Klute*. The end of the film has visual information which partly contradicts the verbal information provided by a voice-over. By which should we be guided? The visual or the verbal? McCabe argued that in such a situation the spectator will always prioritise the visual.
► Do you agree? ●
► Can you think of an example from a different film of this conflict between visual and the verbal information? ●
► What does visual information add to the dialogue? ●

Maurice tries to persuade Roxanne to come back to her party and says of her mother, 'She can't help it, she's never had enough love.' (122.40)

Just as commonly, a character may either tell us how to respond to another character or speak our own response. For example, Beth in *Once Were Warriors* tells her husband, shortly after Grace's death:

'You're still a slave to your fist, to the drink.' (78.00)

And not just in their individuality, but also in their relationships, dialogue is highly revealing both in what it tells us about individuals and what it tells us about their relationships with others. Consider in both *Once Were Warriors* and *Secrets and Lies* the central relationships between husbands and wives, Jake and Beth, and Maurice and Monica.

The dialogue quoted below comes from sequences early in each film. Even without visual information, what does dialogue tell us about these characters and their relationships?

Once Were Warriors (03.15–08.10)

(Beth, Grace and the two youngest children in their garden have been called indoors by Jake who has arrived home unexpectedly. He puts a packet on the table.)
JAKE: Go on, open it … what do you reckon, kids?
CHILDREN: Yeah!
(Opens seafood.)
JAKE: Bloody oceans of the stuff.
(The children, including Grace, take helpings and go back outside, leaving Jake and Beth alone in the kitchen. He goes behind her and starts stroking her hair. She clearly enjoys the sexual attention. Nig comes downstairs …)
JAKE: Where the fuck are you off to? Come and have a feed, boy.
NIG: Nah! (He puts dark glasses on and exits.)
Jake: Fuck him!
(He turns his attention back to Beth. They feed each other and kiss passionately. He picks her up and walks her over to the kitchen table and pushes up her skirt.)
BETH: Not on the table, hon.
JAKE: Oh why not, I want to feel you.

BETH: The kids might come in.

JAKE: Oh, what about the chair. Remember?

(He picks her up and walks backward, sitting down on a chair, Beth now on his lap.)

BETH: So where did all the seafood come from?

JAKE: I got lucky. *(Pause.)* I got laid off.

BETH: What? Jake!

(Beth pulls off him and stands.)

JAKE: Wooh, wooh, woman, let me finish.

BETH: You've got a family to feed.

JAKE: I've signed up for the dole. It's only 17 bucks less than my wages. *(Pause.)* Well, don't look like that – it ain't the end of the world.

BETH: What about our house?

JAKE: We've got a house – and the government aint going to kick us out. The rent's cheap.

BETH: I want us to have our house, Jake. We can't make bloody ends meet as it is.

JAKE: Forget the bloody house. Let's talk about the bedroom.

(Beth moves away.)

BETH: Don't, Jake.

JAKE: You fucking got to spoil everything. Fuck you!

(The door bangs shut.)

Secrets and Lies (13.47–15.41)

(Maurice returns home; Monica is hoovering by the front door.)

MONICA: What do you think you're doing?

MAURICE: Sorry. Didn't hear you. *(Tries to kiss her – she backs away.)*

MONICA: Mind, out the way.

(Maurice walks down the hall and into the kitchen, taking a bottle of wine from the fridge.)

MAURICE: Want a drink?

MONICA: What? If I want a drink I'll get it myself.

(Maurice looks at her from the kitchen.)

MONICA: Since when was hoovering a spectator sport? *(She comes into the kitchen.)* Can I have a glass too, please?

MAURICE: Sorry, I thought you didn't want …

MONICA: I've changed my mind. I'm having milk – not in a wine glass. Give me a high bowl. You don't drink milk out of a wine glass.

MAURICE: There you go, er …

▶ Go through these two dialogue sequences on video and storyboard them. Then consider precise reasons for the decisions made by director, cinematographer and editor. ●

▶ Think about where your sympathies lie in each of these exchanges. What features internal to the film (such as editing, shot composition and performance) influence you? What features external to the film influence your response – that is, things *you* bring to the film? ●

For discussion of issues concerning our identification with film characters and the ways we show allegiance to them, see section 3.5 (p. 76)

See the still reproduced on p. 69.

MONICA: Thank you.

MAURICE: That'll do you good.

MONICA: Meaning?

MAURICE: Nothing. *(While Monica opens the cooker …)* Had a good day?

MONICA: Scintillating. I suppose you'll be starving as usual?

MAURICE: I am a little peckish, yeah. (Drinks his wine) Want me to do something?

MONICA: Like what?

MAURICE: Anything you like.

MONICA: No I bloody well wouldn't. (She gets up.) Alright – fridge – there's a freezer – there's a recipe book – help yourself – don't make a mess.

(She goes back into the hall. We are given a high-angle shot of Maurice which moves closer. Monica comes back.)

MONICA: Unless you fancy a take-away.

(Maurice smiles weakly. Monica's face turns to tears. She goes out and bangs the door.)

One interesting and valuable use of dialogue is to create **dramatic irony** – that is, a pointed contrast between two actions or between what is said and what is happening. Dramatic irony can, but does not have to, be humorous. We find this in various scenes in *Secrets and Lies*, particularly in the interplay between one character's sensitivity and the other's clumsiness. If we take the sequence where Cynthia and Hortense meet for the first time and go to a café to talk, we find a vivid example of this. Cynthia makes references to her past and her present life in speaking to Hortense whom she has just discovered is her daughter. She fails to recognise the sensitivity of the situation so completely that what she says is more comic than cruel:

> (74.30)
>
> HORTENSE: Why didn't you want to see me?
>
> CYNTHIA: I don't want to upset my daughter, do I?

Hortense responds with brief comments and silence to Cynthia's mixture of apology and self-justification.

Another use of dialogue is to create a powerful sense of **pathos**. Here is an example from *Once Were Warriors*. Consider the sadness that lies beneath this exchange between

Grace and her mother, Beth, en route to visiting Boogie who is in the youth custody centre.

(53.30)
(They pull into the car park of the beer hall.)
JAKE: Just one beer, eh?
BETH: One Jake. Just the one. Promise.
(He kisses her.)
JAKE: I promise.
(Cut to interior – he walks up to Bully and some of his other drinking mates.… The following dialogue in the car indicates some time has passed.)
GRACE: How long's Dad going to be?
BETH: I'd get that tone out of your voice if I were you. How many times have you seen your father like today, Grace. Never! That's how many. Just give him a chance.
(Cut to interior – a horse race on television. All the men, including Jake, are completely absorbed.)

It is not a simple sadness we feel at Beth and her children being let down here by Jake. It is the complexity of Beth's struggle, her desperate hope that things can be different – set against the reality of abuse and selfishness which, as the audience, we witness so clearly. Again, we *see* this at least as much as we hear it – we see it in the performance of the actress.

In both films, character change is marked by 'speeches'. These carry information about the themes of the respective films, but they derive very specifically from the accumulated 'weight' of the character who speaks those words.

At the climax of the birthday scene, after Cynthia has told everyone that Hortense is her daughter, Maurice admits that the unhappiness of his marriage is rooted in the fact that Monica cannot have children. They have suppressed this information from everyone. He says this:

(126.14)
MAURICE: There I've said it – where's the bolt of lightning? Secrets and lies – we're always in pain. Why can't we share our pain? The three people in the world I love the most hate each other's guts. Sorry, Hortense – you're a very brave person – willing to find the truth and were prepared to suffer the consequences.

At the very end of *Once Were Warriors*, outside the bar room after Jake has taken his revenge on Bully, Beth says to Jake:

> (93.00)
> BETH: I've found something better, Jake, and I'm going to make damn sure my kids have it all. From now on I make the decisions for my family.
> JAKE: Fuck off then, you'll get nothing from me.
> BETH: You've got nothing I want. Our people once were warriors, but not like you, Jake. They were people with mana, pride, people with spirit …

The authority in these words comes from the respect we have gained for the character who speaks them. The words have an authority which is ultimately rooted in performance.

3.4. Character and performance

We all 'perform' our characters in that we reveal our characters in our actions. (I use the word 'action' in its broadest sense: anything we do – the choice we make in dressing in a certain way, for example, as much as the choice we make in an extreme and dramatic situation. This includes the 'action' of choosing to do nothing.)

In drama, including film drama, characters are very obviously 'performed' by actors. Depending on the style of the enacted performance (see p. 61), we may be more or less drawn into it as a convincing, believable representation of a 'real' person. Narrative realist cinema, of which our two films in this chapter are examples, clearly tries to create the fictional illusion of the 'real' using a certain performance style and a form of film language that appears to correspond to a natural way of seeing. (Or, to put it slightly differently, both acting performance and the 'performance' of cinema use techniques that attempt to disguise their performances.)

As already mentioned, in Mike Leigh–directed films, such as *Secrets and Lies*, character construction often comes from a very distinctive approach in which actors work out of improvisation – although the scenes as filmed have had their dialogue 'fixed' in rehearsal before filming. This means that the actors enjoy a vivid relationship between character and their performance – the character is, to an unusual degree in

---

It has already been suggested above – and will be expanded upon in Chapter 4 – that it is not just actors who give a performance, but also cinema itself. Cinema, through the agency of director, cinematographer, editor and so on, 'performs' the film. *Once Were Warriors* is a much more loudly stated cinematic 'performance' – visually, stylistically – than *Secrets and Lies*.

▶ Is this another example of the contrast between 'histoire' and discourse? See p. 48. ●

cinema, their creation. By contrast, *Once Were Warriors* was scripted and filmed in a much more conventional way. In comparing two scenes – each involving social workers – it may be possible for you to recognise differences in performance style and speculate on how these differences may be the result of different approaches to the building of character/performance.

Hortense meets the social worker Jenny Ford in a scene beginning at 19.26 in *Secrets and Lies*. The performance that follows is wonderfully ambiguous. We are not quite sure how much the social worker cares as she goes through the required questions before handing Hortense the file on her birth and adoption. The performance is edgy, full of hand movements and a straining to be sociable. Jenny represents, in her own words, 'a professional service' straining to personalise its routine contacts with strangers while allocated fixed periods of time for each client. Jenny is sensitive to Hortense's hurt, but has her eye on her watch. Tellingly, she glances over her shoulder near the end of the scene, presumably concerned about her next appointment, while still engaging with Hortense. The performance can only begin to be studied by looking at the words of the script. Meaning is powerfully contained in the visual performances, especially body language.

Compare this with the scene in *Once Were Warriors* between Boogie and his social worker, Bennett, after Boogie's frustration and anger has led him to break a window at the youth custody centre. Compared with the previous example, this is much more direct in its communication – both in the words spoken and the physical nature of the 'performance'.

(47.40)
Boogie has a wooden fighting stick (a taia*). He is smashing windows in the gym of the borstal. The social worker marches up to him very purposefully, grabs the* taia *from him, knocking him to the ground in the process. Bennett communicates considerable power and authority as he says:*

'You think your fist is your weapon? When I have taught you, your mind will be. You'll carry your taia *inside you. Come on.'*

Bennett's authority comes not just from his institutional position, but also from his character, which it seems is deeply rooted in Maori culture. He assumes the role of father

---

Mike Leigh's films thrive on building sharply defined characters out of the raw material of stereotypes. By contrast, Lee Tamahori's film is full of strong visual images typical of a showy cinematic style, appealing to a young audience. (He said he deliberately wanted to avoid the kind of social realism of Ken Loach, another British director, often linked in critical discussion to Mike Leigh.)

▶ Think of an example in either *Secrets and Lies* or *Once Were Warriors* where a stereotype is used as a base, but is then individualised, made more complex. ●

▶ As with the dialogue sequences you were invited to storyboard on pp. 70–1, think carefully about visual elements – cinematography and editing – in both these 'social worker' scenes.

What are some of the ways in which the shooting and editing of each scene differ? ●

Of course, the children and teenagers of *Once Were Warriors* have not the emotional and physical toughness of the adult characters. Grace and her friend Toot provide a dramatic and thematic contrast with the adults. They are gentle, sensitive and 'live' in their minds, somewhere else besides South Auckland.

As a footnote to this, Grace's name points to an idea that is used quite often in this book – she em-*bodies* a range of qualities and values. As an image of 'grace', she undergoes a series of awful experiences. And, after her death, she is invoked by Beth and her children in prayer as they say 'grace'.

▶ Look at the physical performances of the actors playing Grace and Toot. What in gesture or movement communicates innocence (the grace of the characters)? ●

substitute to Boogie – a man in stark contrast to Boogie's actual father, who has no pride, no natural authority except that which derives from his brutality.

The physical body is such a strong source of visual communication. It is usually the most important of all the aspects of *mise en scène*. *Once Were Warriors* is full of physical performances – from the women as well as the men. These performances are tough, hard, suppressing weakness in order to survive the community and domestic pressures of everyday life. By contrast, *Secrets and Lies* finds (usually) a gentle humour in the physical. In *Secrets and Lies*, the vulnerability is there on the surface: insecurities, frustrations, feelings of inadequacy, low self-esteem. Again, we begin to appreciate how much we know a character through their gestures and body movement.

Roxanne has a particularly striking introduction – in Maurice's photograph of her as a schoolchild. Looking at the picture, Maurice pointedly says, she's never smiled since. A cut allows the film to immediately contrast the photograph with Roxanne in the present as a roadsweeper, her face, especially her expressive nose, a wrapped image of unhappiness. Sitting at home on the settee opposite her mother, Roxanne's every small gesture, such as the way she smokes her cigarette, conveys her irritation and frustration.

Paul, Roxanne's boyfriend, is described by Cynthia, following his first appearance, as walking like a crab. Indeed he does, leaning back and walking sideways down the street with Roxanne, twitching his head. He is fairly inarticulate, hopelessly shy and easily intimidated. Through the performance of the role, Paul 'speaks'. There is a wonderful moment early in the birthday scene when even the generous Maurice is moved to spontaneous laughter by Paul's mannerisms and inability to speak more than three words. The actor, of course, communicates much more than these words.

3.5. Getting involved with characters – the cinema way

The characters exist separate from us on screen – constructed by *mise en scène*, by dialogue, by performance. How do we connect with them? How is it that we come closer to some characters, become dramatically and emotionally involved with them?

Our dramatic involvement is very significantly controlled by a film's narration. For example, to refer back to the last chapter, think how *Sliding Doors*'s narration, by means of editing, controls so completely our knowledge and viewpoint. Also, as we saw in Chapter 2, a key question we can ask about narration is whether it offers restricted or unrestricted access to story information. In *Secrets and Lies*, we have a fairly unrestricted view of the unhappiness in Maurice and Monica's marriage. Nevertheless, our knowledge of the cause is restricted until their revelation at the end of the film. In *Once Were Warriors*, the narrative presentation of the rape of Grace is unrestricted – knowing what Beth does not (that Bully raped her and provoked her suicide) – creates a particular kind of dramatic tension for the audience.

Moment by moment, of course, our knowledge of character is dependent on the observing camera. The camera may observe the character in both their public lives – for example, at work – and in their intimate private lives – for example, in the bedroom at home, as it were, behind locked doors. In observing a character, the camera acts as the instrument of **voyeurism**. We may not think of this when the camera tracks a character walking down a public street; we may become a little more sensitive to our viewing activity when the camera takes us into the bathroom. This is the most common voyeuristic act in cinema, simply that of going into the private places of a person's life – the bathroom, the bedroom – and observing the behaviour a character wishes to hide from the world or at least not conduct in front of it.

One of the pleasures of cinema is this opportunity to pass beyond the doors that are closed to us in our real lives – to pry into the private lives and private spaces of others. It gives us privileged access to a character and satisfies our ongoing desire not just for knowledge, but also for the pleasure of investigation which reveals this knowledge. The camera is always voyeuristic, always investigative – and we go along for the pleasure of what will be revealed, perhaps even for the titillation of what will be revealed. We are driven at first by curiosity, but increasingly, as a film proceeds, by a desire to know, a desire to participate in the search for knowledge.

Think of the 'private places' we enter into in the two films under discussion in this chapter. Often the pleasure of this access to the private is mixed with unease, even embarrassment. Consider, for example, Cynthia looking at herself in the mirror (*Secrets and Lies*, 30.40). She holds up her sagging

> The voyeur looks without being looked at. The classic image is the 'peeping tom' who looks through the keyhole, confident that the object of the gaze will not return the look. The voyeur is assumed to be male – the object of his look, a female.
>
> Very early in the development of narrative cinema, it was determined that an actor should not look straight into the camera, at the audience – returning the gaze. We enjoy the privilege of looking without being looked at. It is one of the fundamental pleasures of cinema.
>
> Hitchcock's *Rear Window* (United States, 1954) is all about 'the 'private things' we can see by peering into the private worlds of others – raising what one of the characters calls 'rear-window ethics'.

▶ Go back to what was said about interpellation in Chapter 2 (p. 42). Is it true to say that we are not interpellated into the dramatic world of the film in this scene between Hortense and Cynthia in the café, whereas we are in the scene between Hortense and the social worker?

If we are not, does this mean a different response to the drama is constructed compared with if it were presented in, for example, shot/reverse-shot? ●

breasts and reflects on her ageing. Or consider Beth the morning after her beating by Jake. She sits on the toilet (*Once Were Warriors*, 28.00). One of the most startling ways we can pry is through the simple close-up. There is an intimacy in the close-up and, if we are shown a character – such as Beth or Cynthia – sufficiently often in this kind of shot, we may imagine an emotional and psychological closeness.

Even without this physical closeness, we can gain all kinds of visual insights into character through *mise en scène*, as we have already seen, for example, in our study of *E.T.* in the last chapter. In dialogue sequences, our viewing position will again significantly affect our response. The most common method for shooting a dialogue sequence in commercial film and television is the **shot/reverse-shot** approach already discussed with reference to *Sliding Doors* (see p. 42). In *Secrets and Lies*, for example, the scene between Hortense and the social worker is shot in this way. Of course, there are other ways of filming a two-character dialogue scene, ones which create different kinds of audience involvement. For example, the first face-to-face conversation between Hortense and Cynthia in a café (after they have met outside Holborn tube station) is presented in a **two shot**. The characters remain a steady and equal distance from us. Other than an establishing shot, the entire conversation is filmed in a single take, with the camera positioned directly in front of the actors. The effect is somewhat similar to the 'fixed' position of a theatre experience, except, of course, we are much closer.

Secrets and Lies mixes different approaches to filming characters. This is well illustrated by the climactic birthday party section of the film. It starts with two ensemble **wide shots**. The first (107.55) is a high-angle shot lasting 1 minute 18 seconds, looking down on Maurice and Monica's garden. We watch the characters as a group being introduced to one another, being offered a drink. We are then given a single shot which lasts 4 minutes 46 seconds. The camera is more or less at table height, able to take in all of the characters. This is contrived because Maurice, who would be occupying the nearest chair, is standing behind the group serving food. (The scene closes when he walks around and takes his seat.) Perhaps the justification for these two ensemble wide shots is to convey a sense of a group of people interacting socially. It

1

2

3

4

5

6

7

8

9

10

11

12

Secrets and Lies: Roxanne's birthday, hosted by Maurice. Two different ways to shoot a scene: a single wide shot embracing all the characters (1–5 outdoors and 12 indoors); close ups, tightly edited, with spatial relationships between characters established through eye lines (6–11).

certainly contrasts markedly with the same group of characters as they are presented shortly afterwards.

Everyone has moved indoors. Roxanne has been presented with her birthday cake and Hortense, upset by her sudden and secret involvement in 'family', has retreated to the bathroom. This, incidentally, allows for a repeat of the second wide garden shot described in the last paragraph, this time in the living room. Again, we have a wide shot of everyone sitting around the table, thanks to a vantage point having been created by one person not being in their place – Hortense.

In her absence, a conversation begins which leads to Cynthia blurting out that Hortense is her daughter. This section of dialogue (beginning 116.53) is shot in a series of **close-ups**, cutting from character to character with their physical positions relative to one another established by 'eyelines' – the direction of look of each character. This is not at all unusual in films generally, although it arguably has more impact here because the close-up is used relatively infrequently in *Secrets and Lies*.

If we see a character through the eyes of another character who has a very distinctive attitude, this may influence our view of that character, too. This is, of course, complicated by the fact that we have to take into consideration what we know about this other person and the 'reliability' of their point of view. In *Secrets and Lies*, several characters have a view of Cynthia. Is any of them 'privileged', in the sense that his or her viewpoint will dominate the others and most strongly influence our own response? By comparison with Cynthia, our viewpoint of Hortense is not influenced particularly by strong views of her expressed by other characters. We are much more dependent on our direct and unrestricted observation of her. She appears as a professional and mature woman, independent and emotionally quite strong – except when we are 'privileged' to see her in private, when the voyeuristic camera goes behind the closed door of her private space. There we see some signs of her uncertainty and anxiety.

In *Once Were Warriors*, our viewpoint of Jake the Muss is worth reflecting on. He clearly condemns himself through his words and actions. We have already referred to the words with which Beth sums him up: 'You're still a slave to your fist, to the drink.' (78.00) Yet Beth loves him for much of the film. (Look again at that sequence beginning at 44.45 when, beaten

▶ Think about the ways of shooting dialogue scenes mentioned here. What is the effect of shooting scenes in each of the ways described? How different is the experience for the spectator? Again, think in terms of interpellation (see p. 42). ●

Think of the reliability of information provided in films such as The Usual Suspects.

Be careful to distinguish 'viewpoint' from 'point of view'. In film studies, point of view is a term best reserved for a particular kind of shot – the point-of-view shot in which we see an action as if through a particular character's eyes. If it helps, think of point of view as possibly contributing to our viewpoint.

▶ What do you think of Hortense?
Do you think she has a quiet dignity and is someone to be respected? Do you think she lacks some passion and personality?
When you have decided what your response to her is, think about why you think as you do. ●

and bloody, she kisses him passionately after he tells her he will hire a car so that they can visit Boogie.) Jake feels intensely his lower caste status. When they picnic on the way to visit Boogie, he tells how he was perceived as not 'bloody good enough' in the eyes of Beth's people. While she was 'pride of the fucking tribe', he tells his children he 'came from a long line of slaves'. (52.00) Also, through him, revenge is meted out against the rapist, Uncle Bully. It is he who is left alone and lost at the end, with the police on their way to arrest him. We may see Jake the Muss in his drinking, in his domestic violence, as victim as much as villain. (To see him as victim is not to condone what he does, but it opens up other and perhaps more complex ways of understanding and responding.)

3.6. Text and life – investigating response

In the last four sections, we have considered how character is communicated through:

- visual signifiers (iconic, indexical and symbolic);

- speech;

- performance;

- narration and the cinematic presentation.

All of these are 'textual' ways of making meaning in and around character. But, to go back to a point made repeatedly, we, too, make meaning as we interact with the film text and as we bring our own desires, beliefs and life experiences into the cinema. More particularly, as suggested earlier (p. 64), we 'animate' the character in our imaginative engagement with the film – projecting our curiosity, desire or hatred onto what may be described as nothing more than a textual construct. For a film story (or any story) to affect us rather than simply provide us with information, we will want to be drawn into the emotions and issues – we will want to take sides in a drama. The questions we raised about our response to Jake the Muss at the end of the last section demonstrate how important and complex this process of 'taking sides' can be within a drama where we are given any kind of context. We begin to think about competing calls on our sympathies as we reflect on character histories, character motivations.

In thinking about Jake (and perhaps Cynthia in Secrets and Lies), we may recall what was said at the beginning of the chapter about 'character as fate'. Jake is trapped inside his specific 'formation' – of class, race and gender.

▶ Can this allow us to sympathise with him as a wife-beater, as 'a slave to his fists'?

As with the question posed on the previous page about Hortense, what do you feel and think about Jake – and *why*? ●

Once Were Warriors: Domestic images of violence and love – Jake and Beth. How do we respond to these characters?

See Chapter 2 (pp. 17–21).

One important question to consider in this regard is the relationship between how the film aligns us with the character by textual means, and whether this automatically determines our response – our **allegiance** to that character. We receive all kinds of guidance from the text about how to respond to a character – from their overall place within a narrative cause ➤ effect chain to very specific ways in which the character is positioned in the *mise en scène*. Sometimes a character is 'privileged' in a variety of ways, such as seeing/hearing the story from their point of view. We may wish to consider how dialogue includes 'guidance' from other characters as to how we should respond to the character in question. We may wish to consider the way the character is performed, including the em-bodiment of the character in the body of a particular actor. All of these are ways in which we may be positioned – or aligned – with a particular character.

Alfred Hitchcock was fascinated by this phenomenon in cinema – the capacity of a film-maker to place the spectator in a position of **alignment** with the bad guy and then draw them into allegiance. To take a very obvious example: in *Psycho*, after Norman Bates has committed the famous shower murder, he takes the body in the boot of a car to a lake or pond. He hopes car and contents will disappear under the water. Through careful editing and the use of close-up reaction shots, the spectator is interpellated into the drama in a way that allows us to participate in Norman's anxiety. For several moments, we bite our nails with the same tension Norman feels as the car will not go under – and then we share his immense relief when it does finally slide below the surface. We have become so aligned with his need for the car to sink that we have put to one side any reservations we might have about showing allegiance to a psychopathic murderer. (Or do we think he is protecting his mother?)

There is, however, no automatic linkage between alignment and allegiance. One film that deals with this issue in a very witty (though horrific) way is the Belgian film *Man Bites Dog*. Here we are very closely aligned with a documentary film crew who in turn align themselves very closely with their subjects – a gang of homicidal criminals. The film crew end up helping the killers in their crimes and the film draws attention to the way in which we, as spectators, can so easily be drawn into this kind of allegiance. On the other

▶ In exploring the distinction between alignment and allegiance, is it true to say that there is a matching of alignment and allegiance in the way we respond to Elliott in *E.T.* and the two Helens in *Sliding Doors?* ●

There is, perhaps, more difficulty for the first half of *Once Were Warriors* in committing our allegiance to Beth despite our alignment with her through the construction of narrative and point of view and our dramatic engagement through interpellation.
▶ Explore in detail the ways in which we are aligned with Beth/distanced from Beth in *Once Were Warriors*. ●

hand, if we are not drawn into an alignment with Norman Bates in *Psycho* or the documentary crew and their subjects in *Man Bites Dog*, it means that we have resisted the film text's 'summons' (see p. 42) for whatever reason – moral, psychological or aesthetic.

Equally, it needs to be emphasised that we can accept the 'invitation' despite our personal values. We can knowingly put them to one side as part of the 'what if' imaginative pleasure of choosing to go the cinema and sit in the dark in front of a movie dealing with events and characters way outside our personal realities. Perhaps the most vivid (and disturbing) examples are point-of-view shots of killers – such as the opening of *Halloween*. We are not only aligned with the killer, but also, within the terms of the genre experience we have paid for, we want them to succeed – do we not?

We bring lots with us into the movie – experience; sometimes, as in the last example, we may choose to leave some aspects of ourselves behind. What we bring to character is a vast array of personal experiences and memories that will affect our response, independently of the textual operations of the film. However much we may be aware of the formal functions performed by the character as a type within a textual structure, as spectators, we are most likely to respond to characters in performance, moment by moment, with our feelings. This is perhaps particularly so in response to weak characters or characters who are placed in positions of weakness. Take the mothers in our two films – Cynthia in *Secrets and Lies* and Beth in *Once Were Warriors*. We might – in performance – come to love a character such as Cynthia in her vulnerability and contradictoriness, so much so that we cannot be content with a cool intellectual analysis of what the character represents. In performance, in the space of the movie auditorium, we may arrive at an understanding of Beth's love for Jake – and be forced to look at this woman in a more holistic way. This is where, in film studies, we recognise that our task is not simply to become a smart decoder of meanings, but to reflect on what we bring to the film as human beings.

This is not to say we decide to go to the movies consciously to engage in self-analysis or to develop ourselves as human beings (well, not many people, at least). Our primary motivation is to be entertained. I want to finish this section by

---

In some respects, *Secrets and Lies* presents us with a different kind of film from the other three we have so far studied. We are held more at arm's length in the ways in which we observe characters – for example, in the scene referred to earlier between Hortense and Cynthia in the café.

▶ Does this produce a more 'open' film, one in which there is less obvious attempted textual manipulation of our allegiances? ●

▶ What questions does this raise about the morality of cinema? ●

Certainly it further illustrates the pleasure audiences experience in trying out' other identities, other experiences. The movies allow us – for two-hour stretches – to be bad.

▶ What is the best (or worst) example of you showing allegiance to a 'bad' character? ●

▶ Can you think of an example of the opposite: where you are aligned with a 'good' character, but refuse to give the allegiance that we may assume the film expects us to show? ●

In fact, you really want to slap this character! Personally, I cannot stand Forrest Gump.

What is being implied here is a distinction between a cognitive and an affective response. Arguably, this is false distinction – between intellect/head and feelings/heart. All response is cognitive in as much as it is the result of processing by the brain (see p. 8).

This does not mean that we should discuss film characters as though they are 'real' people. What we should do is talk about the reality of our response to them.

This idea of film as a form of human play is argued for again at the end of the next chapter (p. 132).

suggesting that whether our taste in entertainment is sophisticated or simple, either way, we will want to 'play'. Our understanding of what we do with film characters may benefit from seeing our activity as three overlapping (and often simultaneous) forms of **imaginative play**.

First, characters may be approached primarily as the entry point into **drama** – into confrontation and opposition in ways that may be primarily physical or psychological, but in any case provide excitement and engagement, often of a quite visceral kind. What I am getting at here is that there is an attraction to 'raw' human drama, irrespective of what the drama is about.

Secondly, this drama will be useful to us – offering a **simulation** of situations we may find interesting, even useful, to relate to our own lives. At an extreme, these characters may 'relive' actual experiences we have had – such as falling into and out of love. More commonly these characters will 'enact' some human experience which we can observe and set against our own similar, but far from identical, experience. Sometimes these characters may exemplify forms of behaviour and reactions that we can only imagine, in relation to situations beyond anything we have ever had to deal with ourselves.

Thirdly, arising out of the drama and the simulation we **experiment**. We may, for example, have never had the Hortense's experience of attempting to discover her birth mother in *Secret and Lies*. We may have never experienced anything remotely like the drama contained in the family violence and abuse of *Once Were Warriors*. Nevertheless, the simulation offered by the film is something we are also offered the opportunity to experiment, to push back the boundaries of our own experiences and, in very serious ways, think 'what if …?'

When we participate in these overlapping forms of play, we are most likely to do so with a fair idea as to what we will tolerate. For example, we may wish to uphold our personal values and standards, and, if necessary, resist a film that seems to work against them. We may feel sufficiently provoked by the film for no other option to be possible. At the opposite extreme, we may wish to relax the standards and beliefs that guide our behaviour in our everyday lives outside the fictional world of the movie. Whatever we do, the fundamental point

War films such as Francis Ford Coppola's *Apocalypse Now* (United States, 1979) and Ang Lee's *Ride with the Devil* (United States, 1999) present us with particular problems. We may be thrilled by an attack, experience it from the side of the aggressor, and yet deplore the morality of what we are, so to speak, witnessing.

is that the movies open up for us an alternative space, a point of entry into (simulations of) other people's lives. What we do in that space is complex and fascinating. Films allow us to explore and learn about ourselves in that space – where textual representation comes up against our experience as movie-goers and human beings.

3.7. Character – ideology – response

Our personal response may be idiosyncratic, and will certainly reflect our individuality, our particular background and experience. More often than not, however, this personal response will be shared by a large number of other individuals within the audience. The fact that our 'personal' response can be a 'common' response may be explained in relation to the concepts of discourse and hegemony (see Chapter 2, pp. 48–52). Specifically, this individual-yet-common response can be explained as follows:

- As individuals, our values, even our experiences, are remarkably similar to those of others who live in the same society and are exposed to the same influences, the same hegemonic 'formations'.

- The film itself is likely to reflect and reinforce this 'formation' – either unconsciously because it is itself a product of this formation. More likely, it will do so in a calculated way in order to guarantee that it 'speaks' to the audience and will thus be commercially successful.

- The discourse of the film – its entire textual 'operation' – exerts considerable control, despite our potential resistance as spectators. (This can be seen in areas such as the narrative control of information, the construction of its realist illusion, the emotive effect of soundtrack, interpellation techniques.)

These points are among those referred to by those who argue that popular films have a negative 'mass' media effect. It takes us back to the discussion on first- and second-level engagement in section 2.7 (especially p. 51). Thus, while the audience may be active in all kinds of ways, responding to character and situation, they still do so under the control of the film text – and so tend to respond the same way, more or less. They will not normally be alert to challenging the ideological messages contained in the film's discourse – or be willing to do so.

▶ Consider a film that you have seen recently and which affected you deeply. Try to work through these categories of 'drama', 'simulation' and 'experiment' in order to see how useful they may be in helping us understand our involvement in a movie.

Also, think about the film in relation to this idea of the movie opening up for us an 'alternative space'. ●

Narrative realism is the most common discursive form in cinema. It is discussed in the final section of Chapter 4.

Let me make it clear that this book adopts a somewhat different view. Certainly, the film text is a very popular mechanism for controlling our response. At the same time, we must recognise and give weight to all that we bring to the film, as individuals and as members of communities.

▶ Try to think through your own position on these issues of film text, meaning and response, then read section 3.8 (pp. 88–92). ●

However, where major discourses are competing with one another within a society, a film's apparent adoption of one discourse is much more likely to lead to major public debate. Similarly, what is hegemonic (common sense, normative) to one community may be seen as openly ideological by another whose world view has been shaped by different experiences and values. Within this kind of context, issues of response become particularly complicated (and interesting!).

To give some indication of what a minefield it is to move across this territory, it is useful to look at the huge controversy that surrounded the release of *Once Were Warriors* in New Zealand in 1994. Many critics and academics despised the film. It was accused of reinforcing stereotypes of Maoris held by the dominant Pakhua (white) population – as drunkards and rapists in dysfunctional families. More specifically, it was accused of offering a hopelessly unrealistic 'solution' in terms of Maori people returning to the *marau* (rural homeland) from downtown Auckland. It was accused of failing to offer any analysis of the present in relation to the past – the colonial exploitation and humiliation of earlier generations that had reduced Maori people to the underclass portrayed in the film. Those 'positive' representations of Maori culture were not seen as positive – especially the warrior tradition turned into some glamorous equivalent of LA gangland; the songs, dancers and fighting rituals romanticised or made 'exotic'. The tattoos were criticised either for not being authentic or for betraying or cheapening Maori traditions, or both.

On a wider front, the film was accused of a hypocritical attitude to violence – condemning it, yet offering it as pleasure. The initiation of Nig was a particular focus for this criticism (brutality without blood), as well as the spectacle of the bar-room brawls. More widely, the portrayal of youth culture was seen as 'americanised', playing off hood movies such as *Boyz 'n the Hood*. The violence of the way in which the message of the film was pounded home was criticised nearly as much as the physical violence of the film. Critics talked about being hit over the head by the director, visually and verbally.

Yet the film was New Zealand's greatest domestic hit. In 1994, it outperformed *Jurassic Park*, until then New Zealand's box-office record-holder. It was well received at film festivals around the world and won major prizes. It sold (its critics would say 'as calculated') in the United States, and throughout the major world markets.

So should the film be considered insidious – promoting damaging ideas under the appearance of being a progressive film? Did all white people who went to see the film have their racist attitudes enhanced or confirmed? Did all Maori people who went to see it feel a sense of shame and insult? For those who did like it, was the attraction the violence? Were overseas audiences who enjoyed the film, such as those in the United Kingdom, naïve, blind to the ideological problems identified by critics? Without detailed audience research we cannot say. What can be said is that audiences negotiate meanings, take from films what they need and want. Sometimes we surrender willingly to the persuasive force of the film, sometimes we resist.

In fact there are positive claims to be made for *Once Were Warriors*. Riwia Brown's screenplay is quite different from Alan Duff's original novel. Most fundamentally, it centres more on Beth than on Jake, making the film much more about gender issues. It also is much more concerned than the novel with representing something of the richness of Maori traditional culture and history.

It is also worth bearing in mind in discussions of this sort that a film such as *Once Were Warriors*, for better or for worse, was conceived as a commercial project, designed to make a profit by giving pleasure to an audience. Consumerist criticism would recognise that some of the criteria used to judge a film such as this must be those of the industry itself – dramatic story, engaging characters, vivid spectacle. However, if we contrast just one criticism made of the film set against a 'consumer' set of priorities, we see the problem. The family leaving the "hood' at the end to go back to the marau offers hope of a new start, a kind of promise of a happy ending. This satisfies commercial considerations. As we have seen, however, this was seen by critics of the film as an escapist solution, one that simply avoids addressing the real issues of the Maori urban underclass.

More positive reactions to the film may be explained by a variety of factors – textual, contextual and even intertextual. To take one example, Jake the Muss was perceived as a pathetic character, deserving some kind of sympathy, by many New Zealanders. This was not because they endorsed wife-beaters. It was perhaps partly because of an ability to

How often in film studies we are left making assumptions about audience response. There needs to be much more routine research into *actual* audience response.

The screenwriter also had clearly commercial priorities in prioritising the 'emotional' over the 'political'. As Brian McDonnell wrote in *Metro Magazine* (vol. 101,pp. 7–9):

> She wanted the film to be emotional rather than political, i.e. not as concerned with racial politics as the book. In her view the script needed several key things which the novel had lacked: 'more light and shade', a 'bit more humour and breathing for the audience', and 'a lot more hope'. The other important new aim was to 'show the power and beauty of Maori culture'.

'Victim' derives from the Latin word meaning defeated.

*This is an example of the **intertextual**: one 'text' informs or influences our reading of another.*

▶ Can you refer to a film you have seen from a very different culture to your own in which you were uncertain about how appropriate your 'reading' of the film text was, applying all of the cultural assumptions of your 'formation' onto a very different world? ●
(See also p. 106)

Consider again the distinction between textual studies and response studies (p. 64).

understand that Jake was a victim, an acknowledgment of the humiliating treatment of the Maori male over a very long period of history. Since one accusation levelled against the film is precisely that the film lost all sense of this, then presumably some spectators were able to read this in to the film from their own resources as meaning makers. In New Zealand, the sympathetic response to Jake was also partly attributable to the fact that the actor, Temuera Morrison, enjoyed a very positive media image through his role as a doctor in a daily television soap opera.

Outside New Zealand, Jake may or may not have been the object of sympathy, depending on all kinds of cultural attitudes held by the specific audience – although it is my view that the director, screenwriter and actor have tried to make him appear sympathetic. This raises major questions about the reading of film texts across different cultures – a fascinating and huge topic!

Certainly what this example of the character of Jake illustrates are some of the complex ways in which meaning is the product not just of a film text, but also of personal response. If we hold to the textual study of a film alone, analysis of the meanings and values, especially concerning issues of representation, can give the impression of being fairly objective. We find clues, make sense of them, gauge their significance and arrive at an overview. When we include an assessment of our complicated interaction with characters and the feelings that they and their situations evoke, however, we are forced, sometimes at least, to make quite different statements.

3.8 Making meaning – experience and desire

To repeat what was said near the beginning of this section, meaning is a process – ongoing, shifting, changing – the result of competing claims. Clearly, *Once Were Warriors* has different kinds of 'truth' for different spectators and this is dependent on the 'formation' of that spectator and the specific questions they ask of the film. For some, the emphasis is on the 'truthfulness' of the human drama, the representation of emotions and exchanges between characters; for others, it is on the 'untruthfulness' of the wider context, the representation of culture, politics and history. For still others, a major 'truth' of the film is that it lies!

Underlying this critical debate and reflection are two very

problematic points of reference – one is **realism** (informing what we see) and the other is **experience** (informing how we see what we see). As students of film, we develop an ever greater sense of character (and everything else in a movie) as a construct. As we do so, realism becomes both less and more of a problem. It becomes less of a problem because we begin to recognise that realism is a non-issue: all films are (just!) rule-based meaning structures. It becomes more of a problem when we continue this sentence by saying that films are rule-based meaning structures that attempt to represent aspects of the real world.

Inevitably we ask how a character and the situation they are located within measure up against our sense of the 'real'. Films such as *Secrets and Lies* and *Once Were Warriors* are concerned with observing characters in their social realities. Now, it may seem that within this kind of social realist film, it is important that the representation of the world that we are given seems believable, that our willingness to think about major issues raised by the film will depend in large part on how 'realistic' we find them. But what does it mean to be 'realistic'? For example, the two films we are studying have strongly contrasting styles, neither of which can be said to reproduce reality simply and unproblematically. Indeed, as narrative realist films working more or less as melodramas, they artistically shape and dramatically intensify 'reality'.

We are thrown back on our own experience in two respects. One is our experience of cinema itself – our familiarity with the ways in which story is shaped in conformity with conventions we have been familiar with since we were small children. The other is our experience of life. This does not have to be actual personal experience; in fact, to apply really circular logic, it may be experience of the world we have gained from watching other movies (or television or reading literature). Whichever way we gain our experience of the world, we apply it in our moment-by-moment response to character and situation. Our experience is not a fixed and clearly definable critical tool. Rather, as a reflection of our identity as human beings, it helps explain our choice and use of critical tools in any particular instance.

What a slippery equation: **realism ◄─► experience**! Both are so subjective: one a construct of text and performance; the other a construct of society and culture. And yet we use them all the time as the basis for what we believe is 'objective' interpretation. We are fairly confident about engaging in this kind of 'common-sense' analysis. It seems practical; it is something we do all the time. We trust our own perceptions and instincts. In so doing, we confirm a certain idea of what is real and we confirm the methods by which we approach the real. In other words, we reinforce a certain discourse, a certain hegemony.

Perhaps because we are provided with a security that comes from familiarity, we are (perhaps foolishly) confident about using realism ◄—► experience for getting our bearings in film discussion. By comparison – and this goes back to what was said in the opening pages of the very first chapter – we are much more inhibited and uncertain about working with a different equation: **fantasy ◄—► desire**.

We can think of films as 'staging' our fantasies (and these do not have to be crazy or way-out fantasies – perhaps just the fantasy of living better, being happier). We can also think of our response less in terms of our actual experience of the world (in fact, we may want to leave this well behind!) than in terms of our desire for the world to give us what we want. If films 'stage' our fantasies, then characters are highly significant in 'performing' those fantasies: sometimes by embodying those fantasies in their physical bodies so that we project our desiring selves onto them; sometimes by doing things which enact a different, better, more ideal self that we enjoy imagining.

We may open up a film to a more critical view, gain a critical distance on both the film and our response to it, by working in relation to the fantasies 'performed' by the film and the desires that it provokes. More so, certainly, than if we remain within the circularity of realism ◄—► experience. This second line of enquiry is less secure, more open. It links with the idea of seeing the film text and our response to it as forms of imaginative play. It encourages us to interrogate the messages and values of the film in a much more subversive way – breaking open the film's discourse system. We see the film as a constructed text that, by design or accident, releases a vast array of sensory triggers for our minds to respond to.

For example, if we consider the use of Maori cultural forms in *Once Were Warriors* – such as the facial tattoos – in their **psychological** or mental function rather than their realist or physical function, we may gain greater insight into what the film is offering us as an experience. For some spectators, these cultural forms may trigger macho fantasies, fantasies of group solidarity and independence, a collective pride in difference, 'otherness'. This may be experienced by audiences who have no direct connection with Maori culture, indeed audiences who may live thousands of miles from the location of the film. The visual and aural signifiers of the film are appropriated, translated into a form that conforms to their particular fantasy ◄─► desire trajectory. As a consequence, we can begin to understand better the commercial motivation of the film and its particular appeal to a target audience. With *Once Were Warriors*, we may be able to understand its appeal among Maori audiences, despite the 'realist' objections levelled against the film. We may be able to understand how – at the level of performance, in the 'staging' of desire – the film is potentially more oppositional than it seems to be if analysed in other ways.

We will come back to this in the second half of the next chapter, which considers how films as 'spectacles' stage and perform their stories. This will inevitably require some further consideration of characters who take their places within these stagings. It will also, inevitably, force us to think harder about the issues just raised. How do we really respond to films: in relation to their realism or in relation to their fantasy? How do we really evaluate films: in relation to our experience or in relation to our desire?

What the above discussion clearly illustrates is that when we watch a film with a level of sensitivity to its messages and values, the whole dynamic of our response to character and performance may change. Ideological analysis may put a break on us slipping into simplistic, even irresponsible, emotionalism. Equally, though, it may not. The emotional power of a film may be so strong, may so engage our sense of personal identity or experience, or so appeal to our fantasy that it absorbs or sweeps aside any ideological sensitivity we might otherwise have. (This is quite different from the deliberate 'switching-off' of our critical faculties in order to simply enjoy a film we know to be bad.) One of the long-standing and central criticisms of popular cinema is based on the claim that our critical faculties are swept up in emotionalism – and hence the underpinning ideological

We may also be able to understand better its appeal for specific audiences far distant from the Maori community of South Auckland – whether in Los Angeles, New York, London, Paris or Johannesburg.

As on p. 88, consider the issues involved in cross-cultural readings of a film.

Several times you have been asked to think through your views on the issue of how far the film text determines our response. Here is a further question.

▶ **What determines how we value a particular film?** ●

It may be useful before answering this question to summarise the main points that have been made from the beginning of this section on p. 88.

values and attitudes of the film are not only unchallenged, but also perpetuated.

Each of us is implicated in a whole network of meanings and values circulating in our society – some of them so commonplace that they can appear to be part of our normal everyday processing of our reality. Sometimes in films we encounter characters that we can easily fit within these frames of meaning and understanding. One of the pleasures of cinema is this kind of confirmation – it is reassuring that people and their experiences fit within a frame of reference which we already have. Sometimes we encounter characters that defy such easy categorisation. These characters force us to modify or extend our categories. In so doing, they may make us sensitive to the limitations of those categories in the first place. Perhaps they even defamiliarise these categories.

A film has no absolute truth, no essence waiting to be uncovered. Meaning is a process, a dynamic interaction between a film text and constantly shifting and diverse audiences who bring their particular experiences and understandings to bear. This is the great fascination of studying film. Certainly, meaning is not a fixed object waiting to be found by the 'expert' film analyst.

3.9. Film character and evaluation

Finally, let us consider a critical question. How do we evaluate how well a character works in a particular film? There are at least three broad sets of criteria that we need to consider.

The first is in relation to the internal **textual requirements** of the film. This approach is formalist and asks questions about the appropriateness or otherwise of the character in performing certain functions required to support other aspects of the film. These include:

- contributing effectively to moving forward the cause → effect system of story/plot;

- helping the audience to locate the film within a genre framework;

- providing an adequate focus for the audience to project their emotions and values;

- representing the film's messages and values.

▶ In everyday speech, we often use the term 'hidden meaning' or 'layers of meaning'. Consider the value of these expressions in light of the discussion in this section. ●

The second may appear the same as the first, but it arises from a consideration of **commercial requirements**, rather than textual ones. (The idea of the 'commercial aesthetic' links this to the above.) Is character conceived in such a way as to provide pleasure for the audience – and profit for the industry? Here character will be judged in relation to satisfying audience expectations and desires. Here we may well consider a star (personifying/embodying) as character, defining the role through their distinctive screen image.

A third moves away from the needs of the text and the needs of producers/audiences and asks questions of character based on broader social and political considerations centring on **representation**. This overlaps with the final bullet point under 'textual requirements' (see opposite). The difference here, however, is that we ask questions about representation in terms of how that is of significance *outside* the text. Are the messages and values communicated through a particular character ones that we find challenging or reassuring – are they true or false to our experience of living.

Beyond this, we have begun to question whether our evaluation of character is more appropriately measured in terms of its ability to appeal to our fantasies, to stage our desires, than in terms of its realism. Whether or not a film conforms to our actual or learnt experience of reality may be less significant (or valuable) than whether it opens up a kind of imaginative play in which we can experience drama and simulation, or experiment with other lives.

Finally, I want to raise some difficult questions about evaluation of character in relation to the different levels of **competence** within a film audience. Once we begin to consider levels of competence in different people's response to a film, we appear to be setting up a hierarchy in which some responses are not simply more mature (in terms of understanding), but also more competent (in terms of knowledge and critical application). This may seem to fly in the face of a kind of natural democracy in which everybody's response to the movie experience is equally valued. It is, however, true to say that:

- Some members of an audience are more aware than others of a film as a **textual 'construct'**, are more knowledgeable about the techniques and strategies being employed. As a result, they may take greater delight or show greater

See Richard Maltby's Hollywood Cinema *(Oxford: Blackwell, 1985), pp. 6–9.*

▶ Do you think we apply all three kinds of criteria outlined here when we watch a movie? Which come more immediately? Which only come with reflection? ●
Think about these criteria in relation to your evaluation of the characters in Secrets and Lies *and* Once Were Warriors.

▶ Are there other criteria, other aspects of the process of coming to a judgment on film characters, that you think need to be added? ●

▶ What would be the consequence for film evaluation if we all decided that we make our judgments based on how successfully a film staged our fantasies and stimulated our desires? ●

distaste in relation to the formal and aesthetic means employed in, for example, the presentation of character.

- Similarly, some members of an audience are more perceptive than others in identifying the **messages and values** inscribed in the film in general, and possibly characters in particular, and are more sensitive in their response to these.

One response to this is to say that it is not our response that is more or less interesting, it is simply our ability to articulate it. This again takes us back to the introductory chapter and to the point made there that the gaining of knowledge is often primarily the gaining of a language that allows us to express more adequately what we already feel, already know. Another response is to acknowledge that, as in every other area of human activity, we can become more skilled in what we do. So, in film studies, we can become more skilled in identifying detail, as well as more articulate in describing it. In our response to any art form, these skills cannot be separated from our growth and development as human beings. We become (hopefully) more mature, more sensitive through experience, as part of the natural process of our human development. A far greater problem is actually trying to define what is a 'mature' level of maturity, a 'sensitive' level of sensitivity, a 'competent' level of competence.

In this kind of work as a film student, each of us has two obligations. The first is to be honest to ourselves about what our response to a movie is and as rigorous as possible in analysing the reasons why we respond as we do. The second is to listen to others. Evaluation can only ever be comparative – never absolute.

So when is maturity mature? When is sensitivity sensitive? When is competence competent? We spend our lives becoming more experienced, more discerning, so it is impossible to draw up a defined set of 'standards'. This book cannot talk about your response, your feelings – only you can.

4. Spectacle

This chapter turns to the film attraction *or* spectacle. *Emphasis is again very much on the visual, although some reference is made to sound as an integral element of the cinema of attractions. Specific study is made of sequences from* **A Chinese Ghost Story** *(Hong Kong, 1987) and* **William Shakespeare's Romeo and Juliet** *(United States, 1996). Ideas of performance are carried forward from the last chapter to consider* stardom *and the idea of the 'performance' of cinema itself in the design, staging and* cinematography *of spectacular scenes.* Excess *is identified as one of the characteristics of this kind of cinema 'performance'. The final part of the chapter revisits ideas on how we make meaning and elaborates on the idea of* schemata, *before setting up questions of* make-believe *that are developed by reference to the distinction between* realist *and* fantasy *traditions in cinema.*

4.1. The cinema of attractions

So far in this book we have looked at elements of film – story and character – which are not specific only to film. Story and character are, of course, central to novels and plays (and often songs and paintings, too). Throughout chapters 2 and 3, however, we have recognised that film is a visual medium and this has encouraged our emphasis on visual storytelling and the visual presentation/revelation of character. In this chapter, we will go further in exploring the specifically visual attractions of cinema.

Of course, in discussing dialogue, we have also considered film as an audio-visual medium.

This is taken from the London IMAX Cinema website:

[It] features the UK's biggest cinema screen, soaring more than 20 metres high – nearly the height of five double-decker buses – and stretching more than 26 metres wide; an 11,600-watt digital surround-sound system; and an IMAX projection system, the most sophisticated motion-picture projection system in the world. Working together, these elements immerse viewers in larger-than-life images and ultra-realistic digital sound, making them feel as if they are literally 'in the picture'.

▶ Have you ever had to sit through someone's home videos and begun to wonder when this set of 'attractions' will end? What makes the visual interesting? What makes us care? ●

The '**cinema of attractions**' is a term that has been used to describe very early ('primitive') cinema. The first audiences paid to be dazzled by the visual, by moving images. This most commonly involved trick photography (such as playing a film backwards) or filming movement towards the camera by, for example, a car or a train, giving the spectator the momentary terror of being run down. This was cinema as a fairground attraction, as a novelty. Even in its earliest form, the cinema of attractions was more than a cinema of views – it was a cinema of sensations. One hundred years later, we find that such a cinema of attractions still exists. For example, IMAX cinemas function to offer an audiovisual experience using the very latest technology. Even in our routine film-going, we are regularly offered the choice of a big budget film in which the spectacle (action sequences, special effects) is the principal draw, or 'attraction'.

Right back at the beginning, however, within the first six or seven years of cinema, it became apparent that audiences wanted more than the mere trickery of the 'fairground-attraction' experience. The motivation to watch moving images needed to be driven by desires other than that of simply being delighted and surprised by the mechanical reproduction of movement and the distortions to reality made possible by techniques such as superimposition. The spectacle needed to be driven by a sense of involvement beyond the simple sensation of, for example, being 'run over' by a car or train. In the twenty years between 1895 and 1915, cinema discovered that, for the visual spectacle to be sustained (as opposed to the sudden-impact visual effect), the audience had to be motivated to participate imaginatively and emotionally in the drama.

Although this is not a good analogy for people who really like firework displays, let me compare the visual spectacle of a firework display with that of a tightrope walker. In the first instance, I can take a certain aesthetic pleasure in the pretty patterns formed in the sky and perhaps receive the occasional shock from a particularly loud bang. In the second instance, I am terrified for the tightrope walker, projecting onto him or her all my fears about falling. Simultaneously, I am awed by the person's skill and courage. Whereas the firework display is nothing more than display (unless I start imagining some disaster caused by these fireworks), the tightrope walk triggers desire – in me – desire that the person make it across to the other side safely. Beyond this, I may project myself into the narrative of the tightrope walker's 'journey' or into their state of mind.

The techniques required to draw the spectator into the drama – mainly dependent on editing – developed during the silent era. To create a spectacular attraction *and* position the spectator within that spectacle was a huge evolution in cinema. In films made in the Soviet Union in the 1920s, the cinema of attractions was exploited with the intention of creating powerful effects on the audience. One of the most famous examples in the entire history of cinema is the Odessa Steps sequence from Sergei Eisenstein's *Battleship Potemkin* (USSR, 1925). Here the army restores order among the civilian population of Odessa after they have come out to support the mutineering sailors of the *Potemkin*. Eisenstein uses editing and graphic *mise en scène* in order to create attraction after attraction for the spectator. (You will note that an 'attraction' need not be pleasurable; it can be shocking and awful.)

Watching Eisenstein's Odessa Steps sequence, film spectators are drawn into a cinema of attractions in which each editing 'beat' creates a further intensification of the drama and a sense of physical participation in the event. This was the film-maker's intention – to shock an audience into remembering the suffering of the people in the period before the Bolshevik Revolution of 1917 and to strengthen their support and solidarity for that revolution, eight years on. The Odessa Steps sequence still works today because the images and their sequencing (through montage editing) have immense dramatic power, stimulating our imaginations to project fear, outrage and shock. Perhaps it evokes desire for an end to this butchery, both in the immediate context of the scene and in the broader humanitarian context triggered by the associations these images make with horrors we may have seen on television news or perhaps even experienced ourselves. Perhaps it evokes different desires, ones less easy to talk about and deal with – desires that have to do with the visceral excitement of death and of the exercise of power triggered by the remorseless march of the Cossack soldiers.

The nature of the response will vary. The obvious point to be made here is that the spectacle provokes a response, has an

▶ What is your reaction to visually shocking images, particularly when they accumulate over a whole sequence? Can they be described as providing an 'attraction'? ●

Often we find ourselves watching a dramatic sequence in which two impulses are in opposition – our desire for the sequence to end because the tension, the intensity of the images, is so powerful and our desire for the sequence to continue because it is so spectacular, so imaginatively engaging.
▶ Think of a sequence that has this mixed effect on you. Try to pinpoint your reasons for wanting the sequence to end and your reasons for wanting the sequence to continue. ●

Battleship Potemkin was made in 1925, but in fact examples of feature-length films containing spectacular sequences were established much earlier. For example, *Cabiria* from Italy in 1914 and the Hollywood film it partly inspired in 1916, *Intolerance*, both contain spectacular sequences. An Italian film, *Good Morning Babylon* (Taviani Brothers, Italy, 1987), dramatises this influence of Italian spectacle on Hollywood. Charles Dance plays D. W. Griffith, the real-life director of *Intolerance*.

impact and is therefore in some way dramatically meaningful to each of us. We care. We simultaneously desire that this sequence will end, as the Cossack jackboots keep coming and coming (an example of editing being used to stretch out real time), and want it to continue because it is such a brilliantly created cinematic spectacle.

In *Battleship Potemkin*, the spectacle is an integrated element within the structure of the film and is at the service of the film's messages and values. Further, the film consciously and deliberately constructs the spectator as someone who admires and sympathises with those in revolt and those supporting them. In other words, the viewing experience is much more than that of simply looking at a visual display.

Yet, this argument that spectacle works as an integrated component within the overall experience of the feature film is not the whole story. I have taken the Odessa Steps sequence from Eisenstein's film out of context as an example of the cinema of attractions (Eisenstein called it 'montage of attractions') in mature silent cinema. I have thrown it onto your 'screen' as an image experience. We are now used to this sort of thing – clusters of images competing constantly for our attention alongside other clusters of images, their only context the here-and-now of visual stimulation. Images are played as music is played – constantly, sometimes they are identifiable and familiar, sometimes not – part of the sensory world through which we move. We can easily imagine sections of the Odessa Steps sequence appearing within a music video, as part of a back projection in a club or as part of a fashion-store window display.

This experience of wall-to-wall visual imagery has had a significant effect on commercial cinema. The movies are both a source of much of this visual imagery and its victim, having to extend further and further the possibilities of the cinema of attractions in order to capture interest. This is seen as particularly important commercially since the age group that most frequently goes to the cinema is the same one which is most immersed in this visual culture. A new cinema of attractions has arisen, particularly within action genres, where plot and story are of less importance than the spectacle. Indeed, the function of plot can be seen as offering minimal links and justifications for moving from one spectacle to the next. So, whether the film is a futuristic action movie such as *Men in Black* or the latest James Bond film, spectacle is the dominant element. We may well have forgotten the plot of such a movie within days – but the 'attractions' will remain clear. Devising spectacle in big-budget movies involves a range of commercial considerations, some of which have to do with the production of multimillion dollar spin-offs, such as computer games based on the spectacular locations and hi-tech gadgets of the movie.

The selling of spectacle over narrative is often discussed as a retrograde development, a move back to the idea of cinema as an attraction (although obviously at a much more sophisticated level). A simplistic evolutionary model of Hollywood proposes that Hollywood moved away from spectacle for its own sake very early (certainly by 1920) and standardised its product around the traditional dramatic and literary structures of the melodramatic theatre, with strong emphasis on plot and character. (For example, we looked at a traditional 'three-act structure', typical of nineteenth-century stage melodrama, in relation to storytelling in *E.T.*) So, marks of quality in the narrative realist film were considered to include a coherent plot, believable characters and plausibility of motivation – all evaluative criteria we will find in literary studies. In this context, the blockbuster cinema of spectacle is seen as something of a 'dumbing down', a deliberate attempt to appeal to a very basic craving for action.

Cinema history (its *histoire*) is rather more complicated than this, however! For example, some of the most intellectual arguments supporting cinema as an artistic medium in the 1920s focused on its visual qualities. 'Visual' cinema as varied as Charlie Chaplin/Buster Keaton/Harold Lloyd Hollywood comedy, Soviet montage and German expressionism were praised as contributing to the development of a 'seventh art'. Both theorists and significant numbers of key film-makers spoke of their regret at the coming of sound, which they felt would drag cinema back towards theatre.

In practice, after the coming of sound in the period 1927–1929, Hollywood continued to put great energy into genres of spectacle – the gangster films of the early 1930s and the swashbuckling adventure romances of the later 1930s, for example. Certainly no one who has ever

> Do you agree with this? Is the plot and theme of, say, *Terminator 2* or *The Matrix* less important for the audience than spectacle?

Can you distinguish between films in which the narrative is simply a platform for spectacle and others where spectacle supports, but does not dominate, narrative? ●

> What is the relative importance of narrative and spectacle in computer games? ●

Hindi cinema (Bollywood) is an example of a popular cinema which has never repressed the 'attraction'. Masala movies are best known for the song and dance sequences which erupt routinely and regularly within the melodrama. A recent film such as *Kuch Kuch Hota Hai* shows that, even with the increasing influence of Hollywood values and lifestyles, the conventional ways of staging 'attractions' remain.

> Make some notes towards a critical response to a 'spectacle' film in relation to the ideas raised here. For example, consider *Gladiator* (Ridley Scott, United States, 2000). ●

See Public Enemy *(1931) as an example of a gangster film of the period and* The Adventures of Robin Hood *(1938) as an example of a swashbuckling adventure romance.*

For an example of Busby Berkeley's work, see Gold Diggers of 1933.

seen a Busby Berkeley–choreographed musical from this period could possibly argue that cinema lost its sense of the visual!

4.2 The cinema of attractions – from the visual to the aural

The pleasure of looking – **scopophilia** – has been central to cinema since the beginning. The object of our looking can be anything from a fabulously staged number in a musical to an intimate portrayal of the human body. In Hollywood, especially during the Studio System period, this pleasure was to be found in such things as the choreography of action sequences and the glamour of the *mise en scène*. Most commonly, it was the human being – embodied in a star – who provided a desirable object for the gaze of the spectator.

Scopophilia can be intensely experienced within the darkened space of the movie auditorium. It may override our interest in story, character and theme in ways that have no real equivalent in our experience of literature. Cinema has always been a cinema of attractions. And, where a film is not consciously constructing spectacle-as-attraction, we can make it so. As participating spectators, we have the capacity to energise the image with our desire. Looking is motivated by pleasure and fuelled by desire, desire that we bring with us to the viewing situation and desire that is anticipated by those who have made the film.

► Can you recall any films where you have been aware of how you invest the visual with your own personal desire? ●

We return to these issues in section 4.7 below.

Before moving on, I am going to risk boring you by going back to my prejudices concerning firework displays. I have suggested that, as a 'display', a decorative pattern of red, yellow and white light in the sky, a firework display does not do much for me. I have said, however, that the bangs (and even more the whizz) of fireworks conjure up a mild sense of anxiety which allows me to begin to project fears and fantasies about some awful thing that might result from this display, which does add the ingredient of danger to the event. In fact, large public firework displays today are now conceived as part of a son et lumière (sound and light show). The fireworks are let off in synchronisation to a soundtrack made up usually of a compilation of classical and rock music. The music provides an additional and different sensory stimulation. Our minds, as always, are quick to make meaning as we try to find some form and shape to the combination of sound and light. This may stop far short of a 'narrative', but it nevertheless allows us to imagine shifts in mood and tone throughout the display. More specifically, we imagine the music imposing some rationale on the release of the fireworks, which might otherwise seem random. Sometimes we sense a 'visual' rhythm shaped by the music. Music makes the firework display a richer, more interesting event, most especially because it provides a further source of stimulation for the imagination.

By contrast, I can watch my tightrope walker without any soundtrack besides my ticking heart. Perhaps some tension-inducing music would work – a roll of drums at the beginning; a celebratory fanfare at the end – but it is not necessary. I am watching what I believe to be a person risking their life and music may reduce this to showmanship. (Think how often a 'heartbeat' rhythm is used in tense action sequences in the movies.)

The point of this further digression into the world of fireworks and tightrope artistes is that the cinema of attractions also uses sound to special effect – and has done so right from the earliest days of 'silent' cinema. A study of our experience of the cinema spectacle must include consideration of what we hear as well as what we see.

Sometimes a film is characterised by a particular sound, a few repeated notes – as in *Jaws* or *Halloween*. Most often a film has a series of motifs running through the film, each representing a different character or location or mood. The soundtrack is serving the visual and the narrative, giving greater communicative power to the film as a whole. We find this in *A Chinese Ghost Story*, the first film we will look at in detail in this chapter.

In Chapter 2, we looked at the visual in storytelling by reference to *mise en scène* and editing. In Chapter 3, we looked at the visual in characterisation by reference to *mise en scène* and performance. In both these studies, reference was made to the central importance of signification – the signifier as the basis for the exchange between film and spectator. Meaning is made by the film-makers in the selection of signifiers and by the audience in their decoding of what it is that is signified. Reference to this process of signification will continue to be made in this section as we extend our study of the communication system of cinema, shifting our emphasis

▶ Reflect again on sequences you have already been thinking about in relation to earlier questions in this chapter.

Which of them attempts a naturalistic effect, using little or no music and only ambient, diegetic sound?

Which of them really go for a son et lumière? ●

Melo in Classical Greek meant 'song', giving us the word melodrama. From the very beginnings of western drama, there was the realisation that song/music could enhance the dramatic effect. Melodrama can be seen as the foundation for almost all popular genre cinema — whether action or romance-based — as well as that 'high' culture form, opera.

The 'signifier' has appeared in both chapters 2 and 3. As a reminder:

Signifier The sign (visual, verbal, aural) which represents the signified
Signified The mental concept suggested by the signifier
Referent The thing in the real world which the signifier/signified alludes to

The referent is always absent (see p. 48) and yet apparently present. This apparent presence is intensified by the fact that the most common kind of signifier in film is the iconic sign. The iconic sign (see pp. 65–6) has a very close (photographic) resemblance to the referent.

▶ Take a sequence from a film you know well and reflect on the effect of the music and how it achieves this effect.
Repeat this simple procedure of reading the visual images first without and then with the soundtrack. ●

▶ Is the general point made in this paragraph correct, is music generally symbolic? ●

Here are a few points to consider.
To say that music is symbolic suggests that there is no real relationship between a piece of music and, let's say, happiness. If we decode a piece of music as signifying this state of being, it is purely because we have learnt this code from our culture. This suggests that, in other cultures, happiness may be associated with different sounds, different patterns of music.

▶ Do you agree? Do musical 'signs' have no connection to a state of mind/feeling until we learn the cultural conventions of musical communication? ●

slightly – from *mise en scène* to cinematography. In considering the work of signification, we will move from the actor's performance to the 'performance' of those behind the camera, such as the film director, director of photography, and art designer. Before doing this, let us explore film music a little further, attempting to apply the terminology of semiotics.

In both chapters 2 and 3, we considered meaning contained in the aural signifier, the spoken word. We will now add to this, as the previous section suggested we should, another **aural signifier – music**. How does music signify? Unlike the visual signifier (which most often represents a thing iconically – as it appears in the real world), the musical signifier is more likely to be symbolic, of some general state of being such as sadness or happiness. The symbolic aural sign can transform the otherwise iconic visual sign, turning it from a simple resemblance – such as the visual signifying of a city or a landscape – into a representation of romance, beauty or danger. Watch a sequence of film with a music soundtrack, but with the sound turned off; then watch it with the soundtrack on and consider the difference. For example, however expressionistic the opening shots of *Taxi Driver* may appear to be, without the Bernard Hermann music, these images remain iconic representations of portions of a New York yellow taxi and the 'mean streets' through which it moves. With the music, we are much more inclined to regard the visual signifiers as carrying some symbolic association of a hellish, nightmarish city, associations anchored in Travis Bickle's voice-over.

Of course, the audio element need not be music. To take another well-known example from Martin Scorsese's body of work, the sound montage that accompanies Jake la Motta's fights in *Raging Bull* includes a range of suggestive sounds – howling, groaning, screeching – collectively symbolic of the animal-like savagery and cruelty of the big ring. This is supplemented by the exaggeration of numerous more obviously iconic sounds – such as the repeated soft explosion of flash lamps and the sounds of the gloves making impact. Can it be said that their volume, their texture as sounds, gives them, too, an indexical quality, signifying a kind of madness, a level of reality beyond that which could be captured by a documentary recording of a boxing match?

In some media, such as the music video, the visually spectacular serves the music. The 'attraction' becomes a complex play on our imagination and emotions of musical signifiers (usually with associated lyrics – verbal signifiers) and a dense display of visual signifiers. In its abilities to play on our fantasies and desires via these different channels, it is a potentially very powerful textual system. In looking at *William Shakespeare's Romeo and Juliet*, the second film studied in this chapter, we will be tempted to use a not particularly precise but quite suggestive term to describe the film's style – MTV-style.

4.3. Spectacle, performance, genre

In the process of signification – which is another way of talking about making meaning – our role is clearly crucial. We work with signifiers, identifying one or more iconic, indexical or symbolic functions 'performed' by the signifier. Most of the time our experience as cine-literate spectators will stand us in good stead. This is especially so when viewing or working with a genre film. Our experience of previous films provides a basic mental map (or **schema** – plural, schemata) that we can apply to the particular film in front of us – whether in our working with its visual or aural features or, indeed, the relationship between them.

Much cinema spectacle is genre-based, that is, it has its basis in familiar and easily recognised conventions. Genres generally have a high level of predictability, with just enough variation to surprise and delight the audience (and to distinguish the film from all the others remarkably similar to it). As found in genre films, spectacle, too, will demonstrate a high level of predictability within the apparently new and surprising. In this chapter, we are going to focus on spectacle in one film which works very close to its genre conventions – those of the Hong Kong martial arts/ghost genre. In the other, we will consider a film which exemplifies the mixed genre (hybrid) nature of much American movie-making since the late 1980s. Both films also show the influence of other image-based contemporary media: Manga comic books and animation in the case of the Hong Kong film; the music video in the case of the Hollywood film.

The central ingredient of the genre spectacle will be a dramatic confrontation, whether a crucial confrontation between whole armies or just a single pair of lovers.

If we take a famous example, John Williams's musical motif for *Jaws*, this clearly has no iconic resemblance to a shark swimming through the ocean; however, within the film, can it be described as indexical, once the relationship between music and shark is established? Or, if we take the famous violin shrieks in the *Psycho* shower sequence, can these be described as somehow iconic?

What I am raising here are questions about the adequacy of these basic semiotic terms for describing how music signifies.

▶ What do you think? ●

This is yet another way in which I am using the word **'performance'**. To recap, we have used the word in its most obvious sense to refer to actors in performance. This was then extended in the previous section to consider the idea of others – director, cinematographer – 'performing' their roles behind the camera. Here we consider the idea of the 'performance' of meaning itself by a film's visual and aural signifiers. Below, I will suggest that, particularly in relation to spectacle, we can talk about the 'performance' of cinema as a whole.

▶ Do we, as spectators, have a performative role to play? ●

This is the subject of the final chapter.

Richard Dyer, in a very influential essay *On Entertainment*, lists energy, intensity and abundance as antidotes to the tiredness, routine and poverty of everyday life. He describes this process in terms of a Utopian desire – not so much what Utopia might look like, but what it might *feel* like.

One of my favourite examples of implausible spectacle is in *Speed* when Keanu Reeves accelerates the bus so that it takes off at the end of a section of elevated highway, only to land safely on another section perhaps 80 metres away! What are your favourite moments of crazily implausible cinema spectacle?

▶ If spectacular sequences can be so unbelievable, where does this lead us in thinking about the importance of realism to audiences? ●

▶ Does the term 'pure cinema' mean anything to you? Nominate a genre other than the musical where you believe cinema 'lets go' the restrictions of realism and becomes a more imaginative and creative form of expression. ●

Superhuman skills or impressive technology, or both may be on display. The protagonists will be good-looking movie stars and the location will either be futuristic or exotic, or the ordinary made exotic by the people and technology in it. Fundamentally, however, this **transformation** will be the product of cinema itself – a demonstration of cinema's capacity for turning the world into a more intense, energetic, abundant place where the impossible is realised in moving images.

In exploring film genres in general, definitions of what we mean by the 'real' have to be loose and flexible. Within the genre world, events occur according to templates provided by the internal conventions of the genre at least as much as by external reality. Audiences know this and accept genre cinema on its own terms. (We came across plenty of instances of this in looking at *E.T.* and *Sliding Doors* in Chapter 2). If genre in general requires relaxed definitions of the 'real', then cinematic spectacle located within genre requires this approach even more. Audiences understand this and find pleasure precisely in the elastic way everyday reality and plausibility are stretched, sometimes near to snapping point. Spectacle is about transformation – and audiences buy into the cinematic spectacle for this very reason. Spectacle is cinema at its most resourceful, most ingenious – and most playful.

The musical – whether the classic MGM Hollywood musical, the Bollywood musical or the MTV-style music sequence – is the most common site for this kind of transformation. The musical is sometimes referred to as 'pure cinema', with the implication that, in this genre, it is possible to think of cinema as most successfully escaping the restrictions imposed upon it as a 'realistic' medium. If this is so, then it is significant that music most commonly provides the pretext for cinematic play – for fantasy. Music is a medium of expression that depends less than any other on a resemblance to perceived reality – although it does work within the formal conventions/constraints of (musical) genres. Music operates according to its own internal rules and thus exists as even more hermetically sealed than genre cinema which, in most cases, must demonstrate some external reference to 'reality'.

It is interesting then to look at a non-Hollywood popular genre cinema operating very much to its own internal rules and conventions, and one where cinematic play, the fantastic, is an integral feature. The Hong Kong martial arts movie became hugely popular with Bruce Lee's films of the 1970s. They are characterised by the skills of the performers, which bring a kinetic energy intensified by fast editing. Simple 'tricks' within cinematography such as fast and slow motion enhance the choreographed movement of martial arts performers. The result is highly stylised action produced on very modest budgets. Visual comedy – a kind of slapstick – is often added to this, for example in Jackie Chan's movies throughout the 1980s. This seems to confirm a sense of dissociation between the screen events and any sense of the 'real', rather like the way a lightness of tone always interjects between and sometimes during James Bond action sequences. This is a distinctive kind of viewing experience, one in which the spectator, however delighted by the entertainment offered, remains firmly aware of the movie as a series of attractions celebrating the fantastic and playful potential of cinema. We can cheer and groan as an audience participating in a public and, more or less, predictable experience.

A quite different genre, the traditional Chinese ghost story, offered itself as a base for adding martial arts and slapstick elements – after all, ghosts are potentially phenomena that create havoc, both comic and serious. This genre, with its roots in Chinese folklore and traditional theatre, offered the possibility of two key ingredients. One was the physical representation of the form and movement of the creatures of the spirit world. The other was the pathos of the ghost's situation – the longing from the spirit world for life, for contact with those still living. Take this one step further and imagine the ghost at the centre of the story as a young woman, full of sexual longing and a powerful erotic presence, and there opens up the possibility of a love story. Go one step further again and imagine the forces of darkness within this ghostly underworld and you have not only a pretext for martial arts action, but also horror special effects.

The sleeve to the UK video version of Ching Siu Ting's *A Chinese Ghost Story* (1986) describes the film as:

> *The classic Eastern erotic horror fest*
> *A truly berserk supernatural spectacular*

And that it:

> *… demolishes all genre boundaries'*.

► Should we criticise this as a more superficial kind of experience than that of the spectator caught up in the psychological intensity of identification with character and situation?

Is it fair to say that this is something like the difference between pantomime or circus, and serious theatre? ●

Tsui Hark is generally considered to have been the single most important person in transforming Hong Kong popular cinema into the kind of action spectacle we recognise here. Bey Logan observes that, in 1978, the year after *Star Wars*, Jackie Chan appeared in a movie called *Spiritual Kung Fu*. In order to create the effect of a comet, someone was asked to run in front of a painted starlit sky with a lighted sparkler! Three years later, Tsui Hark was creating Hong Kong's first special effects facility, Cinefax Workshops, with different departments for animation, stop motion and make-up. Tsui Hark's own ground-breaking *Zu: Warriors from the Magic Mountain* was considered by the director to have been imperfectly achieved and he felt that working with imported American specialists (who had worked on films such as *Star Wars*, *Star Trek* and *Tron*) had been difficult. But, by

1986, it was possible to produce a feature-length film using the facilities of the Cinefax Workshop and locally trained labour. *A Chinese Ghost Story* was the result – directed by Ching Siu Ting, who was best known as a choreographer of rapid-paced martial arts fights and wire work (characters flying on lengths of wire in a studio). The combination of traditional elements such as this (although technically much improved) and new techniques such as the stop-motion animating of the zombie figures was ground-breaking.

It is worth noting that, even with the introduction of sophisticated technology, the entire cost of the special effects in *A Chinese Ghost Story* was only £100,000.

A warning! This and the following examples of dialogue from A Chinese Ghost Story *are my transcripts of English subtitles and therefore their accuracy in relation to the Cantonese dialogue cannot be guaranteed.*

You are reminded of what was said about problems of cross-cultural readings of film texts in section 3.7 (p. 88).

The situation of *A Chinese Ghost Story* can be neatly summarised by referring to dialogue between Tsai-Shen, the main character, and Hsiao-Tsing, the beautiful ghost, at 62 minutes 50 seconds into the film:

TSAI-SHEN: Are you a ghost?

HSIAO-TSING: But some men are more harmful, more frightening than ghosts – although not of this world, ghosts can retain human feelings. It is confusing, some ghosts are better than men.

TSAI-SHEN : Then why do you kill?

HSIAO-TSING: The Mistress forced me to. She is a thousand-year-old Tree Spirit. I was murdered. My father buried me beneath that three. The Mistress took control of my spirit and used me to lure men so that she could suck up their youth. She is now marrying me off to a monster … Are you still afraid of me?

TSAI-SHEN : No, I must deliver you from your fate.

HSIAO-TSING: Tomorrow, take my ashes to my family estate before dusk and my spirit will be freed.

TSAI-SHEN : I'll take the urn there. You'll be reincarnated.

Beneath the action and the comedy, there is a rather sombre tone to the film – a tone caught in these words by a character who at first sight seems to be the most exuberant, Swordsman Yen (72.53):

I hide in the temple because I cannot bear man's inhumanity. To men I am as a ghost, before ghosts I am as a man. Am I a man or a ghost? … I do not want to be a man.

Some caution should be shown, however, in thinking this a peculiarly 'dark' film. What Swordsman Yen expresses is typical of his stock character type in stories of this kind. If we are not familiar with a genre, we may think an individual film more 'original' than it will appear to those who are easily able to place character, situation and theme within their previous movie-going experience. This is not to say that *A Chinese Ghost Story* is not a remarkable example of its genre – and a trail-blazing original in its combination of generic elements.

Let us take two short consecutive sequences from *A Chinese Ghost Story* and consider how the genre and spectacle conventions used provide a vivid kind of cinematic pleasure. More particularly, let us see what kind of 'fest' we are being offered.

The hero, young tax collector Tsai-Shen, has arrived at the reputedly haunted Lan Ro Temple to spend the night. (The pre-credit sequence has already identified this as a place where a beautiful seductress draws men to their doom.) Three wolves with glowing eyes are left behind at the gates – presumably these creatures know how unwise it is to go further. The rather stereotypically naïve and cowardly but good-looking hero has hardly set foot inside the grounds of the temple before he is caught up in the middle of a set-piece martial arts sword fight. This is full of impossible athletic leaps and moves between the Taoist Swordsman Yen and a troublemaker called Hsia-Hou. Extricating himself from this fight, Tsai-Shen enters the interior of the temple.

A Chinese Ghost Story – Tsai-Shen at the Lan Ro Temple

(The following are the shots that make up a sequence lasting 3 minutes 50 seconds, starting 13 minutes 45 seconds into the film. Shots are in a dominant blue tone, unless indicated as using natural colour.)

1. Shot from top of stairs as Tsai-Shen ascends
2. Close-up of young female (Hsiao-Tsing) looking in from upper window – hair blowing across face
3. High-angle shot of Tsai-Shen *(her point of view)*
4. Big close-up of Hsiao-Tsing
5. Tsai-Shen steps onto raised section and takes off his rucksack
6. Hsiao-Tsing appears to be pulled backwards from the window – ending in medium shot. The window closes on her
7. *(natural colour)* Tsai-Shen has lit lamp
8. Wide view of zombies lying horizontal on floorboards
9. Closer shot of same
10. A waterfall
11. *(natural colour)* Hsia-Hou is bathing sword wound
12. *(natural colour)* Wider view shows him strapping his arm by a fire
13. Hsiao-Tsing is bathing
14. *(natural colour)* Hsia-Hou reacts to the ghostly sound

▶ In this sequence, carefully consider sound and especially reflect on what is signified by music. Perhaps you can parallel this sequence summary with a set of notes on sound effects and the use of music. ●

▶ What meanings do you make from the first 30 seconds of this sequence (up to shot 7)? Try to pinpoint your feeling(s) – and also try to pinpoint the source of that feeling in the film text. ●

and looks off left (indicating he has seen her)

15. Hsiao-Tsing is up to her shoulders in water

16. *(natural colour)* Hsia-Hou rises

17. Hsiao-Tsing is in medium close-up pouring water over herself (slow motion)

18. Hsia-Hou steps towards her

19. Hsiao-Tsing looks up at him before swimming off left. He follows

20. *(natural colour)* Hsiao-Tsing falls into frame from the right on to the ground in front of fire. She pulls him down on top of her.

21. *(natural colour)* Graphic match as Tsai-Shen puts down his lamp

22. Floor-level shot as he rolls out the sleeping mat towards camera

23. Close-up of Tsai-Shen touching a blood stain on the mat

24. His reaction

25. *(natural colour)* Hsiao-Tsing is under Hsia-Hou as he kisses her

26. *(natural colour)* Overhead shot as Hsiao-Tsing looks over his shoulder up towards camera

27. *(natural colour)* Side-on view of Hsiao-Tsing's leg, which she slowly raises and bends. Her anklet becomes visible – bells tinkle

28. The camera moves through doors – accompanied by sound of rush of wind – towards what appears to be a statue of a seated figure

29. Big close-up of Tsai-Shen looking right

30. Shadow movement across the window behind him

31. Tsai-Shen rises

32. He tries to open window – but cannot

33. Wide shot of dust, leaves blowing into the building – as a consequence of the rush of air

34. The window

35. Close-up of Tsai-Shen, who has pricked his finger trying to open the window

36. Close-up of zombie

37. Tsai-Shen pulls his finger away and walks from the window

38. Wide shot of zombies stirring

39. *(natural light)* Hsiao-Tsing is kissing Hsia-Hou's neck. But she suddenly pulls away. He turns his head to look where she has gone and then turns back

▶ What are the key signifiers you respond to in the 50-second section from the establishing shot of the waterfall (shot 10) to this cutaway to Tsai-Shen (shot 21)? ●

40. Camera zooms in at ground level towards him very fast

41. He tries to reach for sword

42. Back to the camera zoom which goes into Hsia-Hou's mouth and penetrates his body

43. Cutaway to his body thrashing

44. Back to the interior body shot

45. First of four shots of the exterior of Hsia-Hou's body crumbling

46. Second shot of the exterior of Hsia-Hou's body crumbling

47. Third shot

48. Fourth shot

49. Medium close-up of Hsiao-Tsing watching from a tree. She appears to be watching with distaste and a tear is on her cheek as she turns her head away

50. Swordsman Yen leaps down from balcony

51. Swordsman Yen runs across the water towards the camera and the remains of Hsia-Hou in the foreground

52. Close-up of Hsia-Hou's head

53. Low-angle medium close-up of Swordsman Yen. He says, 'You were ambitious, but even in death you are a nobody.'

54. He leans forwards to pick up the body saying, 'I won't leave you unburied.'

55. Wide shot of him rising with the body in his arms

56. Close-up of Hsia-Hou's head – the mouth opens and a gawping sound is made

57. The arms of the skeletal body reach around Swordsman Yen's neck

58. First of four shots of the struggle. Swordsman Yen says, 'Even when you're dead you don't give up.'

59. Second of four shots of the struggle

60. Third of four shots of the struggle

61. Fourth of four shots of the struggle

62. He pierces the skull with a needle, the impact producing a bright white light

63. The corpse is thrown back onto a rock

64. Swordsman Yen lights a Taoist scroll which sets fire to the corpse

At 17 minutes 35 seconds, we cut to Tsai-Shen eating an apple. Although he is vaguely aware of some disturbance outside, his naïvety prevents him from realising the scale of the supernatural violence going on around him! Equally, he is

▶ Discuss the part of the sequence from shot 39 to 48. What is enjoyable about this as cinema spectacle? You may wish to use two ideas that have already worked their way into this chapter: cinema as performance and cinema as transformation. ●

▶ How do you find yourself responding to the mix of comedy and horror here? ●

▶ How far does this sequence conform to the conventions of an American or European horror genre set-piece. What is different? ●

▶ Summarise the key elements of this sequence in relation to a cinema of attractions. ●

unaware of the zombies above him, which the smell of his blood has stirred into action.

Each shot itemised above has one or more specific signifying functions, communicating visually and aurally with the audience. Again, the importance of *mise en scène* is clear, as is editing. (*A Chinese Ghost Story* is particularly sharply edited throughout.) Film-maker and audience share this general level of familiarity with these aspects of cinema language. At a more specific level, they share an understanding of the requirements of a particular genre sequence. Those responsible for making a film sequence such as the one described above 'perform' in relation to the rules of film form and genre. They also 'perform' to the limits of the technology available to them and their ingenuity in applying it. The cinema of attractions is always a 'performance' of cinema. The less bound by requirements to conform to an everyday reality, the more virtuoso can be this performance. Fans of certain genres will hold this cinematic virtuosity as one of the expectations they bring to the viewing event.

In the sequence which immediately follows the one we have just looked at, Tsai-Shen meets the ghost for the first time. He hears movement above him and decides to investigate. He is halfway up a ladder – with the zombies waiting for him – when he is distracted by the sound of singing. He decides to investigate that instead. There is a tracking shot of him moving through the woods. This is preceded and followed by shots of Buddha-like statues. We are then surprised by big close-up shots in natural colour of the ghost woman: her fingers on the strings of the lute; her lips; her eyes. From the sublime to the ridiculous, our hero steps in a puddle and can only comment, 'Fortunately, it's not too deep.' He then comes to two magnificent carved figures that stand either side of a jetty which leads across a lake to a pavilion. There is an overhead shot of the ghost woman playing her lute, followed by one of Tsai-Shen moving down the walkway towards her. Meanwhile, Swordsman Yen hears her singing and suddenly realises 'That boy's in danger' and rushes off to save him.

The first meeting between Tsai-Shen and Hsiao-Tsing (the ghost woman) is full of comic business. First, she tells him to put down his knife and he allows it to slip out of his hand, flying past her into the wall. Then he turns around to reveal a series of protective Taoist inscriptions which earlier in the film he accidentally imprinted on his coat. These so disturb her that she sends her scarf flying past him and, as anticipated, he falls in the lake trying to retrieve it. She stretches out her leg – with the anklet prominently visible – from the jetty so that he can scramble out. The following amusing exchange then occurs:

> TSAI-SHEN: You're colder than I am.
> HSIAO-TSING: That's because you're so hot-blooded.
> TSAI-SHEN : You look terribly pale. You should see a doctor.
> HSIAO-TSING : I need your warmth.

Just as he is about to be kissed by her, he sneezes. This contrives to push her away from him. She blows a magic spell across him which knocks him out and says, 'If only you'd stayed away.' At this point, Swordsman Yen comes charging along and she flies off, managing to kick Tsai-Shen back into the lake – and back into consciousness – as she does so. Scrambling out, Tsai-Shen is concerned that Hsiao-Tsing has left her lute behind. The following sequences involve both him and Swordsman Yen pursuing her through the woods. After this, he still has to contend with the zombies waiting for him when he returns to his sleeping quarters!

In this second sequence, there is the potential for suspense as our hero moves towards the apparently destructive femme fatale spirit – employing a *mise en scène* and editing that will generate maximum tension. There is equally the potential for a touching early love scene as the two central characters tentatively approach one another – employing a style of *mise en scène* and editing which draws out the sexual and erotic. There is the potential for comedy as this naïve young man walks innocently into the lair of the wicked witch – employing a *mise en scène* and editing that will emphasise misunderstanding, clumsiness and the absurd. While the first two are compatible; the third, we may think, undermines both. But this is what we seem to have: 'an erotic horror fest' (to quote again from the video slick) which is played for humour throughout. The film is working within a commercial aesthetic, and one somewhat different from Hollywood, in which broad comedy is a conventional ingredient expected by the audience to be seen alongside action and eroticism.

▶ Think about the staging and direction in this second sequence from the specific perspectives of director, art designer and cinematographer.

What is required?

What are the options?

Why the choices that are made? ●

Mixed genre films are not so unusual in North American or Western European cinema today. The horror film, in particular, often plays on the edge of humour and shock. (Can you think of some examples?) More generally, however, we are increasingly offered films that play with different genre conventions – and so play with our expectations. One mood is undercut by another. Humour, in particular, distances us from the film event, constantly reminding us that we are in fact just watching a film. For example, *Pulp Fiction*, *New Nightmare on Elm Street* or *From Dusk Till Dawn* all mix violence and comedy in ways which alert us to their existence as films – as artefacts constructed by witty and imaginative film-makers 'performing' their skills. This idea of the 'performative' in direction, cinematography and special effects is sometimes presented as a new phenomenon, contrasting with a traditional and still very common Hollywood-style film in which everything is done stylistically to suppress the thought that 'It's just a movie' and maximise the illusion of realism. Coming at this issue less from the direction of narrative and more from the direction of spectacle, it seems clear that cinema has always been very open about its performative function. It is possible to see the medium and its capabilities for providing attraction being celebrated – whether in the famous chariot race in the first version of *Ben Hur* in 1924 or *Titanic* in 1998.

There is a perception that, since the mid-1980s, and particularly throughout the 1990s, the performative in cinema has become more self-conscious, more self-reflexive. This self-consciousness may lie partly in the increasing awareness of film-makers, working with a strong sense of film history, of all the films that have gone before them. It may lie partly in the increasing sophistication of the film audience, especially their capacity to 'place' films within genres and stylistic conventions. A different relationship between producer and audience has evolved, one in which (sometimes) both share a playful, self-conscious take on cinema. In semiotic terms, we might say that the visual signifier and the aural signifier are more vivid than ever, produced through ever more brilliant technological means; however, at the same time, the signified, that to which the signifier refers, has become less certain, less fixed in a simple notion of the 'real'. Films are increasingly seen less as referring

A complication in genre study, especially in contemporary cinema, is genre mixing. The 'hybrid' film is one we are increasingly used to working with, and one that may often also include some intertextual feature (see p. 87). *The Matrix*, for example, is a sci-fi thriller that has lashings of ingredients from the Hong Kong martial arts and action genres. At the same time, it makes subtle reference to a range of earlier sci-fi movies.

out from themselves into a real world than simply circulating images within their own structures of meaning.

In the 1960s and 1970s, some film-makers had a clear political reason for drawing our attention to the artifice of film, of the fact that cinema is concerned with the manipulation of familiar conventions that we otherwise would take for granted. They felt that, by drawing attention to the constructed nature of cinema, their audiences would be more critically alert to the film as representation. By contrast, in spectacle cinema, film-makers have a very different reason for making us alert to the conventions they are using. These film-makers and their audiences exist within a culture today in which the flow of images has become more and more an experience of the play of surfaces, full of wit and irony. This is most commonly referred to in relation to the **postmodern**.

4.4. Spectacle, performance, star

There is not enough space in this book to place contemporary cinema within the context of the postmodern. It is, however, possible simply to talk in terms of a natural development in genre cinema towards the end of the twentieth century, as producers and audiences become overfamiliar with conventions and began to 'play' with them. A sense of cinema as performance (as 'pure cinema', to go back to an earlier phrase) has evolved within Hollywood cinema, moving out from the musical and the animated film to incorporate the action movie. Indeed, one external push in this direction came from the increasing influence of Hong Kong cinema on Hollywood in the 1990s. It is not at all necessary to develop an argument that Hong Kong genre cinema is somehow inherently postmodern in order to see how a different kind of relationship between producers and consumers defines that cinema.

At the same time, the traditional Hollywood-style commercial aesthetic based on the narrative realist film that encourages emotional and psychological identification with characters and their situations remains strong. It is interesting to place the other films studied so far on a continuum from solidly narrative realist to playfully postmodern. Clearly *Secrets and Lies* and *Once Were Warriors* are not playfully postmodern. Neither is *E.T.*, however crazy the story. We are asked to accept the realist illusion and respond to the psychological and sociological circumstances of the characters as if

---

Jean-Luc Godard's attempts to produce a cinematic equivalent of the German playwright Bertolt Brecht's 'alienation' effects provide the best examples of this. See, for example, *Tout va bien* (France, 1972).

Some characteristics of the **postmodern** include:

- **intertextuality** – see p. 5
- **hybridity** – for example, the mixing of elements from different genres
- **playfulness** – including pastiche and self-referentiality
- **signification** rather than meaning – for example, a visual sign may be used without any clear sense of it referring to anything other than its own existence as a sign
- **irony** – the inevitable result of all the above

Quentin Tarantino has played a significant role in promoting Hong Kong popular cinema in Hollywood.

There is an interesting and clear connection between youngish, aspiring auteur directors, the ones who want to impose their distinctive 'signature' on a film, and a cinema of stylistic 'performance'. Working within a popular cinema, it is not surprising that Tarantino and others have found so much in another popular cinema – that of Hong Kong – where the performative is so strongly emphasised. John Woo's 'balletic' urban crime movies have maybe had the strongest influence – with John Woo himself directing such a high-concept Hollywood spectacle movie as *Mission Impossible 2* (United States, 2000).

The most postmodern of Hong Kong directors of the 1990s was undoubtedly Wong Kar Wai. His films (for example, Chungking Express, Fallen Angels, Happy Together) show strong influences from both European and American independent cinema. The flow of ideas in cinema is, more than ever, global. In the case of Hong Kong and Hollywood, it has been much more of a creative exchange than a one-way flow.

▶ *From what has been said so far, and from your own experience, can you pin down what you consider are key ingredients of a postmodern film?*

For example, is Trainspotting *(United Kingdom, 1996) a postmodern film?* ●

The conversion of Shakespeare's play in 1956 into the teenage gang musical West Side Story *was a remarkable example of how the play lends itself to different kinds of treatment.*

'Surfaces' refers to the immediacy, the sensory quality of what is presented. There are no implications of 'depth' in this word. What we see is what we see. In semiotic terms, the signifier can be decoded as you please, or even remain undecoded — like a word simply enjoyed as a combination of shapes. There is no 'deeper' meaning that matters.

▶ *What do you think? Is it possible to watch a film in which meaning does not really matter? You may wish to come back to this question after reading the extract quoted on p. 151.* ●

they were real people. Perhaps *Sliding Doors* provides the most interesting case study from the films we have looked at so far. Do we enter into the worlds of the two Helens or do we enjoy the playfulness and performance of cinema?

The story of Romeo and Juliet could provide a perfect basis for a realistic film set in authentic locations, where we would be invited to engage with characters as 'real' people. Franco Zeffirelli's 1968 film version, for example, does just this and succeeds as a vividly realist production. We could even relocate, recostume Romeo and Juliet relatively easily without undermining its status as realist drama. In fact, nearly all of Shakespeare's plays can – and have been – set in other times and geographical locations from those indicated by the playwright. Whether on stage or screen, this does not mean they are postmodern. 'Romeo and Juliet in Space' or 'Romeo and Juliet on the Titanic' could be played 'straight', with all the emotional intensity and conviction of a realist film. Recostuming or relocating a story may introduce new sets of signifiers (spaceships, ocean liners!) – perhaps to give a fresh take on a well-known story. This does not, however, in itself create that different kind of relationship between producers and audience that we are using here as a thumbnail definition of the playful and postmodern.

In moving to Baz Luhrmann's *William Shakespeare's Romeo and Juliet* of 1996, we encounter a film that needs to retain the intensity of the love story – in other words, it has to take itself seriously if the audience is to experience the film as tragedy. On the other hand, the film wants to reflect the spirit (and fashion) of its time – in which style, action, surfaces, playfulness and visual spectacle are important features. What we get is a film that is not only a generic hybrid – that is, one that mixes elements from different genres – but also a film that attempts to work through two different styles: traditional narrative realism and playful postmodernism. This is particularly interesting when we see it within the context of a cinema of attractions. The spectacle in this version of *Romeo and Juliet* is always, well, spectacular, but sometimes the spectacle works to intensify the psychological realism of character and feeling, and sometimes it works to draw attention to its own wittiness and excess as cinematic 'play'.

Certainly Luhrmann's film reflects visual and aural styles deriving from other areas of commercial culture – perhaps, most obviously, television advertising and music videos. These forms can both be characterised as media of attractions, as spectacular forms intended to provide intense but fragmented visual and aural stimulation. They are intensely performative. The film appears at times to be edited by someone operating a games console (or a television remote) – just as at times the *mise en scène* seems to have been designed by someone perfectly at home conceiving Bacardi or Smirnoff advertisements. If this seems like negative criticism of the film, it is not meant to be. It is simply an attempt to locate the film – to establish what it is, what kind of pleasure it offers.

As with *A Chinese Ghost Story*, let us look at two consecutive sequences running to approximately 10 minutes in total.

After the television newsreader prologue and the credit sequence (itself an opening statement about the film's style, the kind of Shakespeare adaptation waiting for us), we have the 'third civil brawl' sequence. Starting with the introduction of the Montague Boys at 2 min. 05 sec., this sequence is $6^{1}/_{2}$ minutes in length. This time you are invited to do the shot-by-shot record yourself – if you have the patience to do so, as there are more than 230 shots! – or an edit every $1^{3}/_{4}$ seconds on average.

This kind of cutting itself makes the sequence feel very fast. In addition, we have a range of devices such as wipes (at the beginning of the sequence), whip pans, zooms, fast- and slow-motion effects, and a variety of surprising camera angles. Unusually, we also have freeze frames and captions introducing the characters. Collectively, these devices certainly draw attention to this sequence as a 'performance' of cinema.

Generic features are exploited with all the playfulness we expect of a certain kind of 1990s movie. At first sight, we appear to have the teen/gangster movie – urban locations filled with cars and young men with shoulder holsters and powerful handguns (all to the beat of hip hop and rock). Then, both musically (the Morricone-style music) and iconographically (the cheroot, the spinning garage forecourt sign), we move into spaghetti western territory. The gunslinging of Tybalt appears to start in spaghetti Western territory, but it shifts into Honk Kong cinema – if not exactly that of Swordsman Yen, then certainly the quickfire gunslingers of John Woo movies. The Hong Kong influence is, I think, reinforced by the comic aspects – Tybalt's pistol

William Shakespeare's Romeo and Juliet: Two shots, one of a Capulet, the other of a Montague, from the first sequence of the film – made up of 230 shots, each composed as an 'attraction' for the spectator.

As always, where a choice exists, it is important to work with a widescreen version of the film.

One very interesting source for this visual style is, perhaps, Allison Anders's film about girl gangs in Los Angeles, Mi Vida Loca (United States, 1993).

There are many specific borrowings and influences that you may try to spot for yourself. I would like to point out one particular reference (or *hommage*) to an earlier film. When the nun leaves the garage shop and walks across the forecourt, she is mocked. Juliet's Nurse, dressed in nun-like habits ('A sail, a sail'), is mocked in just this way in Zeffirelli's wonderful 1968 realist Renaissance Italian version of *Romeo and Juliet*.

trickery momentarily going wrong and, most of all, one of the Montague Boys being repeatedly hit with a handbag. The Roman Catholic religious imagery is so overdone as again to be seen as a cumulative visual joke – more and more is revealed of Virgin Marys, Sacred Hearts and crosses, most strikingly on the hilts of the guns. Perhaps we have had really enough by the time Abra rolls over the bonnet of a car in the middle of the gun fight to reveal a sacred heart tattooed the length of his back. (Surely our only reaction is to laugh at this 'excess'?) There are other visual jokes – such as the sign, already referred to, which says 'Add more fuel to your fire'. The sequence finishes with something borrowed from an LAPD police action movie as the helicopters come in over the statue of Christ located between the Capulet and Montague corporation headquarters downtown (actually Mexico City).

It could be argued that this opening is primarily a statement of intent: this is the kind of fast, almost delirious Shakespeare we are going to be served up. To the audience, the message is clear: if you were in doubt about Shakespeare, about this old story – relax! This movie is going to be cool! However, this argument implies too defensive a position – that is, that the film has to prove itself not to be dull by adopting attack as the best form of defence. A more positive view would be that the film-makers wish to 'animate' a well-known story, employing a cinema of attractions to surprise and energise. The surprise and energy come from both the specific cinematic techniques already referred to, such as fast editing, and from the 'playfulness' of its surfaces – full of visual and aural signifiers that are delightful in their combination, in their 'play'.

After the scene in which Captain Prince tells Montague and Capulet that he will not accept any more of these brawls between the two families, there is a shift from the city to Verona Beach, where Romeo is hanging out, lovelorn over a girl called Rosaline.

At this point, I am going to call 'time out' from what we have been discussing so far and shift focus for a while. This exploration of the cinema of attractions has failed so far to mention one very important, obvious and central attraction – the movie star. Indeed (with the exception of Gwyneth Paltrow in *Sliding Doors* and, for Chinese audiences, Leslie Cheung in *A Chinese Ghost Story*), none of the films discussed so far has a full-blown movie star. This film is different and the observation that Leonardo DiCaprio was not a major star at the time of the film's release does not alter the fact that we can only now ever watch *William Shakespeare's Romeo and Juliet* in the post-*Titanic* era. Certainly his introduction in the film draws attention to his presence as a cinema attraction – as a spectacle!

At 8 minutes 53 seconds into the film, an overhead shot down past the statue of Christ establishes the Montagues driving away from their meeting with Captain Prince. Benvolio is travelling with them and he is asked if he knows of Romeo's whereabouts. This prompts a 4-second shot of a figure in long shot walking towards the ocean. Another 25 seconds of conversation take place in the Montague car before we cut away to the introductory shot proper. In classic style, it begins (at 9.40) at the feet and moves up to finish in medium close-up on Romeo – with a vaguely James Dean look (or should I say a vaguely Leonardo Di Caprio look, because stars, by definition, extend seamlessly between role and star persona). He is dressed like someone the morning after a night on the town. He takes a draw on his cigarette. This then opens out to a wide shot of him framed within the arch/proscenium which provides the extraordinary centre-piece for the Verona Beach location. After a shot of the cars going by, we have a close-up of a notebook, pen and cigarette. Romeo is absorbed in writing oxymorons, suggesting a romantic, somewhat tortured young man. We then (at 10.03) have a very atmospheric close-up with the orange sun behind Romeo so that his features are not clear – as though he is seen through gauze. In looking inquisitively towards his parent's car, he looks out of the screen almost directly at the audience. He then rises back into the previous wide, extreme long shot. The next medium close-up (at 10.25) is the first we have of him fully lit. It begins with him in left-side profile, but again he turns, teasingly, towards the camera.

There is a right-to-left pan which takes in the beach area in long shot. This produces a composition (at 10.45) in which Romeo is framed in the distance by a prostitute on the right and an old man who is ogling at her on the left. Enigmatically, behind Romeo is a sign reading 'Shoot forth thunder'.

Benvolio tells the Montagues that he will try to establish why their son is moping. When Benvolio gets to Romeo

▶ Look at the star's first moment on screen in a couple of other films, ones you know well.

Are there characteristic ways in which the star makes his or her first appearance?

What range of thoughts go through your head here, at the first appearance of Leonardo DiCaprio? ●

Stars possess four identities:

- real person
- role
- screen persona
- image circulating within the culture

If you go back to what is said about personification in Chapter 3, there is a clear linkage between 'real' person and role. Cumulatively, roles create the screen persona – the recurring signifiers of the star (gesture, walk, voice, manner, style and so on). The image circulating within the media will be a hyped-up version of the 'real' person, with a lot of additional colouring from the screen persona. All of this will, in turn, feed back into further roles, further personification.

▶ Carry out a brief study of your favourite star using this four-part structure. Afterwards, consider how useful you find this approach. ●

By now, you should have some sense of just how difficult it is to define cinematic realism, let alone describe how it works. Stars potentially throw a really big spanner in the works. No matter how hard a film may construct a convincing *mise en scène* and render scenes natural through the use of 'seamless' editing, the star's first appearance immediately declares: 'This is a movie.' It would be just as misleading, however, to suggest that the presence of a star prevents us suspending our disbelief as it would be to suggest that our awareness of a film deploying genre conventions does.

What stars force us to do is to ask yet more questions about the nature of the 'inside'/'outside' manner in which we operate as spectators. They force us to examine how we simultaneously can be absorbed in the fiction and on the outside looking in on it as a movie.

▶ How do you cope with stars in movies? Do they draw attention to themselves and away from the dramatic world of the film? ●

What desires? Well, I could try to suggest that I mean something other than sexual desire. My example at the beginning of the chapter included reference to my desire that the tightrope walker made it safely. This is a wish prompted by the drama of a situation. The situation is sufficiently dramatic to make me a kind of participant observer. Another way of considering desire is by reference to that old Hollywood cliché, 'the dream factory'. Here we could be talking about aspirational dreams – such as wishing to own a certain kind of car or achieve a certain level of career success. Certainly, Hollywood's construction of a Utopia, a world where the problems that plague us in life are wiped away, is common. (See the reference to Dyer's essay above – p. 104.) There is a difference of scale, however, between these dreams and more deep-rooted, perhaps unconscious desires. Tell Sigmund Freud that the dream is separable from the sexual impulse and he would no doubt raise a polite Viennese eyebrow. We dream our sexual longings, our repressed desires. The cinema as dream factory is a conveyor belt of sexual desire.

▶ Do you agree? Is desire always sexual in the cinema? ●

across the beach, we find him (at 11.22) shot from a three-quarter back view – though too low to be a representation of Benvolio's point of view. Again, this position gives Romeo/Di Caprio the opportunity to turn towards the camera as he stands up to face his friend. They walk along the beach in a medium-close two shot until Romeo is distracted by the television pictures of the brawl. In close-up, he once more engages in an outpouring of oxymorons, but this time Benvolio shuts him up by gently laughing at him. They disappear into the Globe Theatre pool hall. (Few opportunities in this film are lost for getting an extra gag out of a 'sign'.)

The visual pleasure provided by the human body in the form of a star may appear trivial or superficial. It is not. To go back to the beginning of this chapter, the cinematic spectacle must speak or enact or embody audience desire. The star is the most obvious of all embodiments of desire in popular cinema – whether it be the desire of attraction, to possess this being, or the desire of aspiration, to be like this person.

Cinema can never satisfy our desires. What it does do is restage them again and again in different fantasy forms – it 'performs' them. This staging of our desires is one of the reason we go to the movies. This is another reason for considering the cinema as always, in one sense or another, a cinema of attractions. It is also, needless to say, always ultimately personal – no matter what generalisations we can make about how cinema works as mental machinery. It is our personal interaction within this mental machinery that determines the impact the film has on our imagination and feelings.

4.5. Design, staging and cinematography of spectacle

In looking at the crafting of spectacle in cinema, we are given an obvious reminder of the fact that film-making is a collaborative enterprise, involving many highly skilled people working in collaboration. It may well be the case that a single person, the director, coordinates all of this in order to try to ensure a consistent and coherent vision. It is the nature of group creative work, however, that ideas interact in a dialectic process in which the outcome is different from, more than, any input taken separately. This is one of the fascinations of cinema that can be diminished by an overemphasis on the director as auteur – as the single controlling authorial force at the heart of the project.

Not only are a large number of people working together, but they are also working within boundaries set by genre, by the kind of film they are making and by the conventions associated with that kind of film.

The more commercially orientated the film, the more creative decisions will reflect what it is perceived the audience wants or will accept. In this respect, film-makers can be said to have been granted more freedom by audiences in contemporary cinema because audiences increasingly appear to want to be surprised, delighted, even awed by amazing spectacle. This may take the form of a film such as *Toy Story*. It has to be said, however, that much Hollywood spectacle is less towards the fantastic than towards the solidly realist, whether in the representation of a sinking ocean liner (*Titanic*) or the re-creation of prehistoric creatures (*Jurassic Park*). To some degree, this pulls the other way from the tendency in cinema towards what was described in the last section as a playful self-reflexive cinema.

On a broader economic front, the more the consumer endorses the cinema of attractions by buying into such film experiences, either at the cinema or through video purchase, the more resources are released by the industry to develop new technologies for creative design and cinematography. In this respect, George Lucas, who created the first *Star Wars* movie in 1977, is an excellent example of someone whose business interests have been based on exploiting the demand for a new kind of cinema of attractions – and, in the process, extending the creative possibilities of the medium.

To pull together what has been said so far in this section, in approaching questions of creativity in the design, staging and cinematography of spectacle, it is useful to bear in mind issues of:

- professional practice – creative personnel;
- genre convention;
- consumer demand;
- technological innovation.

The effectiveness of a sequence will be measured in relation to how well a group of people work together, employing the equipment at their disposal – within the limits of a budget – in order to produce a staged scene that is consistent with the requirements of the film as a whole. Equally, it must

And such films are not just popular, but also highly valued. In a 1999 BBC Millennium Poll in which more than 25,000 people voted, five of the top ten films of all time were sci-fi spectacles – including three Star Wars *films. Other spectacular big-budget films in the top twenty included* Jurassic Park *and* Titanic.

▶ What do you think? Is cinema, by and large, still solidly concerned with the creation of realist spectacle? For more on this divide between realist and fantasy tendencies in cinema, see the discussion on pp. 133–4. ●

▶ Choose an example of cinema technology that was not available to film-makers twenty years ago. What does it do? What difference has it made? Consider its use in a particular film. ●

Film budgets are divided between above-the-line costs – director, stars and the property (book, screenplay) – and below-the-line costs, which include the cost of physically producing and filming the movie. Only blockbusters can afford high costs both above and below. Lower budget movies may commit to below-the-line in order to afford special effects and so on. The consequence is that no big-name stars are in the cast.

William Shakespeare's Romeo and Juliet: A spectacularly staged set piece – Mercutio's performance at the Capulet party: a further example of a cinema of attractions.

▶ What important basic creative decisions were made about staging the party scene?

You may consider some or all of:
- location
- costume
- props
- lighting
- figure movement
- camera position/movement
- camera lens/focal length
- editing speed and rhythm
- sound ●

▶ What do you think were some of the practical difficulties in achieving these shots? ●

▶ What is the importance of editing throughout this sequence? ●

communicate effectively with the audience, providing them with an experience which is comprehensible and vividly engaging. As a set of attractions, it must offer sensory pleasures through sight and sound.

In the two sequences we are going to look at here from *William Shakespeare's Romeo and Juliet* and *A Chinese Ghost Story*, respectively, we will look at the construction and exploitation of spectacle leading up to and including the first kiss between hero and heroine. This reminds us that sometimes we should approach the cinema of attractions literally!

Romeo, at 22 minutes 24 seconds into *William Shakespeare's Romeo and Juliet*, pops an E, having told us that 'his mind misgives' and that he has a premonition of 'untimely death'. A close-up of his eyeball is graphically contrasted with a bursting firework. The next minute-and-a-half of film establish what a wild party the Capulets are capable of throwing, as seen through the subjective viewpoint of a young man reeling under the effect of the drug he has taken. (When Romeo says 'Drugs are quick', we have an example of how the film script sometimes takes liberties with Shakespeare's theatre script.) A wild array of fancy-dress costumes provides a phantasmagorical effect. Mercutio does a drag queen performance on the Capulet grand staircase and Romeo, dressed as a medieval knight in chain mail, ends up submerging his head in cold water. The mood is suddenly altered when Romeo pulls away from the party into a different location within the Capulet mansion. The sequence I wish to concentrate upon begins here at 24 minutes 9 seconds. The spectacle is not that of a big set piece – such as Mercutio's drag queen performance – but the intimate spectacle of the staging of Romeo and Juliet's first encounter.

Romeo pulls his head out of the water; his mask is left floating on the surface. As he looks in the mirror, we hear the first introductory notes of 'I'll Always Love You'. He is attracted by a tank of tropical fish and moves over to it. We observe him through the tank, with beautiful coloured fish swimming around him. It is a striking image. The song begins. Romeo observes the fish, remaining fascinated during a cut away to Des'ree singing the theme song. Suddenly (at 25.12), Romeo and the audience are surprised by an eye looking through the tank at him. He jumps up. We see Juliet's face. What follows is a remarkable set of images of the two of them looking at each other through the tank – ended by the appearance of Juliet's Nurse with her very different face (at 25.58). The 46 seconds that Romeo and Juliet spend looking at each other's refracted images with multicoloured fish apparently swimming in, between and around them is a brilliantly achieved piece of design, staging and cinematography. At times, both faces appear pointed in the same direction; at times, they appear very close to each other; when they attempt to touch, there is the realisation of a solid physical object between them. Space becomes dreamlike – at one moment, Romeo's face comes into frame and the camera pans a distance through the water to Juliet and yet there is Romeo's face as though just next to her. The situation allows them to adopt immediately a playful, inquisitive approach to each other. If the brief of the creative team responsible for designing and filming this sequence was to come up with an original and affecting variation on the love-at-first-sight scenario, then what we have here is a sequence of shots which does this very powerfully. It is simple and yet visually rich. And, of course, it is supported by the love theme playing on the soundtrack. What we have in this sequence is a rich array of visual signifiers, intensified by the aural signifiers of music and lyrics.

The nurse takes Juliet off in her angel wings to dance with an astronaut, eligible-bachelor-of-the-year Paris. Romeo, from behind a pillar, holds Juliet's hand before the pair of them break free to kiss passionately. 'You kiss by the book,' Juliet tells him. (I think this is a compliment!)

It is only moments later, as Juliet is whisked away upstairs by the Nurse, that the pair realises each other's identities. 'My only love sprung from my only hate.' As the Montague boys leave, rather amusingly collecting their awesome firepower from the Capulet cloakroom on the way, and pass out beyond the security men, we have an image of an angel in shadow outline moving rapidly from window to window inside the mansion.

If Romeo and Juliet snatch a first kiss in a dangerous situation for both of them, it is relatively low risk compared with the amazing circumstances of Tsai-Shen's first kiss with his ghostly love, Hsiao Tsing, in *A Chinese Ghost Story*.

Tsai-Shen has followed Hsiao-Tsing through the woods. She leads him on with some humour, for example, imitating

William Shakespeare's Romeo and Juliet: Space becomes dreamlike.

▶ **Consider how effective you find the interplay of image and sound through this sequence.** ●

Costume signifiers are particularly bizarre. Some are carefully calculated. Tybalt is predictably a devil, Juliet an angel, Romeo a knight ... but why is Paris an astronaut? Read again what was said about 'surfaces' (p. 114).

Given the close scrutiny that Romeo is under from Tybalt, it seems most surprising that this angel and medieval knight can passionately kiss in what appears to be full public view.
▶ **How should we deal with aspects of the staging of a scene that appear to test our standards of plausibility?** ●
Shakespeare's entire play tests the normal standards of plausibility and, if anything, a modern-day version makes this more acute. For example, one very simple observation might be how on earth it is that Romeo and Juliet have never seen each other before, even if only in their local media.
▶ **How do we cope as an audience? What do we tell ourselves when films beggar belief, but still absorb our imaginations and feelings?** ●

▶ *A Chinese Ghost Story* is a studio-based film made on what, by Hollywood standards, is a very low budget (see p. 106). On the evidence of this sequence, how important is budget and the production values it buys in creating successful spectacle? ●

▶ As with the previous sequence from *William Shakespeare's Romeo and Juliet*, consider the use and significance of music in this sequence. ●

▶ Freeze frame each shot from this opening ground-level rapid tracking shot through to the first shot of the face of the Dark Lord. What is there to admire about the combination of cinematography, editing and staging here? ●

the sound of wolves just at the moment that he thinks he has escaped them. Even more amusingly, the film immediately cuts to the wolves themselves wrapped around the upper branches of a tree. Tsai-Shen is under ghostly protection! Eventually, Tsai-Shen locates Hsiao-Tsing's accommodation and demands that she let him in (at 37 min. 32 sec.). The 5-minute sequence that follows will be divided into four parts, although it will be sufficient to look closely only at the second and third, from the arrival of the Dark Lord (at 38.17) to the kiss (at 40.22).

ONE As Hsiao-Tsing pulls him into the room, she tells him that he should not have come. Almost immediately, the appearance of three shadows on the other side of a screen door requires her to hide him in a large bathtub in the middle of the room. He is told that her sister will not be able to smell him under water. Sister Ting enters with two servants and immediately establishes herself as both very severe and very suspicious. Tsai-Shen comes up for air and, just as he is going back under, he sees on the wall the portrait he had wanted to buy in the village market. Sister Ting walks close to the barrel and a pattern of near-discoveries is set up for the rest of the sequence.

TWO The blue tone, ground-level camera angle and rapid forward movement indicate the arrival of an evil spirit (38.17). Four very rapid shots follow: of feet landing on the floor, a twisting movement, a slap and Hsiao-Tsing falling backwards to the word 'Whore!' The first shot of the spirit's face indicates an androgynous being dressed in black, with a voice that also shifts between male and female. Hsiao-Tsing is accused of protecting a man and evidence is thrown at her in the form of a note she had written for Tsai-Shen.

The Dark Lord takes out a whip that he wraps around Hsiao-Tsing's neck. She is lassoed backwards, doing a somersault in the process. She is told to obey or her ashes will be destroyed and she will disappear forever. Finally, she is pushed against the wall and, as the whip drops to the floor, she is told to find a living man that night to feed the Dark Lord's hunger and lengthen its life. Again, Tsai-Shen comes up for air and Hsiao-Tsing moves forwards to push him back under, alerting the attention of her sister who moves forwards

A Chinese Ghost Story: Staging and choreography, combined with camera position, produces a visually powerful and dramatic sequence.

▶ What is achieved by using tilted shots at different points during the sequence? ●

▶ What is the importance of the cutaways to Tsai-Chin and the large number of reaction shots of Hsiao-Tsing throughout the sequence? ●

▶ Why do you think floor-level shots are used at certain moments in the sequence? ●

▶ There are few props, simple costumes and a plain location used in this sequence (certainly compared with the Capulet party discussed earlier). Nevertheless, shape and colour are important here. How? ●

▶ Draw a sketch storyboard of the 24 shots from the medium close-up of Hsiao-Tsing immediately after the Dark Lord has told her to take off the dress so that it can be repaired (40.42) to the shot of Tsai-Shen in the water after the long kiss (41.23).

Having done this, what can you appreciate about the shot composition, editing and direction? ●

to investigate. Fortunately, the sister is instructed to get ointments and Hsiao-Tsing takes the opportunity to pull a sheet across the tub. She is told that in three days she will marry the Black Lord, who is very old and very evil, and that afterwards she will never return. Sister Ting dresses the wound caused by the whipping.

Throughout this action, there are several cutaways to Tsai-Shen in the tub, each reminding us of the impossibility of his plight. The sister reaches to pull back the sheet over the barrel. Hsiao-Tsing reaches out and takes her hand.

THREE There is a floor-level shot of a red garment being pulled in (39.53). Three rapid shots show the wedding dress being fitted: Hsiao-Tsing's hand emerges from the right sleeve, followed by two separate shots of the belt being fastened behind. This culminates in a strange tilted, low-angle shot of the red dress, which is pulled out and falls as a train just in front of the camera.

There follows more business around the near-detection of Tsai-Shen. The Dark Lord says he can smell blood and this time Hsiao-Tsing must tear her dress to distract attention. When Sister Ting says she needs to wash her hands, Hsiao-Tsing throws water over her – twice. She is told to take off the red wedding dress so that it can be repaired.

An overhead shot of her disrobing allows the inclusion of Tsai-Shen's face in the top of the frame as he comes up yet again for breath. He sees her naked from the waist. As two servants bring towels, he comes up one more time gasping for air; she takes a deep breath. The overhead angle shows the red dress dropping away from her shoulders. There is a close-up of him under water. Her mouth comes down onto his in a shot that is much longer than any other in the sequence – 13 seconds. Finally, she pulls out and we have a reaction shot of Tsai-Shen with a flower floating just above his head. (40.22)

FOUR Hsiao-Tsing turns elegantly to be folded into the towels that have been brought for her. She announces that she must have a bath if she is to seduce anyone that night. The Dark Lord instructs Sister Ting and the servants to leave her. However, on the other side of the screen, Sister Ting stops one more time, still intent on confirming her suspicions. As soon as everyone has exited, Hsiao-Tsing moves to help Tsai-Shen out of the tub. As she sees her sister's shadow, she pushes him back in, strips off and jumps in the tub. We are given a shot of him in the bottom of the tub looking at her naked lower body. Hsiao-Tsing pacifies her sister, as she sits nonchalantly in the tub, and she then moves rapidly to finally get Tsai-Shen out of the building. (41.49)

As I write this, I feel the basic description of the action is useful precisely because it fails hopelessly to do justice to what is cinematic! However much this sequence may be perceived as escapist popular cinema, there is great sophistication in its creation. At the risk of partly answering some of the question posed on the previous page, I wish to highlight three aspects of the sequence we have just gone through: staging, choreography and editing.

Staging is the work of the director working in association with set designer and cinematographer. A physical space is required for a certain dramatic event to be performed. Consideration needs to be given to camera movement, as well as to the movement of the actors. *William Shakespeare's Romeo and Juliet* uses much more expensive and spacious sets than does *A Chinese Ghost Story*. The achievement of the latter film is partly based on the way very simple design features are used so effectively to accommodate dramatic movement.

Choreography occurs in space and time. What this sequence shows is how a single and quite small, minimally furnished space can be energised with constant movement. This is achieved partly through figure movement that is sometimes athletic, sometimes elegant, sometimes an almost still reaction shot – but always animating the space. The beautiful use of clothing is a feature of the entire film – flowing garments become an extension of figure movement.

This energy and dramatic interest is also maintained through brilliantly effective **editing** which constantly succeeds in putting dramatic contrast and pace into the sequence. As with the opening sequence from *William Shakespeare's Romeo and Juliet* which we looked at in section 4.2 (p. 115), there is a cut on average every $1^3/_4$ seconds; in practice, much of the sequence has a cut every second. The dramatic contrasts achieved through cutting are often no more than graphic contrasts between shapes – a face turned one way, the next turned another – or contrasting shot

▶ As we have already said, humour is an integral part of the generic mix in *A Chinese Ghost Story*. Explore how this sequence balances drama, eroticism and humour by looking closely at staging and editing, as well as performance.

Is there any other ingredient to be considered in thinking about how the film works in creating and moving across rapidly different moods and feelings? ●

Earlier in this section (p. 119), it was said that, in approaching questions of creativity in the design, staging and cinematography of spectacle, it is useful to bear in mind issues of:

• professional practice – creative personnel;
• genre convention
• consumer demand
• technological innovation

▶ Think about this now in relation to the *William Shakespeare's Romeo and Juliet* Capulet party sequence and the bathtub sequence from *A Chinese Ghost Story*.

What kinds of creative input and practical skills are required? What conventions and spectator requirements impose boundaries on what can be done? What technological means make these sequences possible? ●

▶ As a creative exercise, take the basic storyline of either of the sequences we have just analysed and restage it in a completely different location.

Storyboard a small segment of your sequence to demonstrate your staging, as well as more specific creative choices, for example, in the choice of camera angles and editing rhythm. ●

▶ How would you choreograph figure movement within the physical space you have allowed yourself? What music would you use with your sequence? ●

▶ Is there a difference between a movie star presented as an object of visual pleasure and an equally or more handsome/beautiful non-star presented in the same way? ●

angles – sometimes very low, sometimes high – as well as the routine use of eye-level exchanges. A dramatic rhythm is established through the darting looks and glances between characters, contrasted with the 'refrain', as it were, of the cutaways to our hero in the bathtub. This rhythm is also broken at carefully calculated moments by completely contrasting movements of figure, clothing or camera.

4.6. Spectacle, motivation and excess

In the two films we are studying in this chapter, the relationship between narrative and spectacle is always interesting, reflecting the balance that needs to be struck within a commercial aesthetic. This is a term we have been using for good reason. It conveys the idea that aesthetics are important in commercial films, but that this aesthetic is determined by the market place. What works with audiences? What do audiences like? What do audiences want?

An argument could be made for describing all the examples of spectacle we have looked at so far as 'motivated' by the requirements of the narrative in a way we would expect of visual storytelling. But the particularities of both the staging – design and movement, for example – and the cinematography – camera angle and lighting, for example – are in fact always in **excess** of what is needed. The visual display in big-budget commercial films is more likely to focus on production values. If a major investment has been made in the staging of a sequence, then the spectacular set and props will be presented as a source of cinematic pleasure, independently of narrative. Also, the spectacle of the star may exist outside the requirements of narrative. Fans are expecting to buy into that part of the movie experience that involves feasting the eyes (and fantasies) on some gorgeous physical being.

'Excess' is not confined to big-budget popular cinema. In relation to the very simple definition of excess as 'more than is needed', much so-called 'art-house cinema' is full of cinematographic and *mise en scène* display – from Eisenstein's *Battleship Potemkin* (see p. 97) to a film such as Pedro Almadovar's *All About My Mother* (Spain, 1999). These are forms of display, simulations of desire. The problem is in finding a language to talk about these other pleasures – and their underpinning desires – that does not sound like either a fan magazine or a psychoanalytical report. Let us content ourselves here by saying that the spectacle is motivated as much by the need to anticipate and attempt to satisfy audience desire as it is by narrative requirements.

All forms of cinema, from big-budget Hollywood to low-budget art house, are driven by other impulses alongside narrative, offer other pleasures in addition to those of narrative. The nature of the visual (and aural) display may vary in cost and scale, but there will be a clear acknowledgment that the pleasure of looking – scopophilia – is a major aspect of spectatorship. A film such as Darren Aronofsky's π (*Pi*) (United States, 1998), made for just $60,000, illustrates how, even on what may be described as a 'micro' budget, spectacle can be a priority. The film works constantly not just to look convincingly real, but also visually interesting. The wacky DIY computer system, the messy garret and the seedy apartment block visually communicate mood and atmosphere, and, to this extent, can be said to be 'motivated' by the wider requirements of the story. Beyond this, however, the visual display has its own independent existence – one that is simply part of the film's identity, the spectator's experience. What we make of it may be reducible to meaning, but we are more likely just to leave it be, acknowledging that it is an aspect of the constructed imaginative world of the film.

The final examples we will look at in this chapter can be seen in terms of the dictates of the particular commercial aesthetic to which each of our films is working. Narrative and genre conventions 'motivate' the action, but in both cases this action and its staging are truly excessive.

For example, in *A Chinese Ghost Story*, Hsiao-Tsing is sucked into Hell for her wedding and Swordsman Yen and Tsai-Shen must go through to the 'other side' in order to save her from marriage to the Black Lord (at 80 min. 25 sec.). The $6^1/_2$ minutes which follow provide a wonderful example of the ghost/horror spectacle.

The confrontation reaches its most dramatic point when Hsiao-Tsing asks the Black Lord to save Tsai-Shen and Swordsman Yen. He replies that she must break the urn containing her ashes and thus become his forever. She dives towards the Black Lord, sword in hand. On impact, multiple heads burst out from the Black Lord's body, attacking and

▶ Ultimately the art object – and a film can be considered an art object – just is. It 'performs' its own self-justification simply by existing.

   What is your response to this argument? ●
This idea is picked up again in a lengthy quotation on p. 151.

The final battle scene in A Chinese Ghost Story *clearly takes place inside a studio.*
▶ Think again about staging, choreography and camera movement. Has much effort gone into disguising the lack of scale, the absence of backdrops and the relatively simple technology utilised? ●

biting Hsiao-Tsing. She falls back, her hands burnt. Yen is too injured to fight on. Tentacles come out from the Black Lord to tear Tsai-Shen and Swordsman Yen apart, but Tsai-Shen has the Taoist book containing a powerful sutra strapped to his chest. As the tentacles tear away his clothes, the sutra folds out, attacking the Black Lord with its power. With one final sword thrust, Tsai-Shen destroys the Black Lord.

Hsiao-Tsing is pulled back through from the spirit world and disappears back into her urn to be reborn, just as the sun rises. Tsai-Shen and she will never see each other again, but there is the promise, reinforced by the final image of the rainbow, that she will be reborn a 'good person'.

The climax to *William Shakespeare's Romeo and Juliet* (which I will call 'spectacular' even though it is not an action sequence) is also determined by genre. There are additional factors at work here, however, ones that go beyond popular film conventions. The climax is determined by the require- ments of the literary genre of tragedy and, more specifically, of course, by Shakespeare's written text. Technically, the climax of a Shakespearean tragedy occurs at its mid-point, the moment on which the fate of the characters turns. The killing of Mercutio on Venice Beach against the backdrop of darkening skies and racing clouds, followed by the killing of Tybalt in the pouring rain at the foot of the statue of Christ are both dramatically visualised scenes which appropriately cue Romeo's awful line, 'Oh, I am Fortune's Fool.'

After the mid-point climax, Shakespearean tragedy requires the inevitable working out of that 'fortune' through to a largely predictable end. All that can be done is to stage the inevitable in a way that matches our admiration for the characters and our sense of the enormity of their deaths; however, any particular version (or 'performance') of the tragedy is free to visualise the written text as it chooses. This can create a distinctive internal structure based on recurring patterns of imagery, as well as a more general visual style. So, as well as the externally imposed generic structure and text, a distinctive internal weave can run through the production. This partic- ular version of *Romeo and Juliet* certainly does this with distinctive and recurring visual signifiers – particularly guns and Catholic religious imagery (and often the two combined).

The final spectacle of visual display in *William Shakespeare's Romeo and Juliet* is preceded by a more or less continuous action sequence. This extends from Balthasar racing off to tell Romeo at his desert trailer park retreat that Juliet is dead – although, of course, she is not – through to Romeo's crashing the door of the church on his pursuers and collapsing at the entrance to Juliet's tomb. The typical fast rhythms of this section include Romeo accelerating in a cloud of dust back towards the city (and past the postman!); stopping off to purchase poison; and taking a hostage with a police helicopter marksman poised overhead. There are zip pans, jump cuts and hand-held shots, all of which help to produce a sequence that dramatically contrasts with the stillness and quiet of the tomb.

Romeo, slumped by the outer facing door, slowly becomes aware of the light playing on his face (at 96 min. 42 sec.). We see a thin strip of intense blue and white light coming from an inner room. His face moves closer and, as in his point of view, so does this thin slit of light. We then see him in left profile, still holding his gun, followed by the reverse shot (at 97.27) of his eye looking into the space yet to be revealed to us. He begins to push open the door. The reverse of this now becomes not his literal point of view, but a shot from over his shoulder into the room. The light is sharp, but there is as yet no clearly discernible shape. Another reverse shot reveals three-quarters of his face, and we sense on it for the first time his astonishment. Finally, we are given his point of view as the full display becomes clear (at 97.35). We see a pathway with a vast array of blue and white crosses. The next reaction shot includes him raising his eyes and this again prompts the reverse shot of what he sees – a canopied altar structure. Controlled by his point of view, there is a pan down again to the walkway. We look at his face as he begins to move forwards. We then see him from behind with the walkway and the vast display visible in front of him. Religious music becomes more clearly audible. The camera then tracks with him from left to right for 7 seconds before we see him face-on, looking at something in front of him. This shot is held for 16 seconds. Finally, revealed to us (at 98.23) and held for 15 seconds, is the resting place of Juliet surrounded by hundreds of candles. We then go close on Romeo as he steps up on to the raised dais. His face is beginning to break with grief. There is an overhead shot of Juliet (at 98.59) which lasts 9 seconds. During this shot, Romeo comes into frame, putting his gun down to Juliet's left.

▶ This may be Shakespeare, but is the final part of *Romeo and Juliet* any different from *Sliding Doors* in its presentation of blind chance? ●

Again, we return to a discussion that (by chance?) is running throughout this book. Of course, a text, as opposed to the world it represents, is without chance. It is controlled by those who make it. 'Narration is never just "there".' (p. 50)

▶ Track the different emotions you have as the sequence unfolds. Try to consider as precisely as possible what provokes each shift in your emotions. For example, how significant are aspects of film form – such as shot composition, control of point of view, editing and pace? Think particularly about our interpellation into the scene – that is, how we are drawn into the dramatic world of the film through shot/reverse-shot and other techniques. ●

William Shakespeare's Romeo and Juliet: Romeo takes in the spectacle of the crypt; the audience is held anticipating what he is now seeing.

William Shakespeare's Romeo and Juliet: Juliet rests in peace, or so Romeo thinks – at the centre of an extraordinary set.

▶ How successful do you think this staging and 'performance' of the tomb scene is? ●

Compared with the frenetic speed of the sequence leading up to Romeo's arrival at the crypt, this sequence is very slow. In fact, from the first full view of the spectacle of Juliet's burial chamber to Romeo sitting next to his wife, the average shot length is 9.3 seconds, making it by far the slowest section in the film.

The five minutes that follow are made up of close shots that make no reference to the spectacular setting. Romeo takes the poison just as she opens her eyes. We are offered one further wide shot of the crypt after Romeo dies. At the moment Juliet kills herself, we look down from above and behind, back down the walkway. There is one final overhead shot of Juliet fallen next to her husband. (Mercifully, despite the fact that she has used a powerful handgun to shoot herself in the head, there is very little mess.)

How do we relate to such spectacle? I want to finish this section and lead in to the final part of the chapter by extending our central interest in making meaning, posing some questions about another kind of 'making' we do as film spectators.

In making meaning, we rely upon **schemata** – that is, templates or mental maps that help us to relate the phenomena in front of us to previous experience. This allows us to recognise a structure (even if it is one we are imposing on the phenomena from our own imagination) and, as a result, make sufficient sense of the phenomena to feel that we have 'handled' it. We are very stubborn and determined in making meaning and will work quite doggedly to make the phenomena we are confronted with fit within the schema we carry with us.

In making sense of films, we rely on two similar schemata. One involves relating the fiction to something external to it – our experience of the way the real world is, or the way we believe the real world to be. It is our model of what life is 'really' like. In fact, what we are doing is making experience fit into conventional forms and categories that we have learnt through our lifetime of socialisation. So we can, for example, fit even extreme experiences, such as love and death, into structured ways of thinking and behaving. We will call this the **reality schema**. The other schema involves relating the fiction to other fictions, other experiences of the same sort of thing. In this case, we fit the fiction into a different schema – one that allows us to make sense of the internal structures and rules of the fiction, such as the conventions of the genre, the shape of the narrative, the routine characteristics in a certain kind of representation. We will call this the **textual schema**.

The reality and textual schemata are different structures that we impose on experience, in order to pull that experience into shape, into something we recognise and which we can work with. They can be considered as the necessary ground of meaning making. In working as spectators on a movie, we will always use both schemata in making meaning – although we may think we are only using one. For example, we may think that the only appropriate framework within which to place a character is the reality schema. However, we are also simultaneously fitting the character into narrative and genre aspects of the textual schema. Characters are recognisable to us because they have human traits we fix in place from our experience (and mental processing) of the real world. They are also recognisable because they have traits we fix in place from our familiarity with the way they fit within the purely textual world of representation. We are hugely resourceful in making meaning, not least because we feel we have to. We will shift pragmatically between the real and the textual in a moment-by-moment processing of the material before us.

Clearly, the climactic confrontation in *A Chinese Ghost Story* is heavily dependent on an ability to place the action within genre. The motivation of characters, however, their reactions, their feelings – for example, Tsai-Shen and Hsiao-Tsing's love – are things we are also likely to make meaningful from our schema of the real. In *William Shakespeare's Romeo and Juliet*, the tomb scene requires us to work not just from what we bring which is external to the film text – in this case our socialised, learnt ways of dealing with the experiences of love and death. In addition, we are required to work also from our sense of the rules of narrative, genre and other aspects of artistic composition internal to the text. For example, the tomb staging depends as much on our ability to make textual connections through what I described earlier as the 'weave' of religious imagery within the film, as from any sense that this is what a burial tomb might look like in reality.

The scene attempts to carry forwards the dominant (and consistent) Catholic religious imagery. Whereas throughout the film this took the form of figurative representations – sacred hearts and Virgin Marys – the tomb scene is a vast

Compare this idea of the reality schema and the textual schema with the reality ◄ ► experience model of response outlined in the last chapter (p. 89). Just as there I suggested the value of moving beyond this to a model based on fantasy ◄ ► desire, so the move at the end of this chapter is away from trying to appreciate film by reference to principles based on realism towards what I will simply call 'make-believe' (see section 4.7).

Perhaps there is no real difference between these two schemata if we think that the 'real' is itself a text. That is, our working with the daily reality outside of our own consciousness requires a mental processing that is not really any different from that involved in handling the 'reality' of a film. In both, we look for recognisable shapes, patterns based on previous experience or shapes, patterns that we have learnt from our culture.

▶ Does this seem right to you? Are you aware of constantly placing a new film within 'recognisable shapes, patterns'? ●

▶ Do the ideas put forward over the previous page help you in reflecting on how you respond to a film such as *William Shakespeare's Romeo and Juliet?* Try to think through the ways in which you apply mental schemata in making meaning and how you enter into a state of make-believe. ●

This extends the idea of imaginative play from p. 84.

▶ Think of the many kinds of play we engage in as human beings, from making music to competing in sport.
It is a characteristic of our species that we can engage with absolute seriousness, as well as delight, in all kinds of activities beyond those needed to survive. ●

How much this 'agreement' depends on culturally learnt standards of realism. How often a film is condemned for 'not being realistic'. Now this may be because the film has set itself up to represent some aspect of the world and of human experience as authentically as possible and has simply failed because of poor production values and lack of skill on the part of those attempting this representation. But sometimes such a judgment reflects how our understanding of the medium of film and our tastes in film viewing have been profoundly influenced by the discourse of narrative realism. This discourse – and practice – has dominated the first hundred years of cinema with a commitment to the realist illusion dominating commercial producers, film-makers and audiences alike.

neon graveyard, something between a disco and a contemporary art installation. As a signifying display, it has an immediate and superficial impact; (in widescreen) it is, after all, big and brash and tasteless (or beautiful?), in the way many electricity-powered religious artefacts are.

When we work through these complex (and yet usually quite effortless) mental operations, we are not only providing the base from which to make meaning, but also indulging in **make-believe**. You may immediately discount this phrase because of its childish connotations, but it is a vitally important task of the film text to trigger the audience's willingness to surrender to the 'play' of the film, to the fantasy potential of the film text – especially in spectacular cinema.

4.7 How make-believe?

Few activities are as obviously make-believe as the making of a movie. The cumbersome equipment, constructed sets and rehearsed actors, not to mention the generally fragmented shooting schedule, are daily reminders of what seems a quite childlike form of (expensive!) play. For the spectator, too, sitting in front of the finished product, whether at home or in a movie auditorium, there is the need to 'make-believe'. The spectator must suspend their disbelief – that is, suppress their knowledge that the film is just a fictional construct.

From Chapter 2 onwards, we have talked about the 'agreement' that exists between film-makers and their audience in sustaining the narrative realist illusion. This pretence requires us to suspend our disbelief not just about the film drama and its actors impersonating/personifying characters. We are also required to suspend our disbelief about the very nature of the cinematic event – the presence yet absence of the people and places that fill our thoughts. How (and why?) do we make-believe in the presence of characters whose existence is merely that of images projected onto a screen? Beyond this, how (and why?) do we believe in the two-dimensional framed screen as an illusion of a real space with a third dimension?

The simple answer is, to repeat the point made at the end of the last section, because we want to – we are willing accomplices in this form of human **play**. (Perhaps the same could be said of the attention we give to any form of art.)

Whether it came about by design or accident, it can be said

that the form of **narrative realist cinema** that evolved through the first thirty or so years of the history of cinema, and which was most significantly stabilised (for commercial reasons) in Hollywood, made it as easy as possible for the audience to enter into the vital agreement to make-believe. It did so by the application of highly conventional **schemata** that people were familiar with from popular literature and theatre, and through the development of a set of conventions that worked to disguise as far as possible any obvious traces of its own artifice, its own construction. Further, a particular visual 'language' (including devices such as the shot/reverse-shot, the eyeline match and the close-up) determined – for some critics 'overdetermined' – a particular kind of participation in the emotional and psychological world of the film. Arguably, narrative realism closed down cinema's options very early, offering an unambitious, easy kind of make-believe for both producers and audiences based on resemblance to everyday reality.

It is worth a brief detour into cinema history in order to clarify this divide between forms of cinema that are more or less committed to make-believe. French film-makers there at the very beginning of cinema in 1895 were the **Lumière Brothers**, Louis and Auguste, and Georges **Méliès**. While the Lumière Brothers conceived of cinema as largely a documentary medium for representing the real, that which could be 'found' in front of the camera lens, Méliès saw cinema as offering new opportunities for creating fantasy – through special effects, animation and mixed media. The Lumières' cinema dominated, not because cinema became dominated by documentary film as such, but rather by the make-believe 'documents' we call narrative realist fiction films. Good examples of this are *Secrets and Lies* and *Once Were Warriors*, neither of which offers anything that will undermine the illusion that life is being played out in front of us – that the camera is recording the (fictional) real.

Although it is very, very far from the early 50-second films of the Lumière Brothers, *Saving Private Ryan* – and particularly its celebrated opening 25-minute sequence, is a vivid example of the heritage of the Lumières' commitment to documentary-style realism. The staging of the Normandy landing attempts to be meticulously accurate; the filming, using hand-held cameras strives for this documentary-style realism. There is nothing excessive or fantastic here that we

▶ Can we also talk about an 'agreement' in the way we involve ourselves in, and *respond* to, sport? ●
When I watch a football match, I know subconsciously that it's 'only a game', played out according to rules (just as cinema works according to its recognised, taken-for-granted rules). Yet my attention is absolute, the result of the game is important to me.
▶ Compare your experiences as a sport and as a movie spectator. Is it useful to think of them collectively as forms of (serious) human play? ●

This accusation of overdetermination is at the heart of much of the negative criticism of popular cinema already discussed.

Although from a different perspective it can be argued that it was the Méliès' approach to film production which came to dominate – filming in the controlled studio space rather than outdoors.

cannot imagine was part of the experience of coming ashore on the Normandy coast of France on 6 June 1944. Editing is of the traditional Hollywood kind – seamless and intent on interpellating us within the dramatic world of the film. The realist effect is guaranteed by this and a number of other long-established devices of narrative realist film-making (such as those mentioned three paragraphs above).

There is clearly an ongoing drive within cinema to produce an illusion of the 'real' – and not just in terms of a simulation of what an event looked like, but also of how it *felt* like to be involved. New technologies may soon offer us the possibility of the virtual spectacle – which, I guess, we will evaluate primarily in terms of its visceral qualities. Perhaps we will be able to talk, as it were, at first hand about how terrible was it to have bullets whizzing past our heads, to be covered in gore as our buddy next to us is blown to shreds. Equally, however, new technologies within cinema (and multimedia) are being developed to produce ever more fantastic sensory experiences that take us beyond the real – or, rather, redefine the possibilities of what may be real.

The interesting and important point is that these new technologies can be put to work either to create a more

▶ Is it possible to imagine a film without manipulative intentions? Is it possible to imagine a film without expressionist effects – one that simply shows reality? ●

A second divide commonly referred to in film history is that between formalists and realists. In what is sometimes called 'mature' silent cinema, from approximately 1919 to 1929, major film movements explored the creative possibilities of this new medium. Most famous were the German expressionists (with films such as *The Cabinet of Dr Caligari* and *Nosferatu*) and the Soviet montagists (with films such as *Battleship Potemkin* – referred to on p. 97 – and *Man with a Movie Camera*). By the 1940s, however, these kinds of cinema came under attack for their manipulation of reality – be it through the exaggerated sets, costumes, lighting and other aspects of *mise en scène* in German expressionism, or through the dramatic, rapid cutting characteristic of Soviet montage. This was seen, most famously by the French critic André Bazin, as betraying cinema's specific 'mission' to record reality as it is. Italian neo-realism was identified as a perfect example of a kind of cinema that did this, recording the real as found in front of the camera without distortion or manipulation brought about by 'artificial' cinematic devices.

Yet another divide that is partly an extension of the above is the idea that most cinema is either propagandist (in the sense that it is trying to push messages at the audience) or pornographic (in the sense that it is trying to arouse the audience sexually). The implication here is that there is or should exist a different kind of cinema that somehow lacks manipulative intentions.

convincing illusion of the (Lumière) real or to create the very opposite, the (Méliès) fantastic. Compare, for example, the application of new technologies in *Titanic* and *Toy Story*.

Toy Story represents, more or less, the Méliès tendency in cinema. In fact, throughout the history of Hollywood cinema, the Méliès tendency has survived, even if, for long periods, relatively on the margins. Two of my favourite forms of Hollywood cinema date from the 1940s and 1950s. Tex Avery's wonderful cartoons used the film screen as a surface on which the crazy logic and visual transformations of the genre could be played out. During the same two decades, Arthur Freed's production unit at MGM created musicals that actively sought to exploit the capacity of cinema to take off into fantastic make-believe where the rules of everyday reality are stretched or let go of completely.

None of the films we have looked at in detail in this book can truly be said to conform to a Méliès-style make-believe. In this chapter, we encountered one film, *A Chinese Ghost Story*, that has sequences of fantastic spectacle that gives us a sense of cinema's capacity for letting go the normal rules of everyday experience. Nevertheless, this film, like most commercial films, is rooted in a certain kind of narrative realism, out of which the magical and the fantastic erupts. The same can be said of *E.T.* The magical (such as the BMX flight) is all the more magical because it emerges out of a film that conforms to the conventions and practices of narrative realist film making. In a similar vein, *William Shakespeare's Romeo and Juliet* exemplifies a contemporary 'mixed mode' – a fictional 'document' of a world and its characters on the one hand, a wildly playful celebration of cinema on the other.

You may be forgiven for thinking how artificial in the context of today's cinema is this distinction, that of Méliès/Lumière. Contemporary commercial cinema, exemplified by a film such as *American Beauty*, seems perfectly comfortable to employ whatever techniques and devices serve the purpose of the film, confident that the audience is competent in working with the material presented to them. Indeed, within Hollywood narrative realist cinema, which operates in accordance with a commercial aesthetic, there are always in practice going to be **expressionist** features that go beyond a simple recording of the well-crafted simulation of the real. It is part of what the audience pays for, even if this extends little further than visual

▶ 'More or less': are there ways in which *Toy Story* and *Toy Story 2* can be described as regular narrative realist films? ●

At the time of writing, two great video compilation tapes are available: Tex Avery's Screwball Classics (PES 54280) and Screwball Classics 2 (PES 51667).
In fact, even animation can be seen to struggle against what may be called the all-pervasive narrative realist tendency, ever since Disney's first feature-length production, Snow White and the Seven Dwarfs in 1937.

▶ Would you describe more recent Disney features such as *The Little Mermaid* (1989), *Beauty and the Beast* (1991), *The Lion King* (1994), *Pocahontas* (1995), *Mulan* (1998) and *Tarzan* (1999) as raising similar issues as those you have just been thinking about in relation to *Toy Story*? At base level, are they rooted as much in narrative realism as in fantasy? ●

'Expressionist' here means any use of the medium of cinema – be it through mise en scène, editing or cinematography – to 'transform' the real for dramatic or psychological effect.

For another example of the fantastic erupting within the narrative realist film, consider the apocalyptic climax to Magnolia (Anderson, United States, 1999) – although friends have tried to persuade me that a frog 'storm' is a natural phenomenon! In literature, this would be described as an example of 'magical realism'.

▶ In the context of contemporary cinema, do you think these divisions – fantasy/reality or expressionist/ realist – have any value in helping us to distinguish between different kinds of films and cinema experiences? ●

A film studies word used in this context is 'recuperate'. What I am saying here is that the spectacular excess of Natural Born Killers is not recuperated by other, conventional elements such as narrative or genre conventions.
▶ **With what consequence, do you think?** ●

exaggeration in the presentation of the star and some spectacular action sequence. It may extend, as in *American Beauty*, to scenes representing the fantasies of one of the central characters. (Perhaps one of the greatest examples of this is Salvador Dali's surrealist work for Hitchcock's *Spellbound* in 1945.) Some genres are well known for imposing expressionist elements on a realist base – perhaps, most famously, film noir. Within certain genres of popular cinema – the fantasy genres such as horror and sci-fi, for example – expressionist devices will be used routinely. Some horror films use more special effects than others, but would it be true to say that, in general they are like *A Chinese Ghost Story* – eruptions of the fantastic from within a narrative realist base?

Two films from the 1990s that demonstrate how digital technologies can be put to the service of films that defy overly neat realist/fantasy distinctions are Oliver Stone's *Natural Born Killers* and David Lynch's *Lost Highway*. These films represent a kind of cinema to which we cannot apply the reality schema or the textual schema referred to on p. 131 with any great ease or confidence. It may be no coincidence that both were highly controversial films and neither were significant box-office successes. These films, especially *Lost Highway*, destabilise the principles by which we make meaning – such as cause ➤ effect narrative and the use of visual imagery to present a coherent and consistent fictional reality. *Natural Born Killers* offers a kind of spectacular excess that remains outside the orderly management of narrative realism, giving the effect of a visual stream of consciousness (made possible through digital editing and effects) that outruns any attempt to contain it.

All the films referred to in this chapter return us again and again to questions of cinematic make-believe. There are at least two good reasons for pursuing these questions. First, because it leads us directly or indirectly to profound theoretical questions about the very nature of what cinema is and ought to be or could be – which, unfortunately, we can only begin to suggest in this book. Secondly, because it leads us, at a more practical level, to investigate the relative commitment by both producers and audiences to make-believe in cinema – or, to use the title of the next chapter, both their and our willingness to work with the capacity of the film medium for transformations.

5. Transformations

This is a relatively short final chapter that expands the simple idea of make-believe *by posing some basic questions about the nature of* cinema *as a medium with a particular emphasis on different kinds of cinematic* transformations. *This provides a basis for the exploration of* realism *in different styles of contemporary cinema by reference to three films:* **The Matrix** *(United States, 1999),* **Festen** *(Denmark, 1998) and* **After Life** *(Japan, 1998). The interaction between the film as 'text' and the spectator as maker of meaning is continued here by reference to the* mindscreen. *The chapter concludes by going back to the general model of film studies proposed in Chapter 1 and offers some guidelines on how to carry forward your interest in film studies from this book.*

5.1 So what is cinema?

We have talked in the three central chapters of this book about ways in which a film transforms life through providing distinctive kinds of shape (story), performance (character) and visual form (spectacle). All of the films we have looked at in some detail have a screen 'reality' – even *A Chinese Ghost Story*. We accept the world of the film – for the duration of the film – as offering us an experience as real as any other. After all it is! Our senses of sight and hearing do not distinguish between this sensory experience and any other; they process the sights and sounds of the film experience in the same way that they process the sights and sounds we

*There is an increasing emphasis in 'home cinema' tech-
nology – widescreen television, DVD, video projection – on
replicating the quality of the cinema auditorium experience.
You must decide how far you believe the discussion of
the specific qualities of cinema can be transferred into the
home-viewing situation. Perhaps the concept of the
'mindscreen', referred to in the pages that follow, offers
some kind of common ground, shifting attention away from
the technology and towards ourselves.*

▶ **Can you distinguish between different kinds of
transformation in the films we have made specific
studies of in this book?**

  E.T.
  Sliding Doors
  Secrets and Lies
  Once Were Warriors
  A Chinese Ghost Story
  William Shakespeare's Romeo and Juliet ●

encounter walking down the street. What is different is that
our minds are alerted to these sensory experiences occurring
in an unusual, more controlled, more intense environment.
We are alert to a world-on-the-screen that is both 'real' in all
kinds of ways and 'different' in all kinds of ways. We may
respond to characters and emotions with the same humanity
that we would bring to our encounters with people in our
actual lives. And at the same time we are alert to the fact that
these characters, the emotions they have and the emotions
they stimulate in us as are the product of an art form –
something full of artifice (*art*-ifice).

The medium of cinema transforms the world in front of
the camera by converting it into photographic images. In turn
the relationship of these images to one another is changed
through editing. Our relationship to the things that are
shown, which most of the time appears to be 'realistic', is
different from our relationship to them in the 'real' world.
This has something to do with their conversion into image
representations projected onto a large screen in a darkened
space. The way the 'real' of life is changed into the 'real' of
cinema is difficult to put into words – except to say that this
change is like the change that occurs in any art form. We
adopt a different position, attune with a different sensibility
to sounds, visual images and solid objects. We look and see
differently. Both the means of cinematic expression – the
language of film – and the means of cinematic reception –
the movie auditorium – offer us a more intense, more reflec-
tive, more engaged take on some aspect of human experience.

At the same time, cinema seems to replicate some of the
ways we think and process information in our everyday
reality. This has been observed since the very earliest
psychological studies of cinema such as Hugo Munsterburg's
The Photoplay: A Psychological Study, written as early as 1916.
For example, if in reality we are presented with an array of
visual detail, the eye will tend naturally to focus on some
telling detail at the exclusion of other objects within our
visual field. So cinema 'naturally' – it seems – selects the
significant detail within the *mise en scène* by use of a variety
of devices, most obviously the close-up. Also, in our everyday
lives, we constantly make mental connections, perhaps
between a memory from the past and our present circumstances, or we play off different kinds of interrelated

information stored in our brain. So cinema constantly makes connections between different times and place, between different sources of information, through editing.

So what we have is a fascinating combination. On the one hand, cinema, like other artistic work, give us a different 'take' on reality, a distance, allowing us to reflect on aspects of our world as they are represented to us. On the other hand, cinema is very close to our ordinary perceptual experience – it has a directness, an intimacy, a 'naturalness' in the way it conforms to our mental activity in the real world.

I want to finish this short book by raising questions about the nature of the cinema medium which arise from these observations.

- First, I want to consider the reality question a little further by reference to what we may describe as the **virtual reality** of cinema. (See section 5.2)

- Secondly, I want to consider the importance of cinema as a medium that allows us to have a different 'take' on experience, the way it **defamiliarises**. (See section 5.3)

- Finally, I want to consider further the kind of investment of ourselves that we put into the cinema experience, particularly by considering the role of memory and the merging of our imaginary selves with the **mindscreen** on which the film is projected. (See section 5.4)

Each of these sections deals with a different style of cinema determined in large part by the technological resources employed. In section 5.2, we consider a film (*The Matrix*) that represents a product of the very latest high-concept digital simulations. In section 5.3, we consider another film marked by new digital technology (*Festen*), but one which represents work at the very opposite end of the production spectrum – using domestic palmcorders. In section 5.4, we appear to turn the clock back to 16-mm film production in a film (*After Life*) that appears to be wilfully rejecting the possibilities of digitalisation and new media.

From the emphasis within this last paragraph, it would appear reasonable to assume that cinematic transformation is dependent on the technological means employed – with some human creativity or imagination a factor, of course! But before we establish this to be so, I wish to return to Hugo

▶ Do you accept what has just been said? Do you think that one of the reasons for a popular narrative realist film being 'difficult to explain because easy to understand' is that it replicates our everyday mental activities of seeing, hearing and processing information? ●

Munsterburg. Having made a number of points (outlined above) about the correspondence between film communication and the workings of the human mind, he wrote that: 'to picture emotions must be the central aim of the photoplay'.

I quote from Dudley Andrew writing on Munsterburg:

> *Since the materials of cinema are the resources of the mind, the form of cinema must mirror mental events, that is, emotions. Film is the medium not of the world, but of the mind. Its basis lies not in technology but in mental life.*

'Its basis lies not in technology but in mental life.' Hold on to this idea as we move through *The Matrix* and *Festen*, and especially call it to mind in relation to the brief discussion of *After Life*. If technology is the more obvious source of cinematic transformation in each of these films, the less obvious is us – in our ability to respond mentally, imaginatively to the sensory stimuli provided by what Munsterburg called 'the photoplay'.

5.2 Virtually there

Films in the sci-fi genre deal directly with the transformative possibilities of new technologies. When these new technologies – such as digital hardware and software – are applied within the film itself, we find ourselves in a cinema experience that directly confronts us with issues of the transformative capability of technology, even as we sit in front of the images this technology creates. *The Matrix* confronts us with new and different relationships to the 'real'. Its subject of artificial intelligence and virtual realities asks us to see and think imaginatively, and perhaps even critically about what constitutes the real – and it does so as a 'blockbuster' movie from within the Hollywood commercial sector.

The Matrix is particularly interesting because it evokes a suspicion about the reality of reality that goes back all the way to Plato 2400 years ago. Plato argued that we live a delusion that what our senses see, hear and touch is 'real'. He argued that in fact we live in a world of shadows, an illusory experience that could be compared to watching images of real things being projected by a lamp as silhouettes on a cave wall (an amazing anticipation of cinema). Until we attain some sense of truth in another life, the best we can hope for is that some few people, those wise people blessed with superior

Dudley Andrew, The Major Film Theories (Oxford University Press, 1976), p. 20.

The Matrix: Neo in the sequence identified in the DVD scene index as the 'lobby shooting spree'.

I have already made some reference to this – see Chapter 2.6a, where I was reminiscing about my childhood experience of watching projected images of cowboys and indians (pp. 47–8). More theoretically, I referred on p.48 to the idea of the 'referent' of the signifier/signified process as always being absent, as having a 'ghostly' existence.

insight, will be able to warn the rest of us about our deluded sense of reality. Throughout the middle period of the twentieth century, precisely such people of superior insight (mainly social scientists!) warned 'the people' of the false reality they were entering into in consuming the mass media – including cinema. They saw the popular media as creating believable illusions that could significantly influence their audiences' sense of the real. This elite was able to see films for what they really were! Everybody else was confusing filmic representations and real experience!

The Matrix is a variation on this idea. The Matrix is an artificial intelligence that creates the illusion that the world exists as if in 1999. In fact, we learn that the world was laid waste early in the twenty-first century. The citizens of the world are living an illusion of 1999. The reality is that the only function of humans is to breed so that the Matrix can be powered by the energy that comes from the human body. A very small group of people under the leadership of Morpheus are able to see the true state of things. Thomas Anderson, a computer hacker also known as Neo, is identified by Morpheus as the 'One' (notice the anagram of Neo) who will save the human race. Neo is put in touch with Morpheus through Trinity and Neo eventually is persuaded to accept his calling to save the world from its own unreality. He is shot, but, after a resurrection experience, destroys the agents of the Matrix and gets ready to save the world. He will presumably do this by telling all the deluded human beings that they are not actually living in 1999 and that they have to wake up to the idea that they are just fodder for the artificial intelligence that controls them.

Is cinema like this? Are the transformative capacities of cinema such that we are deluded into a confusion of appearance and reality? Are we made blind to the deeper realities that determine our lives? In Plato's terms, are we taken in by the shadows? In sociological terms does cinema contribute to what Karl Marx called 'false consciousness'?

Well, let us take the movie *The Matrix* itself as our test case. It is a film filled with amazing spectacle and has a story and characters with the capacity to absorb our interest. This is seen not least in relation to our allegiance to the star, Keanu Reeves, and our shared sense with his character, Neo, that the situation presented to him/us is all very difficult to understand

Most well known is the work of those social scientists who constituted 'The Frankfurt School'.

▶ My exclamation marks suggest that I think this is a rather wild idea.

But am I wrong? Do you think there is actually a lot to be said for the argument that feature films are dangerous in their capacity to delude us about the kind of reality in which we live? ●

Besides the general comparison that can be made with *E.T.* in terms of the science fiction genre, there are some more particular parallels. The most striking is this use of the Christian story base. In *The Matrix*, we have a God the Father (Morpheus), a God the Son (Neo) and a unifying Trinity! But *The Matrix* is much more knowing than *E.T.* and exploits multiple possible identities from names such as Morpheus, who in Greek mythology was the god of sleep and dreams.

For a sense of what 'false consciousness' is and what its consequence might be, read the words spoken by Morpheus which are quoted on the next page.

We have, for example, the martial arts choreography – with even more impressive stunts than in *A Chinese Ghost Story*. The great Hong Kong choreographer/stunt man Yuen Wo Ping was hired to co-ordinate the fight sequences in *The Matrix*. These and other parts of the visual display are enhanced by an array of computerised effects, such as the now celebrated 'bullet time' visual effect. The movie almost seems in places the product of an artificial intelligence!

For an even more testing experience of virtual reality, try to see the Spanish film Abre Los Ojos *(Eyes Wide Open) (Amenabar, 1997).*

MORPHEUS: The Matrix is a system, Neo. That system is our enemy. When you are inside, you look around. What do you see? Businessmen, teachers, lawyers, carpenters – the very minds of the very people that we are trying to save. But, until we do, these people are still part of that system and that makes them our enemies. That many of them are so inured, so deeply dependent on that system that they will fight to protect it. (*The Matrix* – 54.30)

and believe. Are the film's story, characters and spectacle capable of confusing our sense of what is real? Well, within the film itself, yes. We are constantly challenged by a sense of what is 'real' what is a computer-generated effect. This extends to the identity and role of some of the characters, not least Morpheus and Neo, who may or who may not be just an ordinary guy after all, and not the 'chosen one'.

For the duration of the film, we experience through our eyes and ears sensations that are as real as other sensations that impact upon us outside the movie auditorium. The difference between the experience of the real and our experience of the cinema is a simple one, however – in the latter, we know that we are watching a movie. No matter how close an approximation to the real, no matter how similar the stimulation of our senses, we remain sufficiently self-aware to distinguish between the movie experience and other kinds of experience. We enter as willing accomplices into a game of transformations. For two hours or so, we explore imaginatively the boundaries between the imaginary and the real. And afterwards we leave the auditorium and return to our everyday existences having been entertained by the opportunity to exercise our imaginations. This is not to say films do not remain with us. They do so in all kinds of ways. The phenomena of film can be recalled as vividly as dreams or actual memories – all are of a strange kind of equal status on the mindscreen of our brain. The ideas of a film can also remain with us. We may indeed be more alert to the ways in which we surrender too easily to the 'given' reality of our everyday world having seen *The Matrix*. For example, the film may force us to reconsider theories of hegemony – the idea that we cannot recognise the ideology of everyday life because we live within it, our thinking at one with that of 'the system'.

This last point may take us back to the social science pessimism about film and other media referred to above (p. 141). *The Matrix* may appear to be a perfect dramatisation of the way we are duped by the virtually real, by the virtual experience. After all, the fictional world of the matrix functions entirely on this basis. Despite this, I want to argue the opposite – that we remain capable of distinguishing the real from the virtual. We know when we have taken off the virtual reality visor or whatever gadgetry 'delivers' the experience to us. In fact, it is in distinguishing between the 'real' real and the 'virtual' real that the pleasure of the latter has its source. If we were not able consciously to locate the virtual experience as being different, we would not be able to take pleasure in at as an event. It has significance for us because in a number of ritualistic ways – going out, getting in a queue, buying a ticket, and so on – we are able to see this as a different kind of experience, precisely one that we will want to measure against our sense of the real.

5.3 Working to rule

Just a year before *The Matrix* with its blockbuster credentials asserted one more time the economic and technological dominance of Hollywood, a film representing a very different kind of application of new digital technology was released. Made with small hand-held digital video cameras and then blown up to 35 mm for cinematic release, *Festen* represents a polar opposite of film-making to *The Matrix*. And this is in more than just its 'micro' budget. *Festen* was the first feature-length film produced in accordance with the rules of Dogme 95. This set of rules was drawn up by a group of Danish film-makers in order to produce a 'purer' form of cinema, one more or less dependent on the camera and what is acted out in front of the camera (the pro-filmic) and nothing else. So, for example, additional lighting cannot be used – except for one small light attached to the camera – even if what results is 'imperfect' cinema, such as night-time scenes appearing brown and dull, and lacking sharp definition. Does this combination of hand-held video and the Dogme 95 rules limit or extend further the transformative effect of the cinema?

Let us put this question on hold for a moment while we consider what story *Festen* tells. The film has very close thematic ties with elements of *Secrets and Lies* and *Once Were Warriors*, specifically the exposing of lies and betrayals at the heart of the family, the sexual abuse of children, the suicide of a daughter and the coming to terms with the past. We are provided with an unrestricted narrative, in that we see everything significant for ourselves during those eighteen hours or so which the film covers (which is at odds in interesting ways with the cinéma vérité film style where we might expect to experience the dramatic events in a highly restricted way). Christian, Helena and Michael, the three

▶ Discuss the points raised in this paragraph. Do you agree that we are always able to maintain a self-reflective knowledge of ourselves as spectators, as participants in the 'play' of cinema? ●

It is worth considering that the minimum cost for shooting a feature-length movie on 35-mm is about (US) $200,000 at 1999 prices. On 16-mm (the format used for *After Life*, discussed below), the bottom price is about $50,000. It is possible, by contrast, to shoot a feature-length film on a camera costing less than $1,000 and edit it on a home computer. The most significant cost is blowing it up to 16-mm or 35-mm for cinema release. The price can be as low as $18,000 for 16-mm, but as high as $70,000 for 35-mm.

There have been some celebrated examples of micro-budget film-making recently, the most well known and profitable by far being *The Blair Witch Project*.

▶ What are the consequences for film-making generally following the emergence of these new technologies for making films very, very cheaply? ●

Dogme 95
Film-makers must put their signature to this:

I swear to the following set of rules drawn up and confirmed by Dogme 95:
1. Shooting must be done on location. Props and sets must not be brought in. (If a particular prop is necessary for the story, a location must be found where the prop is to be found.)
2. The sound must never be produced apart from the images or vice versa. (Music must not be used unless it is occurs where the scene is shot.)
3. The camera must be hand-held. Any movement or immobility attainable in the hand is permitted. (The film must not take place where the camera is standing; shooting must take place where the film takes place.)
4. The film must be in colour. Special lighting is not acceptable. (If there is too little light for exposure, the scene must be cut or a single lamp attached to the camera.)
5. Optical work and filters are forbidden.
6. The film must not contain superficial action. (Murders, weapons, etc. must not occur.)
7. Temporal and geographical alienations are forbidden. (That is to say the film takes place here and now.)
8. Genre movies are not acceptable.
9. The film format must be academy 35 mm.
10. The director must not be credited.

Furthermore, I swear as a director to refrain from personal taste! I am no longer an artist. I swear to refrain from creating a 'work', as I regard the instant as more important than the whole. My supreme goal is to force the truth out of my characters and settings. I swear to do so by all means available and at the cost of any good taste and any aesthetic conventions. Thus I make my vow of chastity.

Copenhagen, Monday 13 March 1995

► Why would a film-maker want to sign up to this? What is your response to Dogme 95? ●

surviving children, come to celebrate the sixtieth birthday of their father in his big country house. (Christian's twin, Linda, has recently committed suicide.) They are joined by fifty or so guests for a celebration dinner. The plot is very tight in relation to time and space: the film captures the preparation for the dinner; the dinner itself; the immediate aftermath; and breakfast the following morning.

All of the films covered in this book work according to conventions for creating an illusion, an 'effect' of the real for the duration of the film. The fact that they do it differently, work according to different conventions, demonstrates how flexible we are in adjusting to them. Also, the fact that we respond so readily to their internal rules for constructing a cinematic experience of the real – whether it be the parallelism in *Sliding Doors* or the visual excess in the *mise en scène* of *William Shakespeare's Romeo and Juliet* – demonstrates how accommodating are our imaginations, how adaptable are our skills as meaning makers. *Secrets and Lies* and *Once Were Warriors* use variations on a narrative realist aesthetic form that separates them as film experiences from our everyday reality – allowing us to interact with them as representation. We may be deeply moved by their stories and characters, but, nevertheless, we enter into that distinctive cinematic relationship which keeps the experience on the 'outside', even as we engage fully with the films' emotions and drama (as described at the end of section 5.2 on p. 143). *Festen* requires us to work with its distinctive Dogme rules which create the intimacy and immediacy of cinéma vérité documentary and all the imperfections we associate with home video.

Festen challenges us not because it looks more like reality, but rather because it looks less like a movie. The 'normal' transformative experience we expect to buy into when we go the movies is made unfamiliar here. True, there is a linear narrative that is not at all unconventional – it has suspense and closure – but the hand-held video gives us a different kind of intimacy with characters than we are normally used to. At the same time, the drama often seems 'found' rather than anticipated, as the camera zips from one point in a room to another attempting to capture what is happening. Many critics and spectators alike describe this film as making them 'seasick' with its abrupt lurches and whip pans towards and away from characters. In fact, much of the visual 'disturbance' in *Festen* is the result of camera angle and editing – forms of cinema expression not directly related to the use of hand-held video cameras (except that the camera can take up unusual positions more easily and digital video can be edited more dynamically).

Festen: Christian makes his dinner speech, announcing that his father was a child abuser. The actors in the scene where deliberately not told what Christian was going to say.

Our adaptblility is particularly tested by the recent films of the leading figure of Dogme 95, Lars Von Trier. See Breaking the Waves *(1995),* The Idiots *(1998) and* Dancer in the Dark *(2000).*

Developments in camera and sound recording technology at the end of the 1950s and the beginning of the 1960s produced a new kind of documentary, one which we are very familiar with today. Whether this is referred to by its French name (cinéma vérité) or its North American name (direct cinema), the important characteristic is that it suddenly seemed possible to capture life in a more immediate, 'real' way. The same technological developments were significant in allowing a group of young film-makers in France to develop a less professionally polished, more spontaneous kind of fictional cinema: the French New Wave.
► Do you think there are parallels in the development of cinema in the late 1990s which may allow us to refer to a new 'New Wave'? ●

In fact, Festen uses a whole range of 'expressive' devices that ask questions about the director 'refraining from personal taste'. (See the paragraph at the end of the Dogme 95 manifesto opposite.)

▶ It is interesting to compare the first half hour of *Festen* with the first half hour of *Saving Private Ryan* – already briefly discussed in the previous chapter. Are these films working in very similar ways to produce spectators who have the sensation of being (to use a phrase from documentary film-making) participant observers? ●

▶ And what of that most well known of near-zero budget video films, *The Blair Witch Project*? Is this similar to *Festen* in the way it constructs a different kind of cinematic experience? ●

Let us consider again the final part of the Dogme 95:

My supreme goal is to force the truth out of my characters and settings. I swear to do so by all means available and at the cost of any good taste and any aesthetic conventions.

▶ What does it mean, do you think, 'to force the truth out of my characters'? Does *Festen* succeed in this? If so, does the way in which the film is made contribute significantly to this – or is it mainly down to acting performances? ●

▶ Does *The Matrix* illustrate the opposite to *Festen*: that the 'less real' at the point of production – computer- generated images – appears 'more real' at the point of reception? ●

Perhaps it could be argued that The Matrix *(ironically) is perceived by the spectator as more real because it employs a familiar and conventional film form – narrative realism.*

The ordinary transformation we experience in the movies is from audience member to imaginary participant/observer in the film's drama. *Festen* uses standard methods (such as shot/reverse-shot) to interpellate us into the world of the film. But there is an intensity in the style – whether we call it 'cinéma vérité' or 'home movie' – that seems unlike standard narrative realist films. We are transformed for the duration of this film as people embarrassed and moved and shocked by an experience that is physical as well as emotional. The hand-held camera in constant motion and the rapidity of the editing give us a sensation of intense emotional energy. It is also worth recalling what was said in Chapter 3 (p. 77) about the most routinely shocking kind of cinematic voyeurism being that which simply takes us into private lives, behind closed doors.

The Dogme 95 principles as applied in this film do not produce a greater realism – in the sense that this kind of film style comes closer than others to representing the way we experience the world. For example, as has already been mentioned, the refusal to use additional lighting actually means that the way the camera 'sees' is, for significant periods in the film, far from how the human eye is able to see. Similarly, the jerky movement of the camera does not replicate the movement of the human eye. Our ability to shift viewpoint rapidly is far smoother than anything achievable by the camera in *Festen*. In a curious way, the film exemplifies the phenomenon that sometimes the more 'real' (at the point of production) appears less 'real' (at the point of reception).

What *Festen* achieves is a defamiliarising of our experience of cinema. As 'imperfect' cinema, it does not have smooth dolly and crane shots, perfect lighting and seamless editing. It forces us to look freshly not so much at its subject or its characters, but at the nature of the cinema experience itself. In a different way from *The Matrix*, this – and other Dogme films – asks us to think of the possible directions cinema may develop in response to new technology. *The Matrix* points towards an ever more perfectly 'real' experience, a virtual reality. It points towards ever more specialist forms of production using hi-tech means and dependent on huge budgets. *Festen* points towards an 'imperfect aesthetic' that defamiliarises our assumptions about what cinema should be. It works towards another kind of film-making, a kind possible on tiny budgets using equipment that can be bought in the high street.

One of the fascinations of art is that breaking old rules creates new ways of seeing. New ways of seeing have the potential to undermine an easy-going, conventional set of assumptions that we may previously have held towards the thing being represented. Sometimes the old rules that are broken are ones that have guaranteed a certain kind of 'reality effect'. Seeing in a new way, we have the encouragement to think more critically about the existing conventions for representing the real. Arguably the realism effect of *Festen* is the result of it looking like a home movie/video; a form we associate with a certain authenticity – with 'the real'.

5.4 Transformation and memory – working with ghosts

Cinema is about ghosts – the phantoms on screen who yet look so real that we respond to them as to living people. In Kore-eda Hirokazu's film *After Life*, ghosts are asked to use the ghostly medium of cinema in order to each fix in place a single memory from their lives – a precious moment, a moment of significance, of beauty – which they will then take with them to the 'other side' for eternity. In *After Life*, twenty-two newly dead arrive out of a glowing fog at a very plain public building, perhaps a former boarding school. They have from Monday to Wednesday, with the assistance of case workers, to choose their single memory. On Thursday and Friday, this memory is made into a short film. On Saturday, the screenings take place – on the completion of each film-memory, the possessor of that memory disappears from the movie auditorium into eternity. The following Monday, another group arrives and the weekly process begins again.

The film contrasts aesthetically with both *The Matrix* and *Festen*. It was shot in a realist style using 16-mm film stock and natural light in very plain, wintry surroundings. This gives a documentary look to the image and makes the supernatural seem very ordinary. This effect is enhanced further by the way the film was developed out of hundreds of hours of video interviews, producing very naturalistic dialogue. In fact, some of those interviewed ended up as actors within the film. So, here we have an interesting contrast: the 'after life' is performed (in the sense that we used the word

A book on cinema that I like very much is called The Ghost in the Machine *by George Perez (Baltimore, John Hopkin Univ. Press, 1998)*

After Life appeared on the international film festival circuit in the second half of 1998 and was immediately recognised as one of the key films of the year:

> At the business-orientated Toronto Festival a bidding war broke out between Hollywood companies for the re-make rights. At the more culture-orientated Vancouver Festival audiences seemed so much in tune with the film's humour and pathos viewers clustered around Koreeda [the director] afterwards wanting to touch him as if he were some kind of secular saint. And at the Japanese premiere in the Tokyo Festival anyone arriving less than ten minutes before the scheduled start found it impossible to fight their way into a cinema already way past its legal capacity.
> (Tony Rayns writing about in *Sight and Sound*, March 1999, p. 24)

The point Rayns goes on to make is how, despite this critical and popular attention, no distributor or television company in the United Kingdom seemed interested. Today, a foreign-language film has to be both commercial and lucky to get any kind of distribution in the United Kingdom. In fact, the film did get eventually get a British distributor – a whole year later – and the film appeared at a few art-house cinemas in late 1999 and early 2000.

▶ Why is it so difficult to see films such as *After Life* in the United Kingdom today? Why do you think *Festen* was, relatively speaking, more widely distributed? ●

Iseya, the punky young character in After Life, refuses to choose a memory. Instead, he wants to choose a dream and pushes even further the question of the 'real'. He believes that a dream is at least as real as a memory.

He is condemned to join the other case workers – forever in limbo – until they are able to commit themselves to a particular memory.

After Life: Sugie and Mochizuki, two counsellors in Limbo (Courtesy ICA Projects).

in the last chapter) by actors, cinematographer, designer and director as if part of a believable, everyday reality.

The memories that are filmed at the request of the dead are also surprisingly ordinary. One man chooses a memory of himself as a schoolboy riding on a city tram. A woman recalls a different childhood memory – of eating rice cakes in a bamboo grove after the 1923 earthquake that devastated Tokyo. Although these memories take the form of quickly made shorts – either in the tiny studio or in nearby outdoor locations – in many of them there is an emphasis on the physical senses, such as the smell or the touch or the taste contained in the memory. The artificiality, even the childlike quality of cinema, is also highlighted, especially in the reconstruction of one man's chosen memory of flying through clouds in a small training plane. (Clumps of cotton wool are pulled towards the camera on lengths of wire to give the impression of his flying into cloud.) Vividly, we have exemplified what was said on p. 136 – that few activities are as obviously make-believe as making a film.

The relationship between cinema and memory is a very important part of the mental experience of cinema. Not only do we make sense of a film by actively remembering what has gone before, but also our personal memories become implicated in the lives and situations represented. One of the many remarkable things about *After Life* is how the spectator becomes implicated in the film by being distracted from it. I find it impossible to watch this film without being drawn into asking myself the question of what I would choose as a memory to take with me to eternity. This leads me to think about my own life, even as the film is running. In fact, it is misleading to describe these thoughts as 'distractions' – they are an integral and vivid part of our experience of the film.

At this point, I cannot resist quoting Munsterburg again: 'to picture emotions must be the central aim of the photoplay'.

Cinematic sounds and images evoke a constant flow of places, people and sensations from our mental storehouse of sounds and images. Not only is the film projected onto our mindscreens, but so, too, are our memories. I call them 'memories' in a very loose sense of the word. They are mental images that may derive from other movies, sometimes from our dreams and daydreams, sometimes from our fantasies, sometimes from our actual experiences. What is being described here is a very busy – and interactive – play of mental images, themselves provoking ideas and feelings. The very personal nature of spectatorship can be explained in part by reference to the very distinctive and particular memories that we project onto the film.

After Life, like all films, deals with transformations. What makes it particularly interesting and useful is that it is *about* transformations – from life to death, from lived reality to remembered reality, from memory to filmic representation and back again to memory. At a more simple level, *After Life* illustrates (again) how film can create a completely plausible fiction by establishing and maintaining with its audience the kind of agreement we have talked about at different points in this book. There is no way that we are obliged to believe in the basis of this film – that there is really some sort of limbo run in this sort of manner. Nor, for example, are we really expected to believe, as happens in the film, that videotapes of our lives are available for reference if we get stuck for a memory to take with us into eternity! We are willing accomplices in whatever transformations the film works as we bring our innate sense of imaginative playfulness, which includes our intellect and our emotions, to the movie experience.

▶ Recall a film viewing experience in which you have been particularly overwhelmed by your own memories – from life, from other movies.

What qualities in the film particularly provoked this? To what extent is our train of thought – our 'memory train' – independent of the movie? ●

5.4 So how did you find it?

In the three previous sections – and across the three previous chapters – we have encountered a range of films and a range of ideas about cinema as a medium. How did you find it?

We return to this question raised in the introductory chapter. How pleasurable have you found the films them-selves? And how interesting have you found the information, ideas and discussion that have arisen around them? If you have got this far, I will assume that you are nodding positively – as opposed to nodding off to sleep.

The book has attempted, more or less, to consider the range of issues contained in the diagrammatic model presented in Chapter 1 – although, as stated there, not by any means in equal proportions. There has been a particular focus on the film text and this has provided the basis for launching a series of other investigations. For example, we have begun to consider what we bring of ourselves to the film text in making meaning – how our 'formation' is of vital significance and interest. We have considered how a film text can be opened up by different critical approaches and this has led to some reflection on different levels of 'competence' that we bring to our work on film texts. Film texts themselves have been seen as existing within much larger frameworks – textual frameworks, such as narrative and genre; commercial frameworks in which their function is (most often) to provide pleasure in order to make profit; and cultural frameworks within which films circulate and are used in all sorts of ways. We have considered the kinds of discourse and hegemonic value systems within which cinema, both its film texts and its audiences, is contained.

Let us revisit the model provided in the introductory chapter (p. 11). Use the diagram to help you to map out what you now see as emerging issues in taking forward your own film studies:

▶ What additional knowledge of film form and film aesthetics do you think will be important? ●

▶ In reading about film, which kinds of critical approaches may you particularly look out for? ●

▶ What films should you take an interest in – ones dictated by a film studies 'agenda' or ones that you are particularly fascinated by? (They may, of course be the same!) ●

▶ Have you begun to think more about the kinds of values that inform films and inform spectators in their response? Are their particular social/political/moral values that you wish to engage with more fully? ●

▶ How important is it for you to have additional knowledge of the commercial and cultural contexts within which films are made and circulate? (It has to be admitted that very little of this has been provided in this book.) ●

▶ How do you want to take forward your study of spectatorship and audiences? In particular, how may you relate general models to your particular experience? ●

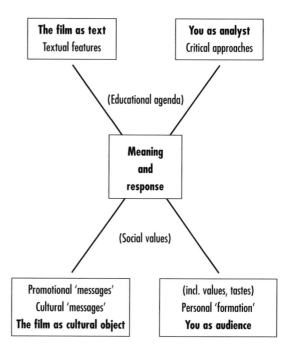

One issue arising from this book is that **film criticism**, an activity that you may have thought central to film studies at the beginning, has not been given much attention at all. Are you disappointed that the chapters have not concentrated on the detailed excavation of film 'texts', identifying levels of meaning not immediately apparent at first viewing? Or are you surprised that there are no carefully argued value judgments on each film's strengths and limitations?

What becomes clear is that making meaning in film studies is about *more* than interpretation and evaluation. A more fundamental (and interesting!) concern is making meaning of the **cinema experience** – in which the film as a text is just one component. Certainly we still want to read detailed studies of individual films, as well as critical reviews of films in newspapers and magazines – reviews that may attempt to explain more complex levels of meaning and even give the film some kind of rating score. And we will certainly in conversation with friends still want to get into debates about what films are about and how good they are. But, as we consider the complex ways in which film communicates and how it affects us as art, we will tend to take our studies into more theoretical and practical areas.

The theoretical and practical may seem at opposite poles. If they are, then they are magnetically attached! Theoretical studies will, for example, take forward questions about the complex interaction between film text and spectator. Fundamental questions around such vexed topics as the nature of cinematic fantasy/desire will be explored. Theoretical studies will consider the film not just as a text but as an event, with social, cultural, ideological impact on the community in which it is experienced. I quote again from Dudley Andrew in *The Major Film Theories*:

> *Film theory is another avenue of science and, as such, is concerned with the general rather than the particular. It is not concerned primarily with individual films or techniques, but with what might be called the cinematic capability itself. This capability covers both filmmakers and audience. While each film is a system of meanings which the film critic tries to lay bare, all films together form a system (Cinema) with subsystems (various genres and other kinds of groups) susceptible to the analysis of the theorist.* (p. 4)

The practical consequence of such theoretical work is a finer appreciation of how the cinema works – what its possibilities are as a creative medium. The better we understand the medium, the more effectively we will participate in it,

It is becoming increasingly common in film studies to argue for a shift away from 'making meaning' toward a more open exploration (and celebration) of the sensory qualities of films – the audio-visual experience not reducible to this or that interpretation. Almost every manifesto for this re-alignment refers to or quotes the following:

Interpretation takes the sensory experience of the world for granted, and proceeds from there. This cannot be taken for granted now ... All the conditions of modern life – its material plenitude, its sheer crowdedness – conjoin to dull our sensory faculties ... what is important now is to recover our senses. We must learn to see more, to hear more, to feel more.

Our task is not to find the maximum amount of content in a work of art, much less to squeeze more content out of a work of art than is there. Our task is to cut back the content so that we can see the thing at all. The aim of all commentary on art now should be to make works of art – and, by analogy, our experience – more, rather than less real to us. The function of criticism should be to show how it is what it is, even that it is what it is, rather than to show what it means.

In place of a hermeneutics,* we need an erotics of art.

Susan Sontag, the end of her 1964 essay 'Against Interpretation', reprinted in *A Susan Sontag Reader* (London, Penguin, 1982)

* Hermeneutics – another word for interpretation

▶ What is Sontag saying? Discuss this statement. Do you agree with her? ●

My own view is that film has been attacked for most of the last one hundred years for the very reason it is so fascinating – its capacity to affect. Music has always been thought of as the great demonic medium of human expression, whether the 'devil's music' of jazz or the excesses of the classic nineteenth century symphony. There is something equally demonic in film, something that moves, shakes, stirs beyond even complex theoretical attempts at understanding – and I'm talking here about films of all kinds – from *Dumbo* to *Billy Elliott*, from *Casablanca* to *American Beauty*, from *Apocalypse Now* to *Natural Born Killers*.

Like the swirling intensities and irresistible rhythms of music, film works outside and beyond meanings that can be expressed (and contained) by spoken or written language. To the extent that film exceeds the verbal, it is dangerous.

The challenge is to reflect on the totality of the film experience – both those aspects that lend themselves relatively easily to verbal description/analysis and those that don't.

whether as film-makers, producers, scholars, critics or audience members.

Going to the cinema, watching a film, is a personal experience dependent on a whole range of factors. As meaning makers caught up in the act of imaginative play, it is inevitable that we become as much interested in ourselves as in the film text. What do we do when we watch a film and how do we do what we do? How, for example, does film trigger certain memories, feelings and emotional states? Again, these are theoretical issues with practical application.

Whichever way we take forward our studies, we should not lose a sense of the cinema/film experience as an important part of our personal lives. You may become a sophisticated textual critic and a theorist, but you will be motivated to do so because you are a consumer and fan of cinema who takes a great deal from the movies (even if it is in the form of 'home cinema'). Making meaning, at whatever level, with whatever tools you have at your disposal, is your work. And it is your passion and commitment that will allow you to mark this work with your personality and identity.

Suggested Further Reading

Below are ten key books for taking forward your interest in Film Studies: (listed alphabetically by author; * indicates more difficult)

Altman, Rick, *Film/Genre* (London: British Film Institute, 1999). *

Bordwell, David and Kristin Thompson, *Film Art – an Introduction*, 5th edn (New York: McGraw Hill, 1997)

Cook, Pam and Mieke Bernink (eds), *The Cinema Book*, 2nd edn (London: British Film Institute, 1999)

Gledhill, Christine and Linda Williams (eds), *Reinventing Film Studies* (London: Arnold, 2000) *

Hollows, Joanne, Peter Hutchings and Mark Jancovich, *The Film Studies Reader* (London: Arnold, 2000) *

Maltby, Richard, *Hollywood Cinema* (Oxford: Blackwell, 1995).

Nelmes, Jill (ed.), *An Introduction to Film Studies*, 2nd ed (London: Routledge, 1999).

Thompson, Kristin and David Bordwell, *Film History – an Introduction* (New York: McGraw Hill, 1994).

Thomson, David, *A Biographical Dictionary of Film*, 2nd edn (London: Andre Deutsch, 1994).

Turner, Graeme, *Film as Social Practice*, 2nd edn (London: Routledge, 1999)

And just two web sites:
Internet Movie Database: *us.imdb.com*
Film Art: Online Learning Center: *mhhe.com/filmart*

Index

Key Terms and Ideas

acting
impersonation 61
Method 61–2
personification 61
audience
activity 7–9, 51, 53, 59, 64,
138, 145
agreement 26, 44, 63, 132–3,
149
competence 2, 52, 93–4, 150
formation 10, 85, 149–50
response 1, 3, 8, 55, 81–5,
112
response to other cultures
88, 106
viewpoint 80
auteur/auteurism 118
binary analysis 49
blockbuster 99, 119
Bollywood 99, 104
business 5
budgets/costs 119, 144
consumer demand 119, 125
distribution / exhibition
147–8
investment 118

character
audience response 59, 76–80
casting 35, 60, 62
causality/protagonist 21
characterisation 57
construction 62–3
depth 62
dialogue 69–74
evaluation of 92–4
fate/chance 58
information 58–9
visualisation 65–9
cinema
experience 4, 138–9, 143,
148, 151–2
medium 47, 74
morality 83
of attractions 95–8, 110
performance 102–3, 109,
112, 115, 127, 130
cinema verite / direct cinema
145
cinematography
camera / composition
119–20, 124, 126–9, 145–6
lighting 120, 126
cognitive–affective response 8,
83

commercial aesthetic 24, 53,
113
commutation test 35, 60
conventions
formal conventions 23
genre conventions 23, 26,
119, 124, 127
costume (see staging)
critical work
critical appreciation 6
critical approach 9, 10
critical judgement 3
consumer criticism 53
explication 3
film criticism 150–1
cultural frameworks 150
defamiliarisation 65, 139, 146
desire 8, 100, 118
(see also fantasy)
dialogue
character 69–75, 85
storytelling 32–3
diegesis 20
discourse 5, 48, 50–1, 74, 132,
150
discourse of Film Studies 4
Disney (feature length films)
135

Dogme 95 143–4
editing 24, 36, 39–45, 78, 97, 110–11, 115, 120, 124–5, 134, 138, 146
entertainment 50, 84
evaluation 3, 8, 52
  of character 92–4
  plausibility 121
excess 126–32
false consciousness 141
fandom 64
fantasy/desire 90–1, 131
  staging of 26, 51
film
  as cultural object 10
  as event 151
film buff 5
film form 6
film history 5
  Hollywood 99–100
film studies 4, 63, 151
film theory 4, 151
flashback 29, 59
film styles
  commercial aesthetic 24, 53, 113
  documentary look 133
  expressionist 6, 134, 135
  fantastic 133, 136
  Hollywood 48, 113
  imperfect 144, 146
  narrative realism 25, 50, 113, 132–4, 136, 146
  neo-realism 65, 134
  'pure' cinema 104
Frankfurt School 141
genre 23, 66, 99, 103, 106, 112, 115
  conventions 23, 26, 119, 124, 127
  hybrid/hybridity 103, 112–13, 115

German Expressionism 134
hegemony/hegemonic 10, 50, 85, 86, 142, 150
hermeneutics 151
histoire 18, 46–9, 51, 74
Hollywood – history 99, 133
home cinema 138
hommage 5, 116
Hong Kong Cinema 103–6, 113, 115
horror 112
iconic (see signification)
iconography 115
ideology/ideological 10, 54, 85, 142
IMAX 96
indexical (see signification)
interpellation 42, 78, 80, 82, 85, 134
intertextuality 5, 40, 112–3
Italian Neo-realism 65, 134
James Bond films 105
location/physical space 67, 120
make believe 132, 136, 148
male look (see spectatorship)
Manga 103
meaning making ix, xii, 3, 8, 34
  and experience 88–92
melodrama 89, 99, 101,
memory and cinema 138, 148
MGM Musicals 104, 135
mindscreen 139
mise-en-scene 24, 34–9, 59, 69, 78, 97, 110–11, 120, 14, 126, 129
motif 36
MTV – style 103–4
music 102–3, 107, 121
narration 19, 29, 46–7, 129
  source 45, 50–1
narrative
  cause–effect/causality 20–1, 82

chance 129
ending / closure 20, 55
design 27–32
motivation 126–7
no-win paradox 52
restricted/unrestricted 22, 44, 77
running time 22
structure 19, 99
suspense 22
narrative realism (see film styles)
New Wave 145
180° rule 42
pathos 72
performance 60, 62, 70, 75–6, 103
  body language 66–7, 75–6
photography–portraiture 65–6
platonism/platonist 48, 140–1
play/imaginative play 25, 84, 132, 143
  playfulness 113
pleasure 4, 8, 25, 52, 126–7, 150
plot 18–19, 59, 144
poetics 6
point-of-view 80
popular culture 53
pornographic 134
postmodern 113–14
professional practice 119, 125
propogandist 134
props (see staging)
realism/realistic 26, 32, 88, 142, 145–6, 148
  conventions 146
  documentary look 133
  experience of 89–90, 131, 146
  virtual reality 139–41
representation 68, 86–8, 93

response/response studies 64, 81–5, 87–94
  cognitive–affective 8 (also see audience activity)
romance 48
schema/schemata 23, 103, 130–3
  reality schema 130
  textual schema 131
sci-fi 48
scopophilia 100, 127
screenplays 70
semiotics 38
signification/signifier/signified 37–8, 48, 59, 65, 102, 107, 113, 121, 128
  aural signifier 102
  iconic signifier 65, 101–3
  indexical signifier 59, 101–3
  referent 48, 102
  symbolic signifier 65, 68, 101–3
Silent Cinema
  Early Cinema 96
  comedy 99
  mature 134
sound 101, 120–1
  aural signifier 102
  coming of 99
Soviet Montage 97, 134
Spaghetti Westerns 115
special effects 101, 105–6, 142
spectator/spectatorship 118
  alignment 82
  allegiance 82
  male look 48
  inside/outside experience 118
  viewing situation 138–9
  voyeurism 77, 146
(see also audience activity)

staging / creativity in 111, 117–21, 125–7, 129–30
  choreography 125, 127, 142
  costume 66–7, 120–4
  design 118–119
  directing 111
  props 120, 124
  set designing 111
stars 64, , 116–17, 126
stereotype 65
story/storytelling 17–32, 52–5
  adaptations 60
  dialogue in 32–4
  visual storytelling 34–45
storyboarding 124–5
surfaces 114, 121
technology / innovation 105, 119, 125, 134, 140
  video technology 143–4
text/textual studies 9–12, 64, 81, 85, 88, 150
time/space 17–20, 44
transformations 104, 107, 137–40
utopia – Hollywood style 104, 118
video (see technology)
virtual reality (see realism)
voyeurism (see spectatorship)

Index–People (selected)

Anders, Alison 115
Andrew, Dudley 140, 151
Avery, Tex 135
Bass, Saul 6
Bazin, Andre 134
Berkeley, Busby 100
Brecht, Bertolt 113
Chan, Jackie 105
Cheung, Leslie 116

Ching, Siu Ting 105
Dali, Salvador 136
Di Caprio, Leonardo 60, 117–18
Dyer, Richard 104
Freed, Arthur 135
Freud, Sigmund 118
Godard, Jean Luc 113
Grier, Pam 3
Hanks, Tom 61
Hermann, Bernard 6, 102
Hitchcock, Alfred 6, 77, 82, 136
Hirokazu, Kore-eda 147
Lee, Bruce 105
Leigh, Mike 65
Levi-Strauss, Claude 49
Lucas, George 119
Luhrmann, Baz 114
Lumiere Brothers 133, 135
Maltby, Richard 93
Marx, Karl 141
McCabe, Colin 70
McKee, Robert 52
Melies, Christian 133, 135
Metz, Christian 4, 7
Munsterburg, Hugo 138–40, 148
Paltrow, Gwyneth 35, 116
Plato 48
Scorsese, Martin 102
Sontag, Susan 151
Spielberg, Steven 12, 27, 48
Tamahori, Lee 64
Tarantino, Quentin 3, 113
Tsui Hark 105
Von Trier, Lars 145
Washington, Denzel 62
Williams, John 103
Wong, Kar Wai 114
Woo, John 113
Yuen, Wo Ping 142
Zeffirelli, Franco 114

Index–Films (selected)

After Life 13, 139–40, 147–9

American Beauty 62, 135–6

Battleship Potemkin 97–8, 126

Chinese Ghost Story 12, 101,
      105–11, 121–5, 127–8, 131,
      137, 142

E.T. – The Extraterrestrial 12,
      27–30, 32–40, 47–8, 51–3,
      82, 99, 104, 113, 141

Festen 13, 139–40, 143–7

Halloween 83, 101

Jackie Brown 1–5

Jaws 101, 103

Jurassic Park 86, 119

Lion King, The 26

Lost Highway 136

Man Bites Dog 82–3

Matrix, The 13, 27, 48, 99, 112,
      139, 140–3

Natural Born Killers 136

Once Were Warriors 12, 64–5,
      67, 68, 69–78, 80–4, 86–9,
      90–1, 133, 138, 144, 145

π 127

Psycho 6, 82–3, 103

Pulp Fiction 2, 19

Raging Bull 62, 102

Romeo and Juliet (1968) 114

Run Lola Run 30–1

Saving Private Ryan 133, 146

Secrets and Lies 12, 64–81,
      83–4, 89, 93, 113, 144, 145

Sliding Doors 7, 12, 27, 29–35,
      39, 41–9, 52, 54–5, 60, 82,
      104, 114

Titanic 8, 112, 114, 117, 119,
      135

Toy Story 119, 135

*William Shakespeare's Romeo
      and Juliet* (1996) 7, 60,
      103, 114–18, 120–21, 125,
      128–132, 138